NEW YORK

AN UNUSUAL GUIDE

T.M. Rives,
Michelle Young and Hannah Frishberg

JONGLEZ PUBLISHING

unusual guide

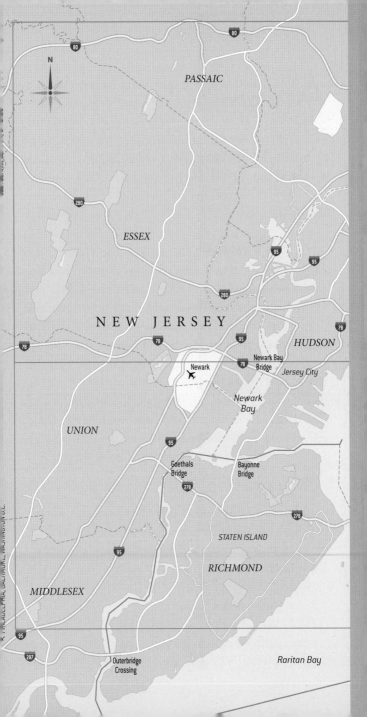

A book of this sort might seem to come with a burden of irony: after all, "secret" is a quality that vanishes with publication. But rather than celebrate the exclusive nature of the hidden, *Secret New York* hopes to use the hidden to trigger a wider curiosity. It offers a parallel metropolis where strangeness, and wonder, and a love of compelling circumstances and people are the norm.

Secret New York favors the walker, the climber, the explorer. But it also sketches a larger portrait, and the reader who never leaves the armchair will find the entire history of New York contained here: the city's deep past, its discovery and development, and the forces that shaped its society and skyline. The writing has been guided throughout by the principle that the city is also the people who live there. You'll hear the voices of artists and administrators, taxi drivers and librarians, paleontologists and park bench bums. These individuals, who generously shared their knowledge and experiences, not only make the book what it is – they make New York City what it is.

Comments on this guidebook and its contents, as well as information on places we may not have mentioned, are more than welcome and will enrich future editions. Don't hesitate to contact us:

Jonglez publishing,
25 rue du Maréchal Foch,
78000 Versailles, France.
e-mail: info@jonglezpublishing.com

CONTENTS

Below Chambers

Chambers to Houston

Houston to 14th

14th to 42nd

CONTENTS

42nd to 59th

Upper West Side (59th–110th)

Upper East Side and Central Park

Upper Manhattan

CONTENTS

Bronx and Queens

Staten Island

Below Chambers

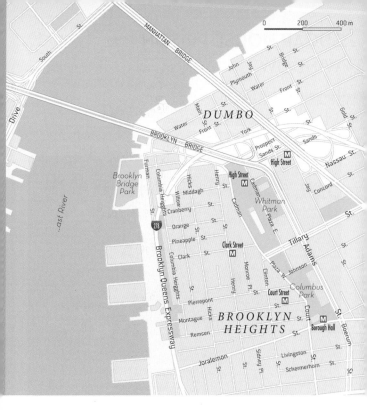

SUGAR HOUSE PRISON WINDOW

Forgotten Patriots

Police Plaza, behind the Municipal Building
J and Z trains/Chambers St; 4, 5 and 6 trains/Brooklyn Bridge – City Hall

SUGAR HOUSE - PRISON WINDOW

This window was originally part of the five story Sugar House built in 1763 at the corner of Duane and Rose Streets and used by the British during the Revolutionary War as a prison for American Patriots.

The Sugar House was demolished in 1892 and replaced by the Rhinelander Building incorporating this window into the facade as an historical artifact.

The Rhinelander Building was demolished in 1968 and the site is now occupied by Police Headquarters.

Despite the historic plaque, there is no conclusive evidence that the building this old window originally belonged to was used as a prison. That the window still exists is a wonder, and regardless of its authenticity, it reminds us of an aspect of the Revolution that is too often overlooked.

Other downtown Manhattan sugar houses were certainly used by the British as holding cells for American prisoners of war. The ominous structures made convenient prisons; first built in the mid-1700s to refine and store sugar, they were five stories of thick walls, low ceilings, and small windows. Prisoner life there was hellish. Starving American soldiers jostled elbow-to-elbow, and contagious diseases tore through them so quickly the corpses piled up like cordwood. If your idea of the typical Patriot is a man with a bandaged head marching into Redcoat bayonets to the tune of "Yankee Doodle," consider this: three times as many Americans died behind bars as did on the battlefield.

The need for some sort of monument was felt early on. A recent book on the subject, *Forgotten Patriots* (Edwin Burrows), tells how a Scottish immigrant at the turn of the 18th century recorded seeing soldiers linger in front of a sugar house to reflect on the horrors they'd suffered inside. As he watched the city busily erase its past, the immigrant wrote that one day "there will not be found a man in New-York who can point out the site whereon stood a prison whose history so feelingly connected with our revolutionary traditions."

This window is all we have left on Manhattan to point to. Both in its original setting in the Rhinelander Sugar House on the corner of Duane and Rose Streets, and afterward as one of a wall of windows retained in the building that replaced it in 1892, New Yorkers reported swirling vapors around the windows and visions of hungry ghosts peering through the bars. The tales are inevitable, but if ever a relic warranted a long and terrible haunting, this is it. In the 1960s the window was embedded in a small brick building in Police Plaza, where it can be seen today.

CITY SEALS OF
THE SURROGATE'S COURT

New York's history in symbols

31 Chambers Street
J and Z trains/Chambers St; 4, 5 and 6 trains/Brooklyn Bridge – City Hall

The city is full of examples of the official seal, but few New Yorkers could describe it to you. Seals are like currency: rich in symbols and so common few notice the details. They're also windows into the past. One of the best places to plot the city's history through seals is the Surrogate's Court Building, in the spandrels of the three arches over the entrance.

The seals are in chronological order. On the far right you see a European man and an Algonquin Indian flanking a heraldic shield. The European holds a sounding line – a lead weight attached to a rope to measure water depth – indicating that he's a sailor, a nod to the colonization of the New World by sea and New York's importance as a maritime hub. The Indian holds a single-curve bow and wears feathers behind his head – both Algonquin style. In the center of the shield is a large X: the blades of a windmill. Between the blades are the beavers that interested early settlers for their pelts – the foundation of New York's wealth and the sole reason for settling the place to begin with – and barrels of flour, a staple that the city monopolized and grew rich from in its early history. Above hangs a half-globe topped with a cocky American eagle.

Interesting, now, to roll back through history to the left. In the next seal the eagle is gone and in its place is the pre-Revolution imperial crown of Britain. The date on the bottom, 1686, marks the year New York was granted a city charter. One more step to the left and we are back in the New Amsterdam of the Dutch; the beaver now basks atop the seal of old Amsterdam. Notice here where the windmill's X came from: repeating saltire crosses in the heraldry of that city. And back one last time: the seal of New Netherland, with the long-suffering beaver and, circling the shield, a string of Indian wampum (see page 92), two forms of local currency in the earliest days of colonization when New York was just a collection of adventuring outcasts on a marshy island, barely an idea let alone a city.

The Surrogate's Court Building was finished before 1915, when New York's official seal was drawn up. You can find the up-to-date version inside on the security guard's podium. Other modern official seals appear on the city flag, on the arm patches of police officers, and behind the health inspection rating in the window of nearly every restaurant.

GHOST STOPS
ON THE 6 TRAIN

They're still down there

6 train (Worth Street and 18th Street also visible on 4 and 5 trains)

Various stops of the century-old New York subway system have been abandoned. Now they live on as ghosts: underground platforms no one waits on, graffiti no one reads, stairways leading nowhere but into the black underbelly of the sealed street overhead. By pressing your face to the train window you can glimpse these old stations as they rush by in the dark.

Three ghost stops can be seen on the 6 train. There's one at the old Worth Street stop between Brooklyn Bridge and Canal Street that is little more than a platform. Further north on the same line is the abandoned 18th Street station. This one is rewardingly creepy, with pillars like stalactites and lonely stairs receding into the gloom. Sub-human cannibals, albino alligators, the rat king: if they exist, they hang out here. But the real show is at City Hall.

City Hall was the starting point of the Interborough Rapid Transit, New York's first subway. Opening day (October 27, 1904) was a spectacle: more than 100,000 New Yorkers descended underground to get a look; passengers sang in the cars, some yo-yoed the line back and forth for hours. Architects Heins & LaFarge wanted to create not just a service, but a monument, and City Hall was the masterstroke of the system. Decked with colored tile, Guastavino vaults, and chandeliers, it's generally considered New York's handsomest station ever. The upper classes used to descend in their evening clothes just to sit after a dinner on the town.

It's still down there. Because the station is on a tight curve that can fit only five cars, when trains were lengthened in 1945 City Hall station was shut down. Today you can see its ghost by staying on the southbound 6 train at Brooklyn Bridge before it makes a turnaround to head uptown again. The conductor will tell you over the speaker that you've reached the end of the line and it's time to get off. That's your cue to move over to the right side of the car, and press your face to the glass.

The New York Transit Museum conducts walking visits down in the City Hall station twice a month, but a membership is required.

If you've wondered what happens to out-of-service trains, they're stripped and dumped into an artificial reef on the southern Atlantic Coast. Old metal hulls attract mollusks, mollusks attract fish, fish attract fishermen.

THE LIBERTY POLE

First blood of the Revolution

City Hall, on Broadway between Murray and Warren Streets
N and R trains/City Hall; 2 and 3 trains/Park Pl;
J and Z trains/Chambers St; 4, 5 and 6 trains/Brooklyn Bridge – City Hall

Perhaps due to the city's long habit of destroying its own past, the crucial role New York played in the Revolution has been strangely subdued in the American imagination. New York was the key to military advantage and the British knew it: taking the city meant splitting the Colonies in half. George Washington knew it too: the first battles were fought in Boston, but when the British were beaten there, the next place the general rushed to defend was this one. Most Americans are surprised to learn that the first blood spilled in the conflict – before the Boston Massacre, and long before the pitched battles of 1776 – was likely spilled downtown. What's more, there's a reminder of it at City Hall: the Liberty Pole.

There were liberty poles in many American cities before and during the Revolution. From an idea originating in Boston's Liberty Tree (an elm where dissenters gathered), they were essentially flagstaffs planted in the ground. New York's pole became the symbol of discord for both sides: the Sons of Liberty kept raising it, and the British kept knocking it down.

On December 16, 1769, an anti-British broadside was circulated to the "Betrayed Inhabitants of the City." It spoke of Tyranny and Despotism, among other fighting words, and was signed "A Son of Liberty." This was too much for the British. Soldiers from the Sixteenth Regiment blew the pole up with charges of gunpowder, sawed it to pieces, and printed a broadside of their own blasting the "real enemies of society" who "thought their freedom depended on a piece of wood." Redcoats hung the insult all over town.

Collectors of bizarre historical trivia will be pleased that a ram's horn, of all things, played a role in what followed. On January 19, New York merchant and patriot Isaac Sears and his friend Walter Quackenbos nabbed a pair of British soldiers posting the offensive broadside. There was a scuffle; when bayonets came out Sears, who happened to have a ram's horn in his hand, got the idea to throw it at one of the soldiers' heads. Support swarmed to both sides, and in the Battle of Golden Hill on present-day John Street several men were wounded and one patriot killed.

Afterward an 80-foot pine mast was sunk deep into private land next to the Common and girded in iron. At the top, as on the one you can see at City Hall today, was a golden vane bearing a single word: LIBERTY.

THE CROWN ON ST. PAUL'S PULPIT

The last surviving royal symbol in New York

St. Paul's Chapel, 209 Broadway
212-233-4164 – trinitywallstreet.org/about/stpaulschapel
Monday–Sunday 10am–6pm (Wednesday 11am–6pm), Friday 3pm free guided tours
A,C, 2, 3, 4 and 5 trains/Broadway – Nassau St; E train/Chambers St; 6 train/ Brooklyn Bridge – City Hall

S t. Paul's Chapel, completed in 1766, is the oldest standing church in Manhattan. Inside you'll find the bench where George Washington attended service, and above it hangs the first known full-color seal of the United States. These relics, along with the fact that Washington prayed here after his inauguration a few blocks south on Wall Street, makes St. Paul's something like the most American church in the country. But one small detail reveals the chapel's – and the city's – colonial past: the pulpit and sounding board (both original) are topped by a white coronet. In all of New York, it's likely the only symbol of British rule that survived the tumult of the Revolution.

The colonial governors got their first taste of an angry New York mob in 1765 during the riots against the hated Stamp Act. But this was just a warm-up for the wreckage that took place after the reading of the Declaration of Independence. New York's Provincial Congress assented on July 9, 1776, and at 6 o'clock the document that announced America's rupture with the Kingdom of Great Britain was read aloud to troops in the Common (today City Hall Park). The reaction was... spirited. "My Lord," wrote the colonial governor William Tryon to the British Secretary of State, "The confederate Colonies have declared themselves independent States: Enclosed is a copy of their Declaration of Independency, which was published through the streets of New York in the middle of last month, where the King's Statue has been demolished, as well as the King's Arms in the City Hall, the established churches shut up, & every Vistage of Royalty, as far as has been in the power of the Rebels, done away."

The "Vistage of Royalty" that was most famously done away was the King George statue and the finials of the iron gate surrounding Bowling Green (see page 50); for a tactile connection with history, run your hand over the uneven tops of the posts: some are still rough from where the hack saws cut the crowns off. The royal coronet on the top of the pulpit of St. Paul's presumably survived when the chapel was shuttered against the ecstatic vandals.

DR. MACNEVEN

THE OBELISK OF WILLIAM MACNEVEN

Kidnapping Canada

St. Paul's Chapel, 209 Broadway
212-233-4164 – trinitywallstreet.org/about/stpaulschapel
Weekdays 10am–6pm, Sundays 7am–9pm
A, C, 2, 3, 4 and 5 trains/Broadway-Nassau St; E train/Chambers St; 6 train/Brooklyn Bridge – City Hall

In St. Paul's cemetery, just to the north of the church itself, rises an imposing stone obelisk, the grave marker of Dr. William J. MacNeven. The inscription reads: "This was erected by the Irishmen of the United States, in grateful acknowledgement of his services to his native land, and of the devotion of his after life to the interests of his adopted country." "After life" refers to his career in the States but, curiously, the doctor contributed in the other sense as well: he helped Ireland from the realm of the dead. The answer to how is the obelisk itself. First of all, it's huge. It's practically *presidential*. William MacNeven, this doctor you've probably never heard of, was a distinguished scholar, author, fighter for Irish liberation before his emigration from Dublin, professor at the College of Physicians and Surgeons, and chief of New York's cholera board. But the grandeur of the grave marker is only partly a tribute: as Hope Cooke writes in *Seeing New York*, "Fund-raising for this obelisk was part of a laundering operation run by the Fenian Society to gather money for guns."

The Fenian Society, more commonly called the Fenian Brotherhood, was an Irish-American group dedicated to the liberation of Ireland from the British. The name comes from the Irish Gaelic *fianna* – small units of fighter bandits who lived, Robin Hood-style, in the forests of Ireland. The guns that the Fenians bought with money laundered through the funding of MacNeven's obelisk were needed for an upcoming invasion. Of Canada.

In the military category of so-crazy-it-just-might-work, the invasion of Canada by Americans is mostly unremembered today. The logic is nice: kidnap Canada, a British territory, and hold it hostage for a free Ireland. The leaders of the movement thought that just a portion of the northern country, or an effective splitting of it, would also do the job. Between 1866 (the year after the obelisk went up) and 1871, the Fenian Brotherhood attacked five times. Thousands of Irish Americans, hardened soldiers still a bit unhinged from the Civil War, took part in these quixotic invasions, most of which were interrupted by the American military. Scores died, U.S.-Canadian relations were strained for years, and the unlikely emblem of this bizarre chapter in American history stands tall in the churchyard of St. Paul's.

HARBORS OF THE WORLD

One of the largest mural cycles ever painted

Three World Financial Center
Corner of Vesey and West Street
1, 2 and 3 trains/Chambers St or Park Pl; A and C trains/Chambers St; E train/
World Trade Center

Three World Financial Center, also known as the American Express Tower, places New York in the context of global maritime trade with one of the largest mural cycles ever painted, Craig McPherson's *Harbors of the World*. The work wraps around all four sides of the tower lobby: linen panels 11 feet high, with a combined width of 318 feet. This sounds big. It looks bigger. Just as photographs can't capture the paintings' scale and atmosphere, neither, as McPherson explained in an interview, can they capture a harbor landscape in the wild. "Forms fall away too quickly and the base line curves," he said, "among other distortions." The artist adopted his own method of perspective using surveying equipment, spending months at a carefully chosen vantage for each scene. The harbors were selected for prominence, diversity, and topography. In addition to New York, there are lustrous and subtly textured panoramas of Venice, Istanbul, Hong Kong, Sydney, and Rio de Janeiro.

Assistants transferred the drawings to stretched linen and did a first pass of grey tints, but McPherson alone, working at a rate of 10 feet per month, did all the painting. Each city has an individual color scheme and feel: Venice is moody, Hong Kong shimmers in furtive blue-greens, Sydney is bright.

Like every building in this neighborhood, Three World Financial Center has a dramatic 9/11 story. Glass and debris tumbled onto the floor where the murals hang, and the Winter Garden on the bay side of the complex was half-buried in smoking girders. A grinning guard notes that, although the murals were unharmed, in the one featuring New York – a glowing skyline at night – the Twin Towers seem to be engulfed in prophetic flame. He adds that the attacks were "God telling us we shouldn't try to reach too far – you know, like the *Titanic*." But the man is obviously sick.

New York is considered the finest natural harbor on the Atlantic Ocean – perhaps the finest anywhere. Sandy Hook and Rockaway Point provide protection from the ocean; from there the Verrazano Narrows calm the waters even further into the Upper Bay where the Hudson River debouches from New York State's deep interior. This arrangement was the key to the city's success; the port and finance were two sides of the same coin until well into the 20th century.

IRISH HUNGER MEMORIAL

All of Ireland hidden above the street

290 Vesey Street
A and C trains/Chambers St; N and R trains/City Hall;
2 and 3 trains/Park Pl

"**W**e stop the Press, with very great regret, to announce that the Potato Murrain has unequivocally declared itself in Ireland." So reads the *Gardeners' Chronicle* of September, 1845. The word "murrain" literally means "death;" the fungus-like organism that causes potato blight is microscopic, but within ten years it had wiped out a large part of Ireland's population. More than a million died of hunger; twice that many emigrated. The disaster, with its themes of nostalgia and displacement, is summarized at the Irish Hunger Memorial in Battery Park City.

There are several spots in New York that create the illusion, often in a very tight space, that you're no longer in the city. The better Vest Pocket parks (see page 228) are based on this idea. The Hunger Memorial doctors the scenery more completely than any corner of New York. Here you aren't just transported to a vague "somewhere else" – you're transported specifically to Ireland. Passers-by who see the monument only from the ground have little idea that, cantilevered 25 feet above their heads, are the ruins of a Famine-era cottage and a path winding through wild grass and along stone walls. All the plants here are Irish natives; scattered about are rugged boulders gathered from all thirty-two Irish counties. Crouch down in the blackthorn and foxglove next to a piece of Limerick or Kilkenny and you can see nothing but Ireland, and sky. Stand up and you can see the Statue of Liberty.

In the limestone tunnel that leads up to the memorial, selections of writing about the Great Famine remind visitors about the misery it caused. There's a list of plants that Ireland's poor ate when the potatoes turned black: nettles, dandelion, tree leaves. During the mass emigration, New York's population became a quarter Irish, most of them desperate. "Foreigners," reads one anti-immigration banner from the period, "are paupers, strangers, sojourners, loafers, and other cattle" – words that have been used by some to describe every wave of immigrants since. It took years for Irish Americans to beat the stigma of Catholicism, poverty, and crime. By 1860 the flood of immigrants had abated. A century later John F. Kennedy was elected president.

Today New York can still claim more Irish-Americans than any other city in the United States.

A SECTION OF THE BERLIN WALL ⑨

A piece of history, separated from its time and place

393 S End Ave, along the building's elevated esplanade and parallel to Liberty Street

While walking the streets of New York, most do not expect to come upon the real remnants of an iconic symbol of the Iron Curtain, Europe's Cold War and the collapse of the Soviet Union. But bits of the Berlin Wall are indeed scattered around the city, far removed from the time and place of which they are emblematic. There were once five portions of the concrete barrier in Manhattan, but today only three remain, and only one of those is freely, publicly accessible.

Located in a quiet corner of Battery Park, the 12-foot-tall slice of history which spent 28 years separating East and West Berlin now stands in the shadow of a luxury apartment complex by the marina behind Liberty Street. The two segments of wall which were previously located in downtown Berlin were donated to Battery Park City in November 2004, on the 15th anniversary of the wall's dismantling. The graffitied slabs were gifted during a concert held nearby, within sight of Lady Liberty – an event which was intended to symbolize how humans, though sometimes divided by walls, are forever united by music.

There are two other portions of the Wall in New York City. One is located in a sculpture garden (named United Nations Sculpture Garden) uptown, on Manhattan's east side, outside the United Nations Secretariat Building near 43rd Street.

The other one is within a Times Square museum, Ripley's Believe It Or Not.

Set among a green plot containing other gifts given to the organization by various foreign nations, this three-segment portion was presented to the UN by then President of the German Bundestag, Wolfgang Thierse, in 2002. On the side of it which faces the East River, beneath the words "trophy of civil rights," there is a painting of lovers reaching over the wall to hold one another. (The garden is not generally open to the public, but is accessible during periodic tours.) The third segment is located at Ripley's Believe It Or Not museum in Times Square. Former Ripley's vice president of archives and exhibits Ed Meyer rushed to Berlin days after the wall fell and managed to acquire sixteen 10-foot portions – 160 feet in all – which were then shipped by barge, ocean freighter and truck so as to eventually be distributed to Ripley's various museums across the nation, including its "odditorium" on 42nd Street.

Portions of the wall which were once displayed on Madison Avenue and on the Hudson-docked former aircraft carrier USS *Intrepid* have since been removed. Those pieces are now, respectively, reported to be in storage, returned to their lender, and at a children's museum in Raleigh, North Carolina.

SIDEWALK CLOCK ON MAIDEN LANE

Time ticking underfoot

Clock: corner of Maiden Lane and Broadway
William Barthman Jewelers: 176 Broadway
212-732-0890
williambarthman.com
4 and 5 trains/Fulton St; N and R trains/Cortlandt St;
A, C, J and Z trains/Fulton St

Williiam Barthman Jewelers on Broadway is the last holdout of a buzzing lower Manhattan jewelry trade that started in the late 1700s. The store has been on the same block for 130 years, a record of service you can see in the historic photos hanging inside, and feel in the unstrained courtesy of the staff behind the counters. But the store's most inspired public relations move was the sidewalk clock on the corner of Maiden Lane. "People know us by that clock," says Connie, the manager.

Founder William Barthman tweaked the concept of sponsored city clocks by placing his underfoot. The sidewalk seems alive on that corner; the glass crystal and the steadily advancing hands bravely submit to endless stomping pedestrians (50,000 in a three-hour period, according to one count). Regularly serviced and synched, the clock is kept going by an electric motor that had to be replaced after 9/11. Guilo, the Barthman's bench jeweler, points out a thin crack in the sidewalk that scribbles from the east to contact the bronze setting at the Roman numeral twelve. "September 11 was like a little earthquake," he says. "The clock is safe because of the caulking, but there's still some water leaking." Connie has a placid outlook. "I think it'll be there long after we're gone."

There are screws around the setting that secure the timepiece to the sidewalk but, surprisingly, the way to get to the mechanism is from underneath. Guilo opens a door on Maiden Lane and leads the way down a hot stairwell to a rare tour of the deeper history of Barthman's: dust, the guts of the HVAC, and wooden cabinets with files going back a century. Under the clock is a small workspace and a desk bristling with tools for cutting, filing, and polishing fine jewelry. Guilo removes a piece of corrugated plastic in the ceiling, and, with pride, reveals the clock's underside. Daylight bleeds around the rim, flickering to the muted tick-tock of heels on the sidewalk overhead. When the 6 train goes by just a few feet on the other side of the concrete wall, everything rumbles.

Back on street level, two cashiers at the vitamin store on the corner who stand not 10 feet from the old clock say they've never noticed it before. "I must have stepped on it a million times," says one. "But that's New York – you get jaded. Hey, put that in the book."

SCALE MODEL AT THE AMERICAN ⑪ INTERNATIONAL BUILDING

An overlooked Titan

70 Pine Street
2 and 3 trains/Wall St

One test of greatness in skyscrapers is if an image of the building can be tastefully included in the decoration. New York's three most famous skyscrapers carry it off: the Woolworth, the Chrysler, and the Empire State Buildings all have depictions of themselves in the murals and details of their lobbies. The Woolworth tells its whole story in stone carvings, including the architect holding the building in miniature, and retail magnate Frank W. Woolworth himself (who began his career as a stock boy) carefully counting coins.

The American International Building on Pine Street took the practice to a new level with the brazen inclusion of a 12-foot version of its own self, carved in stone and to correct scale, on both the north and south façades. At the bottom the stone replica even features a still tinier version: the scale model of the model. This attention might seem out of place in a building most New Yorkers couldn't name, but you can argue that the AIB belongs among the ranks of the skyscraper legends mentioned above. Upon completion it became the tallest building downtown (and regained the title after 9/11); the style is drop-jaw Gothic; snowy mountains are evoked in the white stone of the tower's peak, where an open-air platform offered an unrivaled view of downtown and the Upper Bay. The famous elevators were double-decker, operated by beautiful redheads recruited, according to one account, "from the ranks of unemployed showgirls" – which, with your choice of hair color, apparently weren't lacking during the Depression. What happened? Why didn't the AIB take hold in the public imagination?

Maybe New York was just exhausted. The AIB was begun in 1930, two years into the frenzied "skyscraper race" for the world's tallest building, where the Chrysler competed against the Bank of Manhattan Building (and pipped it at the tape by concealing the addition of a 125-foot spire) until both were creamed by the Empire State in 1931. The finished AIB was likewise taller than the Bank of Manhattan Building – but by then it hardly mattered. The race was over.

Today the Empire State still reigns supreme. For seventy-five years the AIB had the sour title of tallest building in New York that was never the tallest building in the world; that, too, was taken away in 2007 by the New York Times Building. It's still the only skyscraper with the dash to have its own self chiseled proudly over the entrance.

20 EXCHANGE PLACE

Symbols of power

2, 3, 4 and 5 trains to Wall Street; J and Z trains to Broad Street

Anyone in New York will eventually go to Wall Street, if only just to feel the hum of power. It's here you'll find the stock exchange of course, along with the ghosts of Manhattan's very first banks and the Museum of American Finance. Hardly anyone goes one street south to cramped Exchange Place, where finance history is written in metal and stone.

At number 20 rises one of the city's earliest stunners – a skyscraper originally called the City Bank-Farmers Trust Building. Erected in 1930 at the same time as the Empire State Building, during the giddy "skyscraper race" (see page 35), it aspired to be the world's tallest, before the Great Depression put a slump in its budget and it wound up fourth. While 20 Exchange Place remains one of the major towers of the downtown skyline, it's worth seeing up close for the decoration on the exterior of the lower floors.

The architect brothers John and Eliot Cross operated in the sweet spot of Art Deco classicism with its balance of figurative and abstract. This is a building that you can spend time reading. Spoiler: it's about money and authority. The lower floors are clad in Mohegan granite, the upper in Rockwood Alabama limestone. In all it's around 30 million pounds of stone and it took 600 men to put it there. The carvings depict symbols of wealth: giant coins surround the main entrance, one coin for each country with a major banking branch, and a Mesopotamian buffalo head flanked by American rattlesnakes stares from the southern lintel. Look overhead to the nineteenth floor setback where great cloaked figures maintain a gloomy surveillance; according to a contemporary description, these represent the "giants of finance, seven smiling, seven scowling."

The imagery is densest on the massive doors. Here the story of transportation, the lifeblood of international trade and banking, is told in shining nickel silver: hot air balloons, steam ships, locomotives, prop planes. The day it opened, nearly 4,000 visitors every hour trooped through the new headquarters to gawk. Today it seems a little ignored and down-at-the-heels. But that too is part of what this building has to say. You just have to go a little out of your way to find it.

Coded messages from the dead

Trinity Cemetery
74 Trinity Place (Broadway at Wall Street)
212-602-0800
trinitywallstreet.org
Daily 8:30am-4pm
1, N and R trains/Rector St; 4 and 5 trains/Wall St

The oldest tombstone you can find in Trinity Church cemetery is that of Richard Churcher, who died in 1681 at the age of 5. The boy has a small, sturdy stone that is curious for being double-sided: on the back is a carving in high-relief of an hourglass with wings, and below it a skull-and-crossbones.

The message is unmistakable: time flies, and then – *poof*. Some paces away, near the Soldier's Monument at the graveyard's north end, you'll find the stone of James Leeson, a man who died more than a hundred years later. The winged hourglass is chiseled here as well, along with Masonic symbols. But above these, following the stone's natural curve, is a message in a devious code that took nearly a century to crack.

The code takes the form of partial squares. The squares either contain dots – sometimes one, sometimes two – or remain empty. The key to the solution is knowing why the squares are missing sides: they're really just boxes in a tic-tac-toe grid. The dots mark different stages in the alphabet, jumping the letter "j" because it was interchangeable with "i" at the time.

The code freights the message with grandeur, whatever it actually says. Are these last words to a secret lover? Location of a treasure? A zero-calorie apple cobbler recipe?

Disappointingly, the message simply spells REMEMBER DEATH. Why James Leeson took such elaborate pains to conceal a sentiment that can be conveyed neatly (and wordlessly) in a symbol – in fact the only sentiment that absolutely no one who ever entered a cemetery really needs pointed out in the first place – is a mystery. But since the message wasn't for us, we can't complain. The code system is known as a pigpen cipher, which also goes by the name "Freemason's cipher." For what it's worth, Leeson's buddies would have understood.

Ȧ	Ḃ	Ċ	K̈	L̈	M̈	T	U	V
Ḋ	Ė	Ḟ	N̈	Ö	P̈	W	X	Y
Ġ	Ḣ	İ	Q̈	R̈	S̈	Z	-	-

Key to the riddle

BLAST MARKS
ON THE MORGAN BANK

A scar on Wall Street

23 Wall Street
2 and 3 trains/Wall St

At lunchtime on September 16, 1920, a horse-drawn wagon clopped down Wall Street and halted in front of the J.P. Morgan & Company Bank headquarters. The wagon was so ordinary, witnesses later couldn't agree on a description. Inside was a cargo that would rattle history: a timer detonator, jagged slugs of metal, and a load of explosives, probably dynamite. While the bells of nearby Trinity Church were tolling noon, the timer went off.

"I was lifted completely off the ground," a messenger later said, "the terrific force of concussion blowing my hat off my head." The shock wave shook the glass from skyscrapers three blocks away. A reporter for the *Sun & New York Herald* described the scene in language chillingly evocative of another, more recent disaster: "It was a crash out of a blue sky, an unexpected, death-dealing bolt which in a twinkling turned into a shambles the busiest corner of America's financial center." The horse was atomized: its hooves were later found near Trinity Cemetery.

There were thirty-eight dead in all, and hundreds injured, making the Wall Street explosion the worst terrorist bombing in the U.S. until Oklahoma City (1995), and the worst in New York until 9/11. A force of government agencies scrutinized clues and conducted countless interviews in a three-year investigation that stretched all the way to Russia. In the end the bomber was never identified, nor was the group, if any, he belonged to. It's unlikely he was a solitary lunatic: the early 1900s was a period of fire and blood, a battle between capital and labor, and any adult in 1920 could list a number of recent attacks against symbols of American authority: assassination attempts on the President, mail bombs, dynamite on railroads and in factories. Today most people are amazed to learn that the Wall Street explosion ever took place, but forgetting about it is practically a tradition. On the fifth anniversary of the bombing, a *Wall Street Journal* reporter found that passing office workers didn't know why the marble wall of the Morgan Bank was scarred with pockmarks – marks that are still visible today. "How quickly," he wrote, "time effaces the memory of startling events."

THE BUTTONWOOD TREE

A symbol of the formation of the New York Stock Exchange

To the left of the Stock Exchange main entrance
18 Broad Street
J and Z trains/Broad St; 2, 3, 4 and 5 trains/Wall St

The grandness of the New York Stock Exchange on Broad Street with its gargantuan American flag, and Roman façade hinting at gladiatorial bloodbaths of finance, is nicely contrasted by a tiny sycamore tree in the sidewalk down below. For years, this tree has been quietly trying to outgrow its hole in the concrete.

"It's been there for as long as I can remember," says one trader smoking a cigarette as he leans on the fence that closes the main entrance of the Stock Exchange to the public. "That's at least fifteen years. I think it just doesn't grow."

Unassuming though it is, the tree symbolizes the very formation of the New York Stock Exchange. Behind it there's a plaque: "This central market place for the purchase and sale of securities was founded in 1792 by merchants who met daily beneath a buttonwood tree that grew nearby." This is the origin story of the clamorous arena of world finance: a couple of dozen traders who met under a tree. The group, formalized by the "Buttonwood Agreement," wasn't really active until after the War of 1812, and it took a while to find a home: in the early days the stock exchange met in a coffee house on Pearl Street, then at 40 Wall in a building that was destroyed during the Great Fire (see page 260). The current exchange, which less dominates the streets around it than totally overawes them, was built by George B. Post in 1903. One of the architect's innovations was a curtain of glass behind the columns so the trading floor would be flooded with natural light, but the windows have since been darkened so workers can better see the glow of computer consoles. Thus the Stock Exchange has gone from tree shade to coffee house, to temple, to virtual cave.

The original buttonwood (another name for sycamore) grew at 68 Wall Street, a block and a half away from the stubborn sapling you can see in front of the Exchange today.

When traders have been at the Stock Exchange for twenty-five years, they join a group called the Buttonwood Club. There are no privileges, just bragging rights and a numbered pin worn on the vest.

FOUNDATIONS OF LOVELACE TAVERN

New Amsterdam: New York

85 Broad Street
J and Z trains/Broad St; N and R trains/Whitehall St

I n lower Manhattan you can look up at some of New York's tallest buildings, or down at some of its oldest. This is where the city began. The street names offer clues about early colonial life: Stone was the first one with paving, Pearl, once on the waterfront, was named after the oyster shells heaped along it, and Wall Street really was a wall once, built by the Dutch to keep out the English.

At 85 Broad Street you can not only feel history, but peer right through the sidewalk to its bones. Surrounded by an oval brass rail, under a grid of plate glass, are the foundations of Lovelace Tavern, a building that dates back to when the name New York was freshly minted, and most who lived here still thought of the place as New Amsterdam.

The tavern abutted the Stadthuys or old Dutch town hall, the footprint of which is now marked in the sidewalk with pale stone. The Lovelace foundation is the strongest – and practically only – connection to the Dutch period in Manhattan.

The relic was discovered in 1979, prompting New York's first major urban dig. Archeologists found exactly what you would expect in an old tavern's dirt: bottles, glasses, clay pipes.

The building is one we can trace to its inception: there's a record of New York governor Francis Lovelace's petition to "build a howse upon the lott, adjoining next unto the State-house, and to make sd. house to be an Inn." This was 1670.

For perspective, it was also the year of the first published description of the colony in English: Daniel Denton's *A Brief Relation of New York*, with its startling list of local beasts (deer, bears, wolves, foxes, otters) and a depressing account of Indians killing each other while drunk on rum.

Wolves and Indians: just part of the scenery for those first New Yorkers who walked the mud paths of the city, past the wooden ships groaning in the docks, to the lamp-lit windows of the Lovelace for an evening of drink and smoke. The tavern burned down in 1706.

Stadthuys and Lovelace Tavern

ELEVATED ACRE

Unexpected stillness

Entrance at 55 Water Street
Daily 7am–10pm
N and R trains/Whitehall St; J and Z trains/Broad St;
2 and 3 trains/Wall St

It takes a skewed relationship with nature for a city to exalt a small rectangle of plain grass. That's the situation at lower Manhattan's Elevated Acre. The name alone has a worshipful resonance; the secret patch of green might be all that's between the more sensitive of the Financial District office crowd and total melancholy. When the sun is strong, the grass seems a little like a trick, as though at any moment it could shimmer and dissolve into the ugly roof the city wants it to be. It doesn't matter exactly how much nature has been tucked away here, or how many people are enjoying it (in the morning it could be zero) or that the grass is actually permanently emerald astroturf. The attraction is the pleasure in seeing urban traits – height, geometry, modernity – aligned with the concept of the humble lawn. It's marvelous or terrible, depending on your mood.

You enter at the widest, most heavily trafficked section of Water Street, where the buildings are all corporate titans. You ride to the green on a long clean escalator that promises open sky up ahead. The south part of the acre has islands of plants that divide it into more or less private spaces: whatever your neurosis, you'll find a spot to suit you. On the north end are tiered cement steps or seats that lead down to the holy lawn. This is where office workers peering down from the surrounding glass skyscrapers are gladdened and saddened to see sunbathers in the summer, and where you could have a harrowing game of Frisbee. To savor the effect, stand near the rail that keeps you from plunging a couple of stories down into Old Slip: the sight of lawn above and busy street below is truly odd.

But perhaps the best reason to come to the Elevated Acre is the view in the other direction. You can see all of Brooklyn Heights across the East River, down to the cranes of Red Hook. Upriver stretch the Brooklyn and Manhattan Bridges; downriver is Governor's Island. The constant hum of cars speeding on East River Drive and the choppers chuffing at the heliport might annoy you if you seek only peace, but at the rail, looking over the windy river you'll appreciate the acre for what it is: relative stillness in the general whirl.

GEORGE WASHINGTON'S TOOTH ⑱

Odd relics in Fraunces Tavern

Fraunces Tavern
54 Pearl Street
212-968-1776
fraruncestavernmuseum.org
Daily 12pm–5pm
N and R trains/Whitehall St; 4 and 5 trains/Bowling Green; 1 train/South Ferry

Tooth fragment
Dr. John Greenwood
United States, 1789-1798

Contrary to American legend, Washington's dentures were composed of animal and human teeth, not wood. Dr. John Greenwood made five separate sets for Washington, who

Fraunces Tavern, established in 1762, still operates a restaurant and bar on the ground floor. The upstairs has been turned into a museum where you can get a large and personal dose of Revolutionary War – paintings, arms, newspaper clippings, diaries – as well as see two natural objects that are as rare as they are odd: a lock of George Washington's hair, and a piece of one of his teeth.

The tavern bills itself as "the oldest surviving structure in Manhattan" but very little is original. What you see is a faithful restoration completed in 1907, after the building was saved from demolition (the owners wanted to flatten it for a parking lot). Lucky: the tavern is a direct line to post-colonial New York. The address was briefly Washington's last residence as general of the American Revolutionary forces, and he made here his farewell speech to officers at the war's end in 1783. The building's importance goes deeper: in a city that suddenly became the capital of a newly-minted nation, the tavern was used as offices for the first Department of War, as well as Treasury and Foreign Affairs.

The so-called Long Room – site of the farewell – has been preserved to look just as it did on December 4, 1783. In an account by intelligence officer Benjamin Tallmadge, who was present, Washington raised a glass, expressed "a heart full of love and gratitude," and took his formal leave. Tallmadge's diary, permanently opened to the section containing the scene, is on display.

One wonders how Washington would have felt about fragments of his person being offered on display as well. "The first thing people ask," says the young man at the museum ticket counter, "is when we can make a clone of him." The body relics are in a glass case. The tooth, hard to see, is mounted in a pendant; the hair, a surprisingly virile chestnut (Americans might be forgiven for believing that Washington was born with white curls) rests in a round frame. The tooth is a little creepy for being a fragment, as though at death Washington were carefully slivered up like the true cross, but the first president's dental woes are legendary. When he took the oath of office (only a few blocks away on Wall Street) he had only one tooth left. Clinging to it was a frightening contraption made of hippo ivory, gold, human teeth, and spiral springs.

THE FENCE AT BOWLING GREEN

One of the oldest structures in Manhattan

Bowling Green Park
Dawn to 1 pm
4 and 5 trains/Bowling Green

Bowling Green, located at the very end of Broadway, is the oldest park in New York City. The circular green is also the site of the most ironic episode of the Revolutionary War.

In 1765, the Stamp Act went into effect. The act was a way for the British to fund their military by requiring all official colonial business to use stamped paper. The measure was simple, self-enforcing, and in retrospect not too smart: the rage it sparked was the colonists' first step toward open revolt. Here in New York the response was characteristically unsubtle: the royal governor's carriage was set afire, and an effigy of the man was hanged and burned right here in Bowling Green. After the act was repealed, things calmed down. In 1770 the British again showed questionable foresight when they delivered a 4,000-pound equestrian statue of King George III. The statue, paid for by New Yorkers and placed in the center of the green, was made of gilt lead. The gilding was a nice touch; the lead, as will be seen, was a bad idea.

New Yorkers will be cheered to know that graffiti and vandalism have a long history in the city. As tensions rose, the statue was so abused a cast-iron fence had to be built around it. On July 9, 1776, the Declaration of Independence was read for the first time in New York on the Common (City Hall Park today), and a mob of civilians and soldiers with liberty fever stormed the fence and tore the statue down. As King George was being dashed to pieces, some inspired rebel observed that a 4,000-pound lead equestrian statue could probably be melted down into quite a lot of bullets. The exact count came to 44,088. The number of Redcoats killed by a hot flying plug of King George is unknown.

Parts of the statue, as well as the marble slab it rested on, are now kept at the New York Historical Society. The fence is still right here. It's been keeping the roaring city at bay for coming on two and a half centuries, and is one of the oldest structures in Manhattan.

BELGIUM ON THE CUSTOMS HOUSE

A Belgium allegory that was once Germany

One Bowling Green
4 and 5 trains/Bowling Green; 1 train/South Ferry; R train/Whitehall St;
M, J and Z trains/Broad St

Y ou generally don't get to see modern geopolitical tensions written out in city architecture, but the U.S. Customs House on Bowling Green has an odd case of exactly that. High above, on the attic level, stand twelve marble statues representing the great seagoing powers of the world. One of them is ... Belgium. Belgium, you might know, has only about 40 miles of coastline. Here's the story.

The Customs House (now the New York branch of the National Museum of the American Indian) was designed in 1900 to be the most impressive building in the city. The entire world's commerce flowed through this address, and the theme of international trade is permanently fixed in the statuary. On the lower level are female allegories of the four continents by Daniel Chester French; above are sculpted heads of Mercury, the Roman god of trade, and portraits of the "eight races of mankind." From the cornice the twelve great seagoing powers, both historical and modern, strike regal poses. Belgium is third from right. With Portugal and Denmark on one side, and France and England on the other, she's outclassed. The reason: the Belgium allegory was once Germany. After the start of World War I it was decided that a hostile enemy had no place on a government building, and Treasury Secretary William McAdoo asked the sculptor to transform Germany into Belgium. The secretary was unbothered by the fact that Belgium didn't have a navy at the time: she was a U.S. ally, dammit.

Here the story gets even more interesting. Half a dozen different sculptors had worked on the allegories; Germany was the only one sculpted by a native German. Albert Jaegers, an American citizen who had moved from Europe as a boy, was an accomplished artist and favorite for German subjects. When the Treasury Secretary asked him to mar his own work, he refused. The kind of people who get hysterical over this sort of thing immediately got hysterical. Jaegers' refusal was attributed to a latent loyalty to the Kaiser, who had once given the artist a decoration. Called before the National Sculpture Society, Jaegers made the point that the statue's identity couldn't be altered by "a little camouflage with a relabel." No matter: he was widely vilified, the lady was scoured of national insignia, and BELGIUM was chiseled into her shield.

21

MY LOVE MISS LIBERTY

A very odd and very sweet Statue of Liberty

Museum of the American Indian/Alexander Hamilton U.S. Custom House
One Bowling Green
202-633-6644 – americanindian.si.edu/visit/reopening-ny
Daily 10am–5pm except December 25
Free entry
4 and 5 trains/Bowling Green; 1 train/South Ferry; R and W trains/Whitehall
Street; J and Z trains/Broad Street; 2 and 3 trains/Wall Street

The Custom House sits in the heart of the Battery, and arguably the whole city; it was built on the site of the original Dutch fort. Reason enough to go inside: the main rotunda, where the old marble-topped counters and the 1930s murals of harbor life hint at the roaring age of New York shipping. On the front steps are sculptures by Daniel Chester French (see page 299) allegorizing the different continents; America (second from left) has a Plains Indian peering over her shoulder. French couldn't have known – the artist wanted to depict "the American idea of Plenty" – but it's as if he glimpsed the modern-day use of the building as a museum dedicated to Native Americans. That's of course the other reason to go in.

One object in the collection seems to be reaching out to engage the city. It's a Cup'ik doll from Alaska, made, according to the card, from "sea lion fur, sea lion gut, cotton, sealskin fur, glass, wood." You can walk by it a few times before you realize that you're looking at a very odd and very sweet Statue of Liberty.

Any recognition of the original Americans is doomed to the category of "too little, too late," but the permanent exhibit here is one of the best summaries you'll find – from Yámana harpoons from the Tierra del Fuego, to Mesoamerican clay pots and artifacts from the Andes and the Amazon. The best lesson a New Yorker might come away with is how our own nation's paved-over cultures fit naturally within this fascinating patchwork. It can be a little startling to see, for example, a stone cooking pot from Santa Barbara, California, or a place name on a card that seems to have little connection with "Indians" – even when the name itself (for example Oklahoma, or Iowa) is of Native American origin.

"My Love Miss Liberty" was made by Rosalie Penayik, who lived in Chevak in the Yukon Delta. There, doll making goes back as far as the earliest inhabitants, who fashioned figures from coiled grass. Penayik took Cup'ik tradition as a point of departure but incorporated modern themes and humor, passing the style on to her daughters (and grand-daughters) and putting Chevak, Alaska, on the folk art map.

NETHERLANDS MONUMENT FLAGPOLE

22

Twenty-four dollars worth of beads

North end of Battery Park, where Battery Place meets State Street
nycgovparks.org/parks/batterypark/highlights/8094
4 and 5 trains/Bowling Green

On December 7, 1926, the Netherland-America Foundation presided over a ceremony in Battery Park. It was so cold hardly anyone showed up; the members of the brass band huddled in taxi cabs. The occasion was the 300th anniversary of the settlement of Manhattan by the Dutch, and to mark it, a large pink stone flagpole base was unveiled: carved by a Dutchman, and paid for by the good people of Holland. You can still see it today.

If people know only one story about New York history, it's usually the one depicted here: the famed Sale of Manhattan, where the early Dutch settlers buy the whole island from the Indians for a handful of beads worth $24. The legend is savory to New Yorkers: it's about a lopsided property deal where the forward-thinking party wins and the rube loses his shirt. But the legend is wrong, as summed up in a single detail on the pink flagpole: the Indian's war bonnet. It's a mistake you'll find in public images throughout the city. War bonnets were worn by Plains Indians, never by Algonquins. Some might say it's a small thing, but it's a small thing that makes room for everything else.

For instance, there is no document of sale for Manhattan at all. There's a document of sale for Staten Island, and that's where the idea of the fistful of beads came from. Perhaps Manhattan was sold for what Staten Island went for – tools, cloth, wampum (see page 92) – but the legend spotlights those beads, as though the dull Indian was baffled by a gewgaw into throwing away his birthright. "Our people are in good spirit and live in peace," reads a Dutch letter, the only record of the exchange. "They have purchased the Island of Manhattes from the savages for the value of 60 guilders." That's all we know. The exchange for 60 guilders has been forever fixed at $24.

But what's a dollar? The Native American notions of money, not to mention land ownership, were inscrutable to Europeans. To illustrate, the Dutch had to "buy" Staten Island a total of five times. For the Indian, the "sale of Manhattan" was likely at most the "rent of Manhattan" – or he might have been taking goods for land he had no tribal connection with at all. There's reason to think that the Lenape who sold Manhattan returned home chuckling that these pasty, short, soft-bellied seafarers stinking of hogshit and cheese had traveled so far just to get swindled.

AMERICAN MERCHANT MARINERS' MEMORIAL

23

All hands!

Battery Park, just northwest of Castle Clinton
nycgovparks.org
4 and 5 trains/Bowling Green; 1 train/South Ferry;
N and R trains/Whitehall St

Out on a stone breakwater, bronze sailors huddle on the deck of a sinking boat. One tries to save a companion who reaches from the lapping waves; another cups his hands to shout for help. The American Merchant Mariners' Memorial has such dramatic immediacy because – strange among monuments – it's based on a photograph. This photograph has its own rich story of contingency and adventure, and at the center of it all is a man whose name appears nowhere at the memorial.

George W. Duffy was barely 20 when, in September 1942, his American merchant vessel was sunk by a German cruiser off South Africa. The survivors were transferred to an enemy supply ship where they languished for a month. While leafing through the *Berliner Illustrierte Zeitung* Duffy came across a story about a torpedoed U.S. oil tanker; with the story was a photo of seven men in a life raft whom Duffy immediately recognized as fellow merchant seamen. Believing that later they'd be amused by the photo, "and naively thinking," he wrote, "the war would not last very long," he tore the page out and kept it.

Duffy and the other prisoners were turned over to the Japanese. For the next three years – in Java, Singapore, Sumatra – he lived in camps until he was liberated, along with other "walking skeletons," by the British in 1945. All the while, the magazine photo remained stashed in his gear. "After the war," he wrote, "I took this page to as many of the oil tanker companies as I could find in New York. No one could identify the seven men." And so the matter rested for forty years when, in the early 1980s, a historian had the photo analyzed by the FBI. By enhancing a life vest, the name of the merchantmen's ship was made visible for the first time: *Muskogee*. The photo had been taken by a German journalist from the very submarine that had blown the oil tanker out of the water. The shouting sailors captured on film are the last portraits of dead men: records show the *Muskogee* lost all hands. "All hands!" wrote Duffy. "And for all those years I had been searching for living survivors."

French sculptress Marisol used Duffy's photograph to sketch the monument. It was dedicated in 1991.

24

GRAFFITI COLUMNS
OF ELLIS ISLAND

The other immigrants

212-363-3200
nps.gov/elis/index.htm
Daily except December 25
A visit to Ellis Island includes Liberty Island (Statue of Liberty); ferry tickets available at Castle Clinton in Battery Park (first departs mainland at 9:30 am, last at 3:30 pm)

The traditional narrative of Ellis Island is one-way: the Statue of Liberty raises her torch to welcome incoming traffic from afar. You rarely hear about traffic going in the *other* direction: the folks who made it here – also after feats of daring and sacrifice – but ended up getting kicked out again. You can come strangely close to the lives of these other people on the third floor of the main building, just above the great Registry Room. There you'll find two columns that are covered, on all sides and from top to bottom, with penciled graffiti.

Barry Moreno is a librarian and historian at Ellis Island, and author of *The Encyclopedia of Ellis Island* and *The Statue of Liberty Encyclopedia*. He can see the columns from his desk. "The story the tourists get," he says, "is of the thousands of immigrants coming into Ellis Island every day off the ships – the massive immigration. And that story is the major story. But it happened between 1892 and 1924." In 1921 the American government began enforcing immigration quotas; between then and World War II, Ellis Island became a universal detention center for unwanted aliens. "You had prostitutes," says Moreno, "ex-convicts, down-and-outs, vagrants. People who had been in hospital or orphanages, people who suffered from insanity or epilepsy. Alcoholics..."

Some of these people had been living in the States for years; many even crossed over from Mexico or Canada before the borders were enforced. Generally they got arrested for some crime – in Seattle, Kansas City, Chicago – and when they couldn't prove legal entry were packed onto trains. "The train would wind up in New York," says Moreno, "and all of the detainees – hundreds of them – would be brought under guard to Ellis Island."

Just beyond the columns was the Special Inquiry Division, where deportation cases were investigated. Unlike arriving immigrants, who were processed and ejected into the city in a matter of hours, detainees were stuck waiting. To relieve the tedium, and to rebel, and to leave some trace of themselves in the country that had refused them, they would scribble on the walls. There are cartoons of officials, and animals, and faces, and tender portraits of women. One man seemed to want to defend his legitimate entry into America, offering a testimony – in Italian: "Cecchini, Giuseppe," his message reads. "Arrived at the Battery on Saturday, May 18, 1901."

The lost water of Manhattan

The makers of Manhattan's city plan made no provisions for how the island's scores of streams, brooks, ponds and springs should fit within the rigid grid. When the grid was born in the early 1800s, the northern limit of the city was, strange to think, a bridge where Broadway crossed a canal. The canal ran from Centre Street all the way to the Hudson River – the path of Canal Street today. Some of the old streams and inlets were bricked over: hidden below the cobbles and dirt of the streets, the tide would heave underfoot. But the easiest method was simply to fill the water in with earth – a solution New Yorkers would often pay for later on. Generally the only mention of Manhattan's hidden streams and springs were complaints: of sagging foundations, of swamps and disease, of floods. Under Times Square was a spring that fed a stream: it cut an arc down to Fifth Avenue and 31st Street, where it pooled to form the lovely-sounding Sunfish Pond before flowing out into the East River. Years after being filled in and built upon, the old watercourse fell right in the path of the construction of Pennsylvania Railroad tunnels which were delayed by "quicksands and half-dried-up streams." Another stream started uptown at the far west end of 72nd Street and almost completely crossed the island, twisting through the area that would be Central Park (the lower ball fields are actually old riverbeds); when embankments were put in place in 1865 to enclose the park, Fifth Avenue was flooded for months. For anyone interested in Manhattan's lost water, an indispensable reference is the Sanitary and Topographical map drawn by Egbert Viele in 1865. The Viele map is scarcely believable: Manhattan was once a marshland riddled with streams. Some may be flowing still, gloomily, in black channels under the pavement. Here are three of the most interesting.

Broad Street

Historians debate the point, but the Dutch may have chosen Manhattan as the site for their permanent settlement because the inlets and streams made it ideal for carving up with canals: New Amsterdam in the image of the old. Broad Street was once a canal, and its banks were the site of New Amsterdam's first marketplace.

Viele map, 1865

The Collect Pond

Of all of the lost water, the Collect Pond was the queen. The spring-fed lake was the principal source of early New York's fresh water, and so deep it even contained legendary sea monsters. Then tanneries and slaughterhouses turned it into a sewer; the channel that would be Canal Street was dug to drain it. After the Collect was earthed in the area became New York's first violent slum, Five Points. In addition to crowding and poverty, residents had to deal with houses that sank into the oozing ground. Later buildings in the area were raised on piles. The Collect Pond covered nearly 50 acres; the middle of it was at the present-day intersection of Leonard and Centre Streets.

Minetta Brook

This stream, still flowing, is Manhattan's most compelling water mystery. The idea of an underground river is spectacularly eerie: you imagine blind fish nosing the foundations of buildings, or sidewalks vibrating, ever so slightly, with subterranean floods. The Lenape Indians called Minetta Brook Manette, "Devil's Water." It was once full of trout, but got buried by 1820. Kinked Minetta Street in Greenwich Village is said to follow its hidden path, but claims of a Minetta connection can be found all over the neighborhood, from a pump in Grove Court that supposedly drew fresh water directly from it, to a transparent plastic pipe in the lobby of the residential tower at 2 Fifth Avenue that burbles with muddy water after rains: a pressured tendril of the underground waterway reaching up to probe streetside. "A brook winds its erratic way beneath this site ..." reads the plaque, but it never actually says that this is Minetta water. For a stronger connection head to Minetta Tavern, on MacDougal Street since 1937. Weary of floods, the owners recently sealed up and redid the basement plumbing. "Oh, it's active," says general manager Arnold Rossman of Minetta. "When they were digging it up to put in the new piping, they could see the river down there when they opened up the basement."

Chambers to Houston

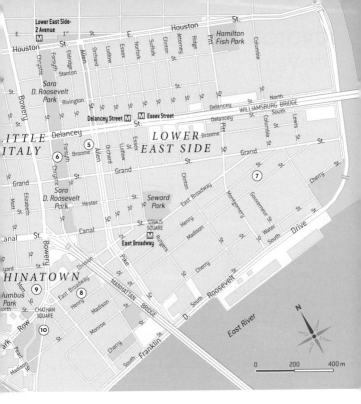

CROTON AQUEDUCT MANHOLE COVERS

Relics of a vast public water project

Below: Fifth Avenue at 110th Street
4 and 6 trains/103rd St

Opposite: Jersey Street
B, D, F and M trains/Broadway – Lafayette

Two manhole covers, hidden in plain sight on Fifth Avenue and Jersey Street in SoHo, are nearly the only ones remaining in the city with the word "Croton" curving around the face. They're vestiges of the titanic engineering project that brought fresh water to Manhattan in the 1800s, and one cover (photo below) is thought to be the city's oldest.

With rivers on three sides, you'd think that clean water wouldn't be a problem in Manhattan. In fact the rivers around the island are salty; two of them, the Harlem and East Rivers, aren't proper rivers at all but tidal straits. The springs and streams that supplied fresh water to the colonists gradually became polluted and were filled in, and most of the growing population came to rely on cisterns, wells, and rain barrels. Some of the effects of this you can guess: illness, disease, increased fire risk. Others not so much: alcoholism (liquor was cleaner than water) and the formation of the Chase Manhattan Bank, which began as a

mostly phony water distribution service for the wealthy.

The Croton Aqueduct changed everything. Using technology that would make an ancient Roman yawn, the aqueduct relied on simple gravity to channel fresh water from the most suitable natural source, in this case the Croton River 40 miles to the north. Construction began in 1837, and just five years later 60 million gallons a day, descending at a rate of 15 vertical inches per mile, began flowing into Manhattan. There were two reservoirs in the city; the furthest south, the Croton Distributing Reservoir, was a magnificent aquatic fortress with granite walls 50 feet high and 25 feet thick. New Yorkers used to take promenades along the rim for an overlook of the entire city, and the beguiling sight of moonlight sparkling on the 4-acre lake within.

The reservoir, built to echo the staid architecture of ancient Egypt, was intended to meet the city's water needs for centuries. It was overwhelmed in fifty years. A parallel system followed (still supplying Manhattan with 10% of its water today), but the enormous Croton Reservoir was razed for the construction of the main branch of the New York Public Library.

Traces of the aqueduct – paths, gatehouses, bridges – can be found throughout the Bronx and Manhattan (for an impressive example, see page 348).

THE NEW YORK EARTH ROOM ②

Three decades of just dirt

141 Wooster Street
212-989-5566
diacenter.org
Wednesday to Sunday 12pm–3pm and 3:30pm-6pm
Admission free
B, D, F and M trains/Broadway – Lafayette St; N and R trains/Spring St

If the story of New York City is the story of real estate, then the *Earth Room* on Wooster Street is a tale of horror. In a second-floor loft of a Renaissance Revival building in one of the city's hottest areas lives ... a roomful of dirt. The dirt covers 3,600 square feet to a depth of 22 inches and weighs 280,000 pounds. According to commissioners Dia Art Foundation, *The New York Earth Room* is "an interior earth sculpture" – but mostly what it is is a roomful of dirt.

Cobbled Wooster Street is lined with shoe stores and boutiques; the only hint that number 141 houses a work by a major American artist is a plaque directing the visitor to ring bell 2B. As soon as you enter the narrow stair, you can sniff what's in store. "That's good," says William Dilworth behind the counter of the reception area. "I was afraid the smell had been fading over the years." Dilworth is the full-time curator of the sculpture. He has a mild smile and the contemplative air you might expect from a man who passes his days tending 140 tons of mute soil. "I water it, I turn it, I rake it." He also plucks out the green shoots that sprout from time to time, for this is real, living earth. It's dark and moist. There is nothing else in the large white space, and nothing between you and the earth but a knee-high glass barrier.

The work's creator, Walter De Maria (b. 1935) is a Minimalist and Land Artist perhaps best known for *Lightning Field*, an array of 400 stainless-steel poles planted upright in the New Mexican desert. Dilworth can answer any question about the nuts and bolts of the project, but leaves you to judge for yourself the mesmeric properties of dirt. The floor is sound: holes are dug to check. The earth goes all the way down. Where it came from is uncertain, but Dilworth's best guess is "somewhere in Pennsylvania." De Maria chose it for the color.

Dia Art Foundation pioneered the retooling of urban industrial spaces for art and has made a mission of funding site-specific installations like the *Earth Room*, on continuous exhibition at the present site since 1980. *The Broken Kilometer*, another Dia-commissioned work by De Maria, can be seen just two blocks away at 393 West Broadway. The work is composed of 500 polished 2-meter-long brass rods arranged on the floor.

THE FLOATING MAP ON GREENE STREET ③

Milling ants or electrons

110 Greene Street
N and R trains/Prince St

There's an alien scrawl in the sidewalk of Greene Street that takes a moment to puzzle out. At first it would seem to be a blown-up flowchart or circuit board, and these guesses are close to the mark. The stainless-steel pattern is a work of urban art by Belgian artist and architect Françoise Schein, and has long held the title of New York City's largest subway map.

"My life as an artist began," says Schein in her project notes, "on a sidewalk in SoHo." The artist had come to New York in 1978 to study urban design at Columbia. Immersed in the literature of mathematics and the dawning information age, she became bewitched by the brute force of New York transit. "This subway fascinated me: its filth, its life, its graffiti, the millions of travelers who used it every day like milling ants or electrons in a computer ..." She had a creative flash flying into New York, watching from the jet window as the city's strings of lights approached: it was like plunging into an enormous microchip.

Schein would get the chance to translate these impressions into work when real-estate developer Tony Goldman asked her in 1984 what she would do with the sidewalk in front of his building on Greene Street. Schein proposed a project called *Subway Map Floating on a New York Sidewalk*; Goldman immediately answered: "I'm buying it."

Illustrating the New York tenet that no one ever got anywhere by being timid, Schein spent the next year presenting her map to a jury of the SoHo community board; she then had to endure the mocking eye of the Department of Transportation officer, who made the young architect in tee-shirt and tennis shoes return dozens of times to explain why New York needed a gigantic puzzle of urban philosophy underfoot. Once the map was approved, Schein got to work cutting and welding stainless steel, pouring terrazzo, blowing her own glass for the station roundels. The finished project earned her the 1985 Award for Excellence in Design from Mayor Koch. Schein went on to make a niche of urban art in subways, with works in Lisbon, Brussels, Berlin, Paris, and Stockholm.

THE HAUGHWOUT BUILDING

The recipe for the skyscraper

490 Broadway
4 and 6 trains/Spring St and Canal St; N and R trains/Prince St and Canal St

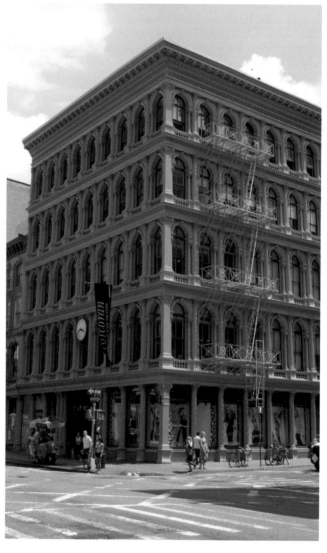

The Haughwout Building on the corner of Broome Street and Broadway may be the most important New York building you've never heard of. Constructed in 1857, just after the city's foray into structural cast iron (see page 292), its metal shell was nothing new, but being located on a corner meant not one but two heavy façades. Architect John P. Gaynor and iron maker Daniel Badger convinced the owner to ease the stress on the structure by letting the iron take some of the weight instead of hanging it on the brickwork, thus advancing New York architecture one step closer to the structural metal frame. But the building's real innovation lay not in the realm of brute pressure and forces, but human convenience. The Haughwout is the location of the world's first passenger elevator.

The story of how it came about illustrates a quality practically standard in your 19th-century entrepreneur: showmanship. The world had known elevators before the Haughwout went up, but no one trusted them. The fear was exploited in the brilliant shtick of Elisha Otis when he presented, at the 1853 Crystal Palace Exhibition, his game-changing product: the safety brake. Otis had himself hoisted on an elevator platform high above the murmuring crowd, then told an assistant to cut the cable. The platform dropped, the crowd gasped, the brake kicked in and the inventor, unharmed, jolted to a stop. Watching all this with a wise eye was china and glassware merchant E.V. Haughwout.

A showman in his own right, Haughwout made the elevator, now proven safe, a central feature of his dignified new cast-iron store on Broadway. He had a steam engine built in the basement to power the lift (which traveled all of five floors) and New Yorkers flocked to witness a changed world. A structural metal frame and an elevator: E.V. Haughwout, looking for the best way to sell more fancy plates, unknowingly wrote the recipe for the skyscraper.

Although you can still see the entrance on Broadway, the elevator is currently boarded up.

The 1853 Crystal Palace Exhibition was held where Bryant Park is today, under a great dome constructed entirely of iron and glass. The combination was hailed as fireproof – until a lumber room went up in flames and the whole thing burned down in about half an hour.

KEHILA KEDOSHA JANINA SYNAGOGUE

The only Romaniote synagogue in the Western Hemisphere

280 Broome Street
212-431-1619
kkjsm.org
Museum and Tour Inquiries: museum@kkjsm.org
B and D trains/Grand St; J train/Bowery; F train/Delancey

Of the hundreds of synagogues that used to fill the Lower East Side in the late 1800s and early 1900s, only five remain that still function as free-standing houses of worship. Of these one is rarer still: the Janina Synagogue on Broome Street. It's the only Romaniote synagogue in the Western Hemisphere.

If you don't know what a Romaniote Jew is, there are good reasons. A small group outside of the major factions in Judaism, the Ashkenazim (originally centered around Germany) and the Sephardim (Spain and Portugal), the Romaniotes settled in Greece, and have traditions that go back to Roman times. As a group they were sometimes marginalized even by other Jews – who might have known better – and in predominantly Ashkenazi New York they were even scorned. "They tended to look down on this community," says Marcia Ikonomopoulos, the Janina Museum director. "How could you be Jewish if you don't speak Yiddish? Well, we were. And we're still here."

Janina can be contrasted with the neighborhood's most regal house of worship, the Eldridge Street Synagogue. Eldridge offers a sweeping story that touches literally millions. By contrast, Janina's appeal is fine-grained. It's small. It's humble, even a little dowdy ("They were decoratively challenged," says Ikonomopoulos.) The main hall is divided, as is customary, with women seated above and men below, but the room is narrow and filled with sunlight pouring through the central skylight. "If a man was sitting over here," says Ikonomopoulos, "his wife would be up there opposite, and they could look upon each other. He could tell her to be quiet if she was talking with her friends, she'd be able to tell him to stop reading the newspaper. I like to define this community as less-neurotically-Orthodox."

For Ikonomopoulos, this understatement is key. Even the synagogue's principal Torah has a utilitarian simplicity: the decorative crown on the olive-wood case is a simple brass cutout with a Star of David punched into it with what might have been a nail. "They weren't looking to impress anybody," she says. "They were looking for a place where they could feel at home."

The Greek Romaniotes are the longest continuous Jewish presence in the European Diaspora: over 2,300 years.

HUA-MEI BIRD MEN
OF SARA D. ROOSEVELT PARK

⑥

A corner of the park, a thousand years of tradition

Chrystie Street at Broome
nycgovparks.org/parks/saradroosevelt
Birders meet fair weather mornings until late fall
F train/2nd Av; 4 and 6 trains/Spring St; J train/Bowery

I n the dark and exciting 1980s, Sara Delano Roosevelt Park in Chinatown was a grey, trashy place, full of drug dealers and nodding junkies. Then, slowly, a group of pioneering Chinese immigrants began claiming a section of turf for their incongruous hobby: the breeding and showing of songbirds. Now on any given morning you can see the bird men smoking or chatting, leaning on the rails as they watch over dozens of exotic birds in carved bamboo cages. The practice goes back a thousand years.

The birding area is closed off by a rope, from which tiny songbirds hang in small cages. Behind, on cobbles, stand larger cages: these contain dark yellow birds just under a foot long with bright beaks and amazing eyes. "That's the hua-mei," says Tommy Chan. "It's the main attraction bird." The hua-mei is a thrush native to China, where its song evokes romance, something like the nightingale's does in the West. Chan is a breeder and collector. He wears his long black hair in a ponytail, topped by a fur cap, and silver rings on his fingers; the wisps of his graying beard are tied off with a rubber band. He's the man you'd naturally, and accurately, finger for top bird man. "In Ming Dynasty," he says, "the famous poets, they are using the eye of this bird to describe a pretty lady. They say: 'how pretty your eyes are, like *hua-mei*.'" (In Chinese *hua-mei* means "painted brow.") "And if you're a good singer they say: 'you can sing like a *hua-mei*.'"

If one hua-mei singing is poetry, twenty or so together sounds like it would be hell. But strangely, it's not. The birds are very active, dodging, twisting, the more energetic clawing backflips along the inside of the cage. Some even twist their heads sideways to press their remarkable circled eyes to the bars to get a better look at you while they trill, or thrust their open beaks through the gaps around the door. Each hua-mei has a distinct song. "This is different from most birds," says Chan. "If you hear your own bird for a while, when it sings, you know it's yours." Asked if the bird he holds is one of his own, he blinks, and explains Rule Number One. "You never touch another man's bird."

THE SLAVE GALLERIES AT ST. AUGUSTINE'S

A pew for the hidden

333 Madison Street
staugnyc.org
Call to arrange tour: 212-673-5300
F train/East Broadway or Delancey St; J, M and Z trains/Essex St

St. Augustine's Church on Henry Street has pews on the ground floor, and a gallery overhead. In the back, above the upper seating on either side, there is yet another level tucked up behind a kind of open transom. These recessed spaces, original to the church's construction in 1828, have been called the slave galleries. They were designed to seat black churchgoers with the idea of making them as difficult to notice as possible.

A visit of St. Augustine's begins with a historical outline of the building and the area; everyone sits in the relative comfort of the lower pews, sunlight angling through the lancet windows and fans humming from the corners. Then things take a sensory turn: visitors are invited to file up the cramped stair at the back to the separate galleries, sit on the bare wooden platform seats, and try to grasp the feelings of the people who were made to accept this concealment as their natural due. "Just close your eyes for a moment," says Reverend Hopper, the church deacon, "and imagine." On this visit, the temperature in the gallery is well over 100 degrees: the visitors are sweating through their clothes. The view down to the lower levels of the church is framed by the transom, with only half the pulpit visible, but the effect is more than visual. The open area down there feels like another, distant dimension.

Deacon Hopper has worked with the Lower East Side Tenement Museum to restore the galleries. Every board and nail has been preserved, and the western side has been painted, based on expert analysis, to match how it looked 180 years ago. The term "slave gallery" is culturally correct, but this one raises questions. New York abolished slavery on July 4, 1799, according to a system of "gradual emancipation:" males born before that date would remain slaves until the age of 28, and females until 25. St. Augustine's was constructed a year after the last male slave was freed, but the existence of the galleries demonstrates that freedom can lag behind emancipation.

39-41 HENRY STREET

Figureheads and Green Men

4, 6, N, Q, J and Z trains/Canal St; B and D trains/Grand St;
F train/East Broadway

One of the major shifts in New York was the loss of any connection to harbor trade. The city's wealth was built on shipping, both on the Atlantic and the Hudson, and the first difference that jumps to the eye when you see photos of Manhattan in the 1800s is the forest of masts that crowd the waterfront. When the tenements of Henry Street on the Lower East Side were built in the first half of the 19th century, many of the tenants made a living from the sea, and at numbers 39 and 41 you can see an architectural detail that was made to attract them: decorative corbels flanking the front door, carved like buxom figureheads from a ship's prow.

The sailors and shipwrights who once swaggered in this neighborhood (caulkers, sawyers, axmen, carpenters, blacksmiths) brought their own rambunctious shorefront culture with them, and may have left an enduring print on the language. The term "hooker" probably originated here. *Bartlett's Dictionary of Americanisms* (1859) gives this definition: "a resident of the Hook, i.e. a strumpet, a sailor's trull. So called from the number of houses of ill-fame frequented by sailors at the Hook (i.e. Corlear's Hook) in the city of New York." Corlear's Hook is the nearby bump of land where the East River turns north.

Strumpets, sailors, ships, boatyards...19th-century Lower East Side was a loud, crowded, dirty, exciting place. The buildings on Henry Street teem with decorative flourishes, as if the liveliness of the period crawled into the very architecture. The figureheads at 39 and 41 are the least of it: walk from Montgomery to Catherine Street, and you'll see dragons, screaming monsters, screaming men, caryatids, festoons of fruit, acanthus, floral patterns, and eerie leafy faces.

Green Man

Leafy faces were a popular decorative element of the Gothic revival period, but their history goes back thousands of years to the forest-themed decorations of European pagans. The leafy face has countless variants, and a name – the Green Man. Look for him on the keystones above windows and arches.

DOYERS STREET TUNNEL

An escape passage from the "Bloody Angle"

Tunnel entrance at 5 Doyers Street; exit on Chatham Square
N, Q, R, J, Z, 4 and 6 trains/Canal St; B and D trains/Grand St; J and Z trains/
Chambers St

Chinatowners strike a fair pact with non-Chinese New Yorkers and tourists: you have the right to look around, and they have the right to pretend you're not there. The civilities of shop owners and waiters aside, the residents have always made a policy of keeping to themselves, and among the city's cultural perks can be listed climbing out of a Chinatown subway and immediately getting the buzz of being a foreigner. One street in particular has a romantic (and bloody) Chinese history that can be easily explored: crooked little Doyers Street.

Once the location of the first Chinese opera house in the United States, Doyers is best known for murder. The zigzag path – unique in Manhattan – is said to foil flying spirits, but the street's nickname, Bloody Angle, refers to its long career as Tong War gangland. Here there have been more violent deaths – by gun, hatchet, knife – than at any other crossing in the country. The wars broke out in the early 1900s, but adjacent Pell Street was the headquarters of the Hip Sing Tong until only twenty years ago, and the area still has an allure in a darker key than the hubbub and dim sum of Mott Street.

The feuding gangsters used a network of underground getaway tunnels. One tunnel has since been turned into a commercial space of fluorescents and tile, and while you can freely enter, you won't exactly feel welcome. There is a grab bag of activity down there: reflexology clinic, employment center, a workstation advertising marine crabs but filled with file cabinets. At one blinded office offering "Metaphysics," a partial woman answers the bell by peeking out – and then shakes her head and shuts the door again without a word.

The only person talking in the tunnel is the owner of a tombstone business. When asked if he sees many non-locals down here, he says, reasonably: "No. We cannot expect a tourist having a tombstone." The man knew the history of the place, and helpfully gave the translation of the word tong (organization, not necessarily criminal). "About a hundred years ago," he says, "a lot of Tong, when they commit crime, they just run away here. Get away from being caught." There are still other tunnels on Pell Street, he claims, "but they won't let you in there." And he was right.

America's other Pilgrims

55 St. James Place
shearithisrael.org; 1654society.org
J and Z trains/Chambers St; 4, 5 and 6 trains/Brooklyn Bridge – City Hall

This simple plot is not only the oldest colonial landmark in Manhattan, it's the oldest Jewish cemetery anywhere in the United States.

The first Jewish New Yorker on record is Jacob Barsimson, who arrived from Holland on the ship *Pereboom* (Pear Tree) with a mission that would resonate through the city's – and the nation's – history: to find out whether a larger Jewish population would be welcome in New Amsterdam. The short answer was yes; the long answer reflects the familiar pattern of harassment. Governor Stuyvesant (see page 108) wanted no part of the "deceitful business" of Jewish settlers, and clergyman Johannes Megapolensis delivered a rant that will bring a grin to the face of anyone who revels in New York's incurable variety. "For as we have here Papists, Mennonites and Lutherans among the Dutch;" he wrote, "also many Puritans or Independents, and many atheists and various other servants of Baal among the English, it would create a still greater confusion, if the obstinate and immovable Jews came to settle here."

They came; they stayed. Two months after Barsimson the first group arrived from Recife (now in Brazil) following a sequence of trials that read like a historical thriller: escape from the Inquisition-crazed Portuguese, a desperate dash for Europe, capture by Spanish pirates, and finally rescue by a French privateer. A group of wealthy Jewish merchants and their families arrived from Holland in 1655; in the same year the Dutch West Indian Company granted the new community the right to "reside and traffic" in the city. You can judge from the record how eager these pioneering Jews were to have their own cemetery: the first petition for one was refused on the grounds that nobody had died yet.

The very first Shearith Israel Cemetery dates from 1656; its exact location is unknown, but it was likely very near or on Chatham Square, a stone's throw from the second cemetery we can see today. For a spot so charged with history, it seems willfully unromantic now. A handful of grave markers, half of them illegible, behind a fence. Across the street is the Chinatown Martial Arts and Fitness Center; south are the baleful Chatham Green Apartments snaking along the square; north is a traffic cop on the corner of St. James Place and Oliver Street, wheeling her white gloves and shouting "Come on, pick it up! Pick it up people, let's *GO!*"

MMUSEUMM

Exhibits in an abandoned freight elevator

Cortlandt Alley between Franklin and White Streets
mmuseumm.com
Admission free
Private visit by appointment
N, Q, R, J and 6 trains/Canal St

Mmuseumm is an exhibition space, little more than 5 feet square, that occupies an abandoned freight elevator shaft in a downtown Manhattan alley. You can only enter on the weekend, but the steel doors come equipped with viewing ports and a number to call to learn about the odd objects that line the walls (all visible at once), making it the only 24-hour museum in the city.

"Welcome," says Alex Kalman, springing the padlock on the doors and sweeping his arm with self-mocking grandeur. The first thing to say about the tiny space is: it walks a narrow line of what constitutes "museumness." Trim design, white molding, rich velvet, etched brass plaques. There's even a "café" (a narrow electric espresso machine) and a "gift shop" (a foot-wide shelf with pencils printed with the tasteful Mmuseumm logo). Because the trappings are so finely observed, it's a challenge to figure out whether you're in a parody or not. Kalman comes clean: "We're absolutely playing with the idea of a museum," he says. But it's thoughtful play. Kalman founded the space with his business partners and friends since high school as another outlet for the ideas the trio explores at Red Bucket Films (the offices are around the corner on Broadway). "We're saying: Why can't we call this a museum? But at the same time trying to really respect the key ingredients."

All of this falls apart if the exhibits fail to intrigue, and that you'll decide for yourself. But expect objects with built-in riddles. Why is that plain brown shoe here? It's the one hurled at George W. Bush by an Iraqi reporter in 2008. Come also to see ornate soap carvings by gifted neo-Nazi zealots with eternities of free time in prison. Or probably the only collection of Disney-themed children's bulletproof backpacks. "No art for art's sake," says Kalman, stating a cardinal rule. "These have to be artifacts, things that have kind of passed through society as part of our nature. And it's up to us to look at society through them." Kalman, curious and good-humored, has created a testing ground for what we consider worth elevating. Mmuseumm isn't a comment on what an exhibition space should be, only on what it could be if he and his buddies ran it. Which, lucky for Cortlandt Alley, they do.

CORTLANDT ALLEY

Hollywood's New York alley

The alley starts on the south side of Canal between Broadway and Lafayette
4, 6, N, R, Q, J and Z trains/Canal St

Hollywood screenwriters have a constant need for slip zones in the city grid: alleys, preferably steamy, where they can dump their murdered bodies, stage knife-fights, and provide vulnerable women in high heels with the perfect echo chamber for gradually noticing, somehow without seeing the source, a follower's footsteps. If the movie is set in New York, this is a problem because New York has really only one suitable alley: Cortlandt Alley off Canal Street.

The problem is felt most keenly by location scouts like Nick Carr, who has become a spokesman for the trade through his blog scoutingny. com. "I try to stress to these directors in a polite way that New York is not a city of alleys," said Carr to the *Atlantic*. "Boston is a city of alleys. Philadelphia has alleys. I don't know anyone who uses the 'old alleyway shortcut' to go home. It doesn't exist here." If you don't live in the city, this isn't something you'll necessarily care about; if you do, you might not have noticed yet. To one degree or another we've all been fooled by the movies into believing that every downtown New York apartment has a fire escape over a trash bin, a steaming grate, a cat, and a bum. Hollywood makes it exist. "It's this self-perpetuating fictional version of New York that just kills me," said Carr.

So if you want to try your luck at being the victim of an authentic-feeling mugging (difficult since New York's violent crime plummeted), or just want to promote a West Coast film and television cliché, Cortlandt Alley is the place. It runs from Canal to Franklin Streets with a dogleg on the way: three brooding blocks of grime and graffiti and entire walls mazed with black fire escapes. It's where someone might look down indifferently while you're running from villains. Or hiding a gun. Or sleeping in the *New York Times*. Or overturning your co-star's goggle-eyed corpse.

In Cortlandt Alley you'll often see no-parking notices from the Mayor's Office of Film, Theatre, and Broadcasting to keep it clear for production companies.

HOLLOW SIDEWALKS

A transparent sidewalk

Greene Street at Canal Street
N and R trains/Canal St

On the east side of Greene Street where it starts at Canal, for decades there have hung notices alerting pedestrians and drivers to watch out for "hollow sidewalks." The handwritten signs are a little alarming, as though locals are in a fight with a menace that claws hungrily under the city crust. But hollow sidewalks are just a feature of the neighborhood architecture.

SoHo was once filled with genteel brick houses. The area began to fall out of favor with the city's wealthy in the mid-1800s when retail and wholesale businesses moved in and south of Houston gradually became a universal supply center: dry goods, glassware, fur, tobacco. A building type emerged to suit these forces, a kind of combination office, manufacturing and retail space. Builders split the difference between cheap and elegant through use of the hot new material, cast iron. A businessman would sit in his offices on the top floor while a hive of immigrant workers buzzed below, and at the same time on the street a colorful awning shaded tall display windows where the enterprise put its best face to the public. Below all this – below street level – is where hollow sidewalks come in.

Keep your eyes on the ground here and it won't be long before you notice a characteristic pattern: a metal lattice of hexagons with – where the whole thing isn't tarred or painted over – circlets of scarred glass. The technical term is "vault lights," and essentially what they are is a transparent sidewalk. The multi-use buildings include underground storage that extends all the way to the street; the circles of glass let the sunlight in. They're even cleverer than that: in some vault lights, the glass stem is angled at the bottom so light will be prismed into the basement's deeper and darker recesses.

One effect of vault lights is more fragile sidewalks; the notices are to keep heavy machinery off. It's not an empty precaution: sidewalks have caved in before. One of the uglier details of the 1911 fire at the Triangle Shirtwaist Factory – the third most lethal disaster in New York's history – was bodies falling from the burning building, and right through the ground to the basement. Another effect: Greene Street has no green. Hollow sidewalks are dirtless, and so treeless.

WAMPUM

The strange quasi-money of Native Americans

American Numismatic Society
75 Varick Street, floor 11
212-571-4470
numismatics.org
Admission: free permanent exhibition open to visitors, call ahead; special
permission required to see objects in the vault
1 and 2 trains/Canal St

The American Numismatic Society, perched eleven stories above Varick Street, houses the foremost currency collection in the country. "It's the most comprehensive," says fair-minded curator Robert W. Hoge, "but it's not the largest of any one given area." He then adds: "not necessarily."

Hoge, an intelligent man with glasses and graying hair, is soft-spoken in the manner of people who command more subtleties about their field than you have any hope of grasping in a short period. Among other specialties, he's the Society's expert on Native American currency, which falls in the shady area of quasi-money. Today he's willing to break out the Society's string of rare purple wampum.

Wampum beads were drilled from a variety of quahog clam which proliferates in Long Island Sound. From New England down to the Carolinas, the beads were used by Native Americans as a medium of exchange, strung together and woven into designs on belts. With enough wampum you could get what you wanted, but you can't really call it cash. "The Indians didn't have a concept of money," Hoge says. "But they did have a concept of status and honor and symbolism, so that's how the Europeans tacked onto it."

The colonial Dutch were the first to get it: they readily used wampum in their business with the natives. Peter Minuit, in his famous "purchase" of the island of Manhattan (see page 57), likely paid in wampum (along with cloth, kettles, tools) and the beads were common enough to warrant a wampum counterfeiting operation where the Dutch, in a feat of special depravity, used their advanced porcelain techniques to mimic the look and feel of polished clamshell.

Hoge walks along the thousands of flat metal drawers in the Society vault. The strangeness of quasi-money is illustrated by his personal favorite piece, a donut-shaped stone from the island of Yap. The stones can reach 12 feet in diameter, and when a particularly large one fell into the bay during transport, the Yap islanders still used it to make deals because everyone knew it was still down there.

"This is true wampum," Hoge says, shaking a string of beads from a small plastic bag. The beads are purple, about an inch long. "These are probably the finest ones you will ever see." And he holds his hand out, cradling a whole vanished and mysterious system in his palm.

THE SPRING STREET SALT SHED ⑮

A house for salt

336 Spring Street
1, 2, A, C and E trains to Canal Street

At Pier 34 on the west side, where the Holland Tunnel dives into Manhattan, passers-by have long wondered about the matching pairs of bare brick towers that rise several stories at the water's edge. They look important, but clearly weren't built for housing people: no balconies, few windows, no lights. The towers (one pair visible in the background of the photo) are in fact ventilation shafts for the unseen tunnel, but their status as reigning enigmas was recently demolished. In 2015 this giant block of brute concrete, faceted like a crystal, rose at the same location. Both old and new are humble infrastructure – but how far we've come. The towers are of warm brick with subtle detailing to satisfy the elegance demanded by the 1920s. The new building looks like it fell from Planet X. What is it?

A place to store salt. Around 5,000 tons, or a small mountain. When snow and ice hit Manhattan, sanitation trucks – "salt spreaders" – stock up here on their rounds. The volume and jutting angles are inspired by the structure of salt itself. Here the concept of form following function is taken to a literally granular level; the salt shed is a blown-up crystal. The building follows a manifest logic, but its beauty seems detached from comfort and emotion. This is a house for salt. It's looking out for salt. It does what salt wants. The side facing the river is taller than the other, and the walls slope out. Yes, this decreases the footprint to leave more room for pedestrians, but the slope is precisely calculated from the angle that a mountain of salt assumes when the crystals naturally stack on one another in repose. Again, the tiny grain is the determining factor.

The work of Dattner Architects and WXY Architecture & Urban Planning, the salt shed has bewitched architecture fans and won numerous awards. Richard Dattner stresses the hidden power in the humble (the next time you don't skid into a pole, thank the Sanitation Department) and seems to be just getting used to the idea that his building has become an object of wonder. "It's a form that is so abstract," he says, "Everybody can read their own meaning. I love hearing different interpretations."

DREAM HOUSE

Eternal buzz

275 Church Street, No. 3
917-972-3674
melafoundation.org
Thursday to Saturday 2pm–12am
Admission free
1 and 2 trains/Franklin St; 4, 6, A, C, E, N, R, Q, J and Z trains/Canal St

*D*ream House on Church Street delivers the most intense version of a certain kind of New York experience: entering a perfectly normal, even run-down building, and finding that it contains its own bizarre universe. Number 275 has been rented, for the last twenty years, by pioneer minimalist composer La Monte Young and his wife and collaborator Marian Zazeela. The main event is on the third floor, but you can feel it already on the stairs: a powerful, low-frequency hum that makes the very walls buzz.

"La Monte Young is considered the godfather of western minimalist music," says Rob Ward, who monitors the *Dream House* environment. He explains the history of the project: "The original idea was that you would have a place where musicians lived, and twenty-four hours a day there would be performance – always some music going on." This was attempted downtown, but limited by human endurance. Then Young discovered synthesizers and began realizing compositions that are virtually eternal. Since 1989, night and day, the building on Church Street has played a single sound – the buzz – composed of thirty-one sine waves, and while Ward talks calmly about it, the door leading to the environment – just a plain white residential door with two locks and a peephole – seems on the verge of shaking off its hinges. "In most western music you have horizontal motion, melody, whereas with this," Wards nods at the beast on the other side, "you're able to get inside the sound in a way that you can't in most normal traditional music."

All you need to do is remove your shoes, and walk through the door. The main room, the size of a large bedroom, has pillows arranged in a circle on white carpet, and spotlights above sear the walls with an acid bath of purple. The windows are completely covered with magenta gels, so the buildings on the other side of the street, while visible, are transformed into a dark, candied hellscape. But this is just dressing for the sonic assault that blasts from 6-foot-tall subwoofers in the corners. The sound is so intense it erases the skull: the *whoom-whoom-whoom* seems as much a part of your brain as the air outside it. As you move your head you can pick up different frequencies – earthquake, hair dryer, crickets – but it's all one thick, deep buzz that goes on, and on, and will never stop.

CRIMINAL COURT

For once, the real thing

100 Centre Street
646-386-4511
nycourts.gov/courts/nyc/criminal
Courts open at 9:30 am; criminal trials on weekdays, arraignments on weekends
4, 6, N, Q, J and Z trains/Canal St; 4, 5 and 6 trains/Brooklyn Bridge – City Hall

The Criminal Court Building is tall, and solid, and ominous. The street rumbles with underground trains as you look up at it, pigeons wheel endlessly in the air next to it, at the top is a simple, impregnable pyramid of stone. It truly looks like a place where the fate of New Yorkers is decided. Inside are twenty floors of court rooms where all the human drama of the justice system is neatly laid out. You're not only permitted to walk into and freely observe the trials – your right to do so is protected by the First Amendment.

With the number of New York court scenes that saturate film and television, finally seeing the real thing is a worthwhile activity. Still, you'd never mistake it for entertainment. On the tenth floor is the Clerk's Office, where on a dry-erase board are listed trials in progress, with the room, floor number, and crime. It's a menu of felonies. 59, 16, Assault. 22, 9, Drug Sale. 32, 13, Enterprise Corruption. With a list of trials, you might spend hours going from one polished corridor to another. The officers are courteous, even encouraging. "Attempted murder," says one. "Go right in, just turn your cell phone off."

The rooms are paneled in wood, with half a dozen pews on either side of a central aisle. Between an American flag and the flag of New York State sits the judge, and on the left are fourteen jurors in rows. Lawyers stand and ask questions in a voice that has been professionally scrubbed of all suggestive nuances. What comes out of the mouths of the defendants in the witness box, however, is as vivid as anything you'll ever hear.

"I was high as a kite." *What were you high on.* "I had marijuana, I had beer, I had dust." *And dust is* ... "Angel dust. PCP."

"I kind of fell asleep on the train, and then when I opened my eyes, I was in somebody's apartment, and there was a naked lady in there, yelling 'Don't hurt me, don't hurt me!' I still didn't really, like, register what had happened." *And were you convicted of rape that time.* "Yes, I was."

"I punched him and said 'What are you doing?' And then he threw a bottle at me. So I punched him again." *Did you punch him in the face.* "Yeah. Like this ..."

The man on the stand rises, and after tucking in his shirt, mimics holding someone by the neck, and driving his fist into the face, again and again, very exactly, as if a perfect recreation of the event will earn him some clemency.

Audrey Munson

Audrey Munson: even if you don't know the name, you've seen her. She was a model of a beauty so magnetic, she became the favorite of New York's prominent sculptors. In 1913, the *Sun* wrote: "One hundred artists claim that if the name of Miss Manhattan belongs to anyone in particular, it is the young woman with the laughing eyes, smooth, sleek hair and features that lend themselves to everything from the blessed damsel to a floating dancing girl." In all there are over a score of statues based on Munson in the city, and her fame outgrew it when she was chosen as the principal model of the 1915 Panama-Pacific International Exposition in San Francisco. Everywhere you looked, in murals and statues, was Audrey Munson. Her nickname was the American Venus.

It seems curious that a person who specialized in standing still – in doing nothing, in principle – would be so elevated. But how seriously Munson took her profession can be read in her ascetic advice to other young women wanting to take it up: no staying out late, no makeup, no strenuous exercise ("The swimmer or the dancer would be hopeless as a Grecian Goddess"), no false modesty. Study art until you understand it, or you'll never be able to inspire it. Be open. "You come into contact with cultured minds," she said of the studio, "able and willing to impart the spirit of the lands of music,

Municipal Building   Firemen's Memorial

art and literature." Whatever she did, it worked. "I know of no other model," said Daniel Chester French (see pages 53 and 299) "with the particular style that Miss Munson possesses...It is a great satisfaction to find so much grace and fineness of line combined."

But French also mentions "a certain ethereal atmosphere" and on the subject of ineffable allure Munson has no tips to give: it's something you have or you don't. The woman's effect on people – or at least artistic men – was almost eerie. She moved to New York City from Rochester with her single mother; one day when they were out shopping "a man kept following me and annoying me, not by anything he said but by looking at me." The man was Ralph Draper, a photographer. He excused himself and told Munson's mother that he had been tailing them because he longed to photograph the girl's face. This connection would start Munson's career. She was only 15.

Munson's later life seems equally guided by strange fate. In 1915 she became the first woman ever to appear nude in a film (*Inspiration*); in 1919 the lovesick (and crazy) owner of Munson's New York boarding house murdered his wife so he would be free to pursue her; in the early 20s she moved from New York, attempted suicide, and gradually became paranoid. She was committed to an asylum in 1931, where she lived out the rest of her life – an incredible sixty-five years in all – until dying at the age of 104.

Manhattan Bridge   *Plaza Hotel*

Houston to 14th

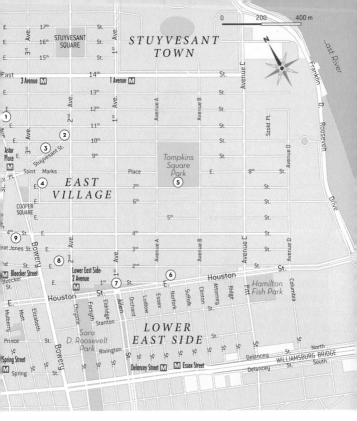

FACE OF ST. ANN'S ROMAN CATHOLIC CHURCH

①

A holy mayhem of new beginnings

12th Street between 3rd and 4th Avenues
N, Q, R, L, 4, 5 and 6 trains/Union Sq; N and R trains/8th St – NYU; 4, 5 and
6 trains/Astor Pl

On the south side of 12th Street stands the face of a noble old church. Just the face. It's all that's left of St. Ann's.

As mother of the Virgin Mary, St. Ann is a Catholic symbol for the shift between old and new. Throughout the history of this particular church the symbol has been stretched to a degree that verges on the delirious: St. Ann's is a holy mayhem of new beginnings. Try to keep up!

During the mass Irish immigration following the Great Famine (see page 28), there was urgent need for new Catholic houses of worship, especially below Union Square. St. Ann's began in 1852 on 8th Street: an impressive stone building that had been moved, block by block, from another location downtown. But the building wasn't Catholic, it was the Third Presbyterian. After reconstruction the church had been taken over by Episcopalians, then reclaimed by Presbyterians, then retaken over by Episcopalians, then offered to Swedenborgians, who in turn offered it to the Catholics, who rededicated it St. Ann's. That's the capper on seven "new beginnings" if you're counting. Protestants grumbled that the old place had fallen to the "Scarlet Lady of Rome," and Catholics didn't like the arrangement much either. Soon afterward St. Ann's moved to its current location – or the location of what's left of it.

The church builders laid the cornerstone on 12th Street in 1870. But instead of creating a whole new structure they followed the pattern of adopting the old: standing already at this location was the Twelfth Street Baptist Church, which, to make things especially confusing, had recently been converted into a synagogue for the Emanu-El Congregation. The front wall of that building survives in the shell of the present one. "It is an edifice," reads a guide printed on St. Ann's centennial in 1952, "that makes no sense without faith, and it is a church that faith will keep meaningful in the years that lie ahead." Or at least until 1983, when it became St. Ann's Armenian Catholic Cathedral, or 2004, when it was finally deconsecrated.

After the property was bought by NYU it was decided – perhaps out of pity – to keep part of the church where it was. The last new beginning of St. Ann's is as Gothic frontage to a towering university residence. The students, who rarely pause long enough to ponder the old stones, call it "the half-church."

A.T. STEWART'S BROKEN VAULT

His body was stolen

St. Mark's Church-in-the-Bowery
131 East 10th Street
212-674-6377
stmarksbowery.org
4 and 6 trains/Astor Pl; L train/3rd Av

At St. Mark's Church-in-the-Bowery there are flat stones arrayed in the ground: the covers of burial vaults. One of these lies in a privileged spot near the center of the East Side, but it's a shambles: there's no inscription and the stone is broken to pieces. On the map distributed by the church this plot is marked 9D, Alexander T. Stewart, with the titillating note: *His body was stolen.*

Dubbed the "inventor of the department store," A.T. Stewart was one of those charmed and driven New Yorkers who manage to strangle every advantage the city offers. The Belfast immigrant made his fortune in textiles; when he turned to luxury shopping he built a marble palace near City Hall that was so lovely the *Herald* wrote: "We hope Mr. Stewart doesn't mean to disfigure his beautiful edifice sacred to the mysteries of Dry Goods with a sign." Stewart didn't need a sign. That store was followed by an even more spectacular iron and glass emporium further uptown, and when he was buried in St. Mark's in 1876, Stewart's fortune was judged at $40 million – the equivalent of about $800 million today.

On a November night in 1878, Stewart's crypt was broken into, and his remains hauled out. It wasn't easy: the deft robbers had to get past the stone, unscrew a cedar chest, cut through a lead box, break a copper coffin, and stuff the dusty old millionaire in a sack – and all without waking the neighbors. There were no suspects.

When the bodysnatchers came forward (through a lawyer) they demanded $250,000 for the remains. During the next two years the executor haggled while Stewart's wife had ghoulish nightmares. Finally a relative of the widow met three masked men on a lonely country road in Westchester and traded $20,000 for a gunnysack. Inside were human bones and a piece of cloth lining from Stewart's casket. The bones – never proven to be Stewart's – now rest on Long Island.

You can still see Stewart's Marble Palace filling the entire block of Broadway between Reade and Chambers Streets. Five stories of Italianate elegance, it was America's first commercial establishment with a lavish exterior. Note the bronze clock bolted to the corner, a relic of the *Sun* (the newspaper's genial slogan "It shines for all" appears below the dial) which bought the palace in 1917. It's now known as the Sun Building.

STUYVESANT STREET

The only true east-west street in Manhattan

N and R trains/8th St – NYU; 4 and 6 trains/Astor Pl

Stuyvesant Street is the one true, compass-tested east-west street in Manhattan. New Netherland director Peter Stuyvesant, who despised disorder, would be pleased.

Stuyvesant is the closest thing New York has to a mythical founder. Sent here in 1647 by the Dutch West India Company to put the fear of business into the locals, he managed within a few years to convert the lower Manhattan landscape of hogs and mud into a profitable port town, with row houses, canals, a stockade wall, and a stone fort. He had only one leg – the other was pulped by a cannonball – and stumped about on a piratical peg, sword hanging at his side. Clues to the man's puritanical nature and the general tenor of New York life at the time are found in his first decrees: outlawing drinking on Sundays and knife fighting in public, and stiff fines for sex with Indians. His farm bordered much of today's Bowery (old Dutch *bouwerij* means "farm") and he and his family came to own virtually all of what we now call the East Village.

The street named after "Pegleg" Stuyvesant has an almost cosmic authority: it flouts the grid plan, making St. Mark's one of the only churches in Manhattan besides Trinity that command a street approach. The church stands on the site of the chapel of Stuyvesant's manor house, where the director lived after his surrender of New Amsterdam, thereafter called New York, to the English in 1664. Stung by how readily the city accepted English rule, Stuyvesant played out the rest of his life in the pastoral doldrums of what was then the city's far outskirts. He died in 1672.

By the early 1800s a small community called Bowery Village had formed around Stuyvesant's old manor. Petrus Stuyvesant III, the director's great-great-grandson, anticipated the grid by laying out a street system in the area that was faithful to the compass. When the Commissioners' Plan of 1811 was put into effect, magnetic north was discarded so avenues would follow the natural cant of the island: 29 degrees. Because Stuyvesant Street was by then heavily trafficked – and because you don't mess with the Stuyvesants – it was allowed to stay true.

NEARBY

You can see Stuyvesant's tomb at St. Mark's Church-in-the-Bowery, built into the east side of the foundation. The stone says he died at 80, but it's twenty years off: Stuyvesant was born in 1612. He was only 35 when he first terrorized New Amsterdam.

THE REWARD POSTER FOR JOHN WILKES BOOTH

$100,000 reward

McSorley's Old Ale House
15 East 7th Street
212-474-9148
mcsorleysoldalehouse.nyc
Monday to Saturday 11am–1am, Sunday 12pm–1am
6 train/Astor Place; N and R trains/8th St – NYU

A ccording to legend, nothing has been removed from the walls of McSorley's Old Ale House since 1910, when founder John McSorley died. It's an easy legend to believe. The bar, New York's oldest, is heaped with an attic's worth of beautiful junk. Even the dust is respected. "The health department made us clean them off last year," says the young lady behind the bar; she's nodding at an old gaslight fixture – the same one you can see in John Sloan paintings of the bar from the early 1900s – decorated with wishbones. Over her shoulder on the wall is a yellowed poster, a broadside of the sort that hasn't been used in a hundred years. "$100,000 REWARD," it reads, "THE MURDERER of our late beloved President, Abraham Lincoln, IS STILL AT LARGE." The date at the top: April 20, 1865, five days after the president was killed.

Broadside and alehouse both strengthen a remarkable connection between Lincoln and New York City. Rural simplicity was central to the president's appeal, but he didn't become a contender until this quality was thrown into relief in America's biggest and dirtiest city. In late February of 1860, a beardless Lincoln stood before a crowd at Cooper Union and delivered a soaring speech that would fix his destiny. "No man ever before," reported the *New-York Tribune*, "made such an impression on his first appeal to a New York audience." Afterward Cooper Union founder Peter Cooper escorted Lincoln across the street to the bar, then only a few years old. The chair Lincoln used, cemented in a pile of cobwebbed miscellany, is now also part of the permanent decor.

Five years after Lincoln raised a glass here, he was shot by John Wilkes Booth. Secretary of War Edwin Stanton relayed descriptions of the assassin and his accomplices, as well as the unprecedented reward, starting a breathless manhunt that lasted ten days. Is the McSorley's broadside authentic? It doesn't matter: the bar has character to burn. The poster is slightly different from other versions you'll see, but several were issued, and the text, spelling errors and all, exactly repeats the War Secretary's telegram. There's a broadside in the Ohio Historical Society that is so identical to the one in McSorley's it's fishy: even the wrinkles and ink smudges match. But if one is a copy, which one? At a bar that drinks this deeply from history, it's a fair question.

THE HARE KRISHNA TREE

Where the sect began

Tompkins Square Park
Dawn to 1 am
L train/1st Av

The Hare Krishna movement is based on 5,000-year-old Hindu scripture, but it started in the East Village. The founder, Srila Prabhupada (born Abhay Charan De in Calcutta), a scholar and translator of Vedanta texts, arrived in New York in 1965 as many do: with little money and big ideas. He rented a storefront at 26 Second Avenue and, relying mostly on charisma, immediately began gathering disciples for his spiritual revolution. The movement was incorporated in the summer of 1966 under the name International Society for Krishna Consciousness, and so a mystical tradition of "Would you like to buy some of our literature?" was born.

The American elm tree in Tompkins Square Park, already venerable in its own way (the elms here date back to the park's official founding in 1873), was the backdrop of the defining event of the Hare Krishna movement. On October 9, 1966, Swami Prabhupada, encircled by followers, led a collective chant of the Krishna mantra for the first time outside India. The mantra, of great antiquity, goes: *Hare Krishna, Hare Krishna, Krishna Krishna, Hare Hare, Hare Rama, Hare Rama, Rama Rama, Hare Hare.* Prabhupada called it "the sound representation of the Supreme Lord." The swami died in 1977, but the shop front on Second Avenue, now the Hare Krishna Temple, is still there.

Other notable trees in New York

New York City has several notable trees. An English elm in Washington Square Park nicknamed "The Hanging Tree" due to an (unfounded) reputation as a site of execution, was planted in 1770 – the oldest living thing in Manhattan. In 1936, on the centennial of the opening of Madison Avenue, a tree from former president James Madison's estate in Virginia was planted on the east side of Madison Square Park and lives there still. For years a legend has persisted (often in the mouths of Conservancy guides themselves) that a mulberry tree in the Shakespeare Garden of Central Park was a graft from one planted in Stratford-on-Avon by the Bard himself. Not only did the tree blow down in 2006, analysis determined that the Shakespeare business was balderdash. The pear tree that Peter Stuyvesant brought from Holland in 1647 stood on the corner of 13th Street and Third Avenue for 200 years before it was knocked down in a horse cart smash-up. A replacement pear tree, and a plaque, mark the spot now.

LENIN ON NORFOLK

Communism, New York style

178 Norfolk Street (Old address: Red Square, 250 East Houston Street)
F train/2nd Av

The bronze statue of Lenin, 18 feet tall, arm raised to salute the Workers of the World, crowns the roof of a luxury apartment building on Houston Street. The father of communism faces south, and as you gaze up at him, it's hard to overlook that within the scope of that confident salute teems the original hive of unchecked Kapital, Wall Street. In fact, a New York monument to Lenin pointing any direction but upside down is hard to reconcile. The statue, then, is some kind of joke.

Not quite. Lenin is a later addition to the building, which was constructed in 1988 when Houston Street fell on the fault line between gentrifying East Village and a much poorer Lower East Side. The 70s were hard on black and Puerto Rican communities here; with a hot real estate market in the 80s, the money marched in and the streets became a class war battleground. M&CO, the design firm that created the building's "identity," thought the name should have a touch of dread to attract those magical New York animals, "people with resources who wanted to live in a hip, extreme and even dangerous neighborhood." The name they settled on: Red Square. The Lenin statue, then, is nothing more than marketing savvy.

Not quite. The developer of Red Square, Michael Rosen, was once a NYU professor of radical sociology with a course called "Power and Politics." A guy like that knows from Lenin. Also, Rosen's post-Red Square activity – subsidized housing for the poor, persons with AIDS and battered women – is not the résumé of a cynic. The 18-foot statue, then, is more like the icing on a luxury apartment publicity stunt by a developer with an eye on a longer goal of social responsibility.

But where did it come from? In 1994, an associate of Rosen's found Lenin in the backyard of a dacha near Moscow. Originally commissioned by the Soviet state, it was hardly finished when communism went south. When you already have a quirky luxury building in Manhattan called Red Square, you snap your fingers at the shipping costs.

In 2016 the statue was moved just across from the Red Square to the roof of 178 Norfolk Street.

ROOF HOUSES

A home in the air

Corner of First Avenue and East 1st Street
F train/2nd Av

There are top dwellers in the city who take the idea of a penthouse a step further and actually build a house – that is, a nice little house like one you'd expect to see on the ground – on a roof. It's like a patch of suburbia in the shadow of a water tower. The highest are undetectable from the street, but you can see two low ones within walking distance of each other in the East Village, and one on a ten-story building on the Upper West Side.

The first, on the corner of East 13th Street and Third Avenue, is perched atop a famous address: the original home of Kiehl's apothecary ("Since 1851") and the site of Peter Stuyvesant's pear tree (see page 112). The elevated home, with its chimney and windows and clapboard siding, is a fake: according to *Time Out*, the "house" contains not an eccentric family, but only boiler rooms and roof-access stairwells.

The second (pictured) looks like it was lifted in a tornado from a whaling village up north and dropped on the corner of First Avenue and East 1st Street. Shingle siding, crawling ivy, an octagonal pilot house with a weathervane on top: it has the hallmarks of habitation. All that's missing is a bearded man in oilskin flaking scrimshaw on the taxis below. Whether or not the little house is currently tenanted is uncertain.

The third roof house is further uptown, on the top of 210 West 78th Street (best seen from Broadway and 77th). There's no doubt this one was built as a dwelling: in 1997 the *Times* interviewed the builder/dweller. Andrew Tesoro converted a tiny 400-square-foot penthouse into a three-story "ski chalet" with a copper roof pitched 60 degrees. His front porch drops ten floors straight down. "I love the view," Tesoro said, "because you feel like you're kind of on top, but you also feel like you're embraced by all of it."

Roof life

The Ansonia residence at 2109 Broadway used to have a farm on the roof, with a "small bear" available for parties. The Pan Am Building's helicopter service (midtown to JFK in 7 minutes) ran in 1977 until an accident killed five people. Both best and worst rooftop idea: the Empire State Building pinnacle was originally designed to serve as a zeppelin dock. A landing was only attempted once: no one had figured on the stiff winds.

NEW YORK MARBLE CEMETERY

A realm between realms

41 1/2 Second Avenue
marblecemetery.org
Open fourth Sundays, April to October from 12pm–4pm; check online schedule for off-season visits
4 and 6 trains/Bleecker St; F train/2nd Av

Two obscure cemeteries can be found only a couple of blocks from each other in the East Village. One is generally overlooked – the other might as well not exist. If you don't live next door or habitually pore over the city map, you'll be surprised to learn that in the middle of a block on Second Avenue you can walk through an iron gate, down a narrow passage, and emerge in a half-acre of emerald quad surrounded by old brick walls. Even the address, 411/2, suggests that the spot is a realm between realms.

The New York Marble Cemetery, incorporated in 1831, is the oldest non-sectarian burial ground in New York. The nearby and similarly named New York City Marble Cemetery on 2nd Street was founded later the same year. "It's totally confusing," admits Caroline DuBois, NYMC president. She parses the difference between the two. "We haven't had a burial here in seventy-five years. The other one has had one every single year. They're twice as large, twice as many families, and you can see them all. They haven't disappeared from memory. We really disappeared." She means not only disappeared from the map: she means you can't see a single gravestone. All of the bodies – a little over 2,000 – are in underground marble vaults. Six columns in twenty-six rows, 10 feet deep, but with roofs just inches under the grass. The cemetery's lawn is interrupted only by shrubs and trees; the names of the dead appear on plaques embedded in the brick walls. You'll find a former mayor of New York City, founders of New York University, and names associated with the city or written into the map: Varick, Scribner, Olmsted.

Today the cemetery can be visited, but only once a month, usually the fourth Sunday, and only during the summer. It's worth having to wait for a chance to stroll for a few minutes in this secret patch, which has been narrowly saved from a kind of double oblivion. "You should have seen it ten years ago," DuBois says, rolling her eyes. "It was a vacant lot full of dead cats." She rotates in place, pointing out the neighboring buildings: "This is a homeless shelter. That's a methadone clinic. That's a hotel. They come in at night through a hole that they punched through our wall. Used to be, when I came in to do any kind of event, the first thing I'd do is pick up the hypodermic needles and the whiskey bottles and the underpants."

MERCHANT'S HOUSE
AND THE GHOST
OF GERTRUDE TREDWELL

This damn stove was moving that day. You think I'm joking?

29 East 4th Street
212-777-1089 – merchantshouse.org
Wednesdays, Thursdays, Fridays, Saturdays and Sundays: guided tour on 12pm or free visit 1pm-5pm
4 and 6 trains/Bleecker St or Astor Pl

The thing about the Merchant's House is, it's haunted. The ladies in the office pretend to be coy about it, and the visiting high school kids pretend to be freaked out about it, and the very walls seem to suffer from performance anxiety. There's a booklet available in the office that describes what to expect if you're lucky enough to piss the ghost off: blasts of frigid air, disembodied footsteps, rattling chinaware. You might catch a whiff of violet toilet water or toasted bread. When the ghost's presence is visible, it manifests as a swinging chandelier, or floating orbs of light, or – the jackpot – a tiny old woman in a floral hoop dress with a stormy look in her eyes that says: *Get out.*

The creepy old woman is Gertrude Tredwell, and her connection to this place is so personal, so organic, as long as the house stands the ghost stories will go with it. The youngest child of a wealthy importer, Gertrude was born in a canopy bed in the front bedroom on the second floor and lived in the house her entire life. As the rest of the family died off and New York society migrated north, she became increasingly isolated. At the end she rarely opened the front door, stuffed the windows with newspaper to keep out the drafts, and let the furniture turn slowly pale with dust. Just shy of 93 years old, she died in 1933 – in the front bedroom, lying in the very same bed she was born in.

Construction of the building dates from the distant period when washing water was drawn from a nearby well; thanks to Gertrude's uninterrupted tenancy, today the Merchant's House is a historical bonanza. Everything here – furniture, carpets, draperies, glass, china, clothing – is original. The only changes made after the old woman's death were electrical wiring and plumbing, and the addition of a cast-iron stove in the kitchen.

This foreign stove is one of the things that pisses Gertrude off. Clarice, a Jamaican woman who has been caretaker here for twenty years, tells the story: "I was down alone in the kitchen, and the stove started to move. I got scared, and I run up the step here and waited outside for 40 minutes in my smock and slippers! This damn stove was *moving* that day. You think I'm joking?"

SYLVETTE

Monumental Picasso

Silver Towers/University Village
Between Bleecker and West Houston Streets at LaGuardia Place
B, D, F and M trains/Broadway – Lafayette St; 4 and 6 trains/Bleecker St

Large-scale Picasso sculpture is a small category. America's first was erected in Chicago's Daley Plaza; at 50 feet tall, it's not often missed. The second was dedicated only a year later in 1968 but concealed in the Village, at the center of three humorless thirty-story residential towers.

In truth it's only *almost* a Picasso: the master oversaw the project, but the concept and execution are the work of Norse artist Carl Nesjar. "I'm like the conductor of an orchestra," Nesjar said. "The composer gives me a piece of music and then it's up to me to see what I can do with it." Nesjar kept Picasso connected through drawings, photos, and samples of concrete. Cast first in black Norwegian basalt, the angular block was then coated in light-colored cement and sandblasted by Nesjar to create dark, permanent lines. The 30-ton sculpture rests on a hidden cement base ("Picasso doesn't like pedestals") to keep it from sinking into the underground parking garage directly beneath.

Picasso's trademark games of perspective are on display. The sculpture is a plane of two dimensions folded to create three, but is best experienced in four: the double-sided portrait invites you to circle around it, and as you do the woman's features change with the shifting vantage, creating a new portrait at every step. The original sculpture copied here was just a little over 2 feet tall; Picasso folded it from paper, then a sturdier version was cut from sheet metal and painted. Entitled *Sylvette*, the subject is Sylvette David, Picasso's muse during 1954. David was only 17 when Picasso first saw her; the smitten artist convinced her to pose as a model when he gave her a portrait drawn from memory. Later a painter in her own right, David is thought to have started the vogue, through Picasso's adoring portraits, of the high ponytail later worn by Brigitte Bardot.

Nesjar's 36-foot-tall *Sylvette* is hemmed in and shadowed by the buildings around it, which house NYU faculty and graduate students. On a warm afternoon the young son of residents warily eyes a group of rowdy kids on the lawn. When his mother asks him if the kids are "too big" to play with, he shrugs her off and spends the next 15 minutes alone, ringing a soccer ball from *Sylvette*'s monumental face.

TIME LANDSCAPE

A living recreation of past Manhattan

Corner of West Houston and LaGuardia Place
B, D, F and M trains/Broadway – Lafayette St; 4 and 6 trains/Bleecker St;
A, C and E trains/Spring St

There are three places in the city that specialize in getting the visitor closer to the vanished landscapes of New York before Europeans. One is wild (the primeval forest of the New York Botanical Garden, page 362); one is well-preserved (Inwood Hill Park, page 344); the third is artificial. *Time Landscape* on LaGuardia Place is part garden, part public art project. You might mistake the fenced trees for another of the several small decorative parks in the Village, but this spot has a hook: the plants within have been carefully selected as representatives of the Manhattan of half a millennium ago. It's a haven for the imagined past. As such, one of the goals is keeping you out: there are no benches, and no gates.

Bronx-born artist and designer Alan Sonfist conceived the project in 1965, very early days for the Land Art movement of the 60s and 70s. In his plan to create a patch of accurate ecology in the middle of the most man-made city on Earth, the first phase involved researching the botany and geology of untouched Manhattan marshland – the proto-Greenwich Village of sandy hills and streams, the one known to Lenape Indians. Sonfist then marshaled local residents to plant the wild grass, shrubs, flowers, and trees, evoking, according to the stated mission, "the hidden narrative of the Earth." The idea was to establish a foothold for a living recreation of the past: among the trees planted in 1978 were beech saplings that are today fully grown; the groundcover of wildflowers, aster and milkweed continues to flourish beneath them.

Time Landscape is too small for the visitor to project a wider Manhattan of virgin nature. It's an 80 by 40 foot rectangle that keeps to itself, crowded by asphalt, architecture, and constant ruckus. The work is like a zoo for plants: the trees grow in their artificial habitat, looking out on an environment they have no organic connection with. The visitor will be struck by an irony: recreating everything like it was took a lot of special work. If the *Time Landscape* has a point, this is it, and the pains taken to create and maintain it underline how completely that unspoiled landscape has been buried.

The Lenape Indians called Greenwich Village *Sapokanikan*, "tobacco fields," either because they grew tobacco here or saw the early Dutch do it. For more on tobacco, see page 364.

THE MEDALLIONS OF
THE AVENUE OF THE AMERICAS

An avenue for a hemisphere

6th Avenue from Canal to Washington Place
Several options, a good starting point is A, C and E trains to Spring Street

Y ou might have had this experience: you're waiting on the corner to cross Sixth Avenue and you look up to see that, for some reason, the country seal of Honduras hangs over your head. Or the seal of Cuba. Or Venezuela, or Grenada (which you weren't completely sure was a sovereign country), or Dominica (which you had scarcely heard of). Or even Canada, which seems frankly out of place. These medallions, bolted onto light posts, mark the whole lower part of the avenue. If you're still puzzled, know that you're not really on Sixth Avenue at all. Officially, you're on the Avenue of the Americas. In fact, for decades after it was named such in the 1940s, the words "Sixth Avenue" didn't appear on signs at all, until finally the Department of Transportation threw in the towel and put up both versions. The country medallions didn't help the idea of an Avenue of the Americas take hold. Here's the story:

"It was good, old, Sixth Avenue ever since that memorable day in 1811 when the city fathers changed the name from West Road." So begins a 1945 *Times* article. The tone is a little bitter – opposition to an Avenue of the Americas was widespread. The new name was confusing, awkward, and expensive – 1,700 subway cars would have to be remarked, for example – as well as an insult to the nations involved because so many of the buildings on Sixth Avenue were "eyesores."

Mayor Fiorello La Guardia, who signed the bill to make the change, left no room for argument, asserting that the idea had general approval ... "in this city, in this country, and in the entire hemisphere." What was the purpose? In short: business. The U.S. had goods to sell to Canada and Latin America, and recognized the need to be a buyer in return. It was thought that if the name came first, the trade would follow. In addition to consulates along the avenue, the Sixth Avenue Association envisaged a sort of open market for the entire hemisphere, with buildings "physically and psychologically designed for this purpose."

The medallions went up with the new aluminum lampposts in the 1950s.

IFC CENTER'S PEEPHOLES

Spyholes hidden in plain sight, redefining a sneak peak of a film

323 6th Avenue

On Greenwich Village's particularly New York corner of West 3rd and 6th Avenue, pedestrians can expect to watch a basketball game, a person eating a Papaya Dog and a street fight – but few realize they can also watch a picture free of charge. Though millions pass it annually, the peepholes on the side of art house movie theater IFC Center remain a well-kept secret hidden in plain sight.

To find them, face the cinema's entrance and walk to the right; next, carefully scan the space between posters for two metal circles, set within a larger metal circle, about five feet off the ground. Now, slide up the tops of the smaller circles and take a peek into them: You're watching what's playing in theater five. "It's something that we've never drawn attention to," the cinema's current general manager, Harris Dew, said of the structural delights. "It's just something that people discover or they don't."

The architectural Easter eggs are the creation of the cinema's designer, the late Larry Bogdanow, who had "a playful sense of humor and thought it would be a fun sort of secret surprise for people to stumble upon occasionally" Dew explained. They were built in 2009, when what was previously a ground-floor cafe was converted into two additional theaters for IFC, which Bogdanow designed in the hull of the old Waverly Theater when it closed after six decades in business back in 2001.

"The Waverly was a mess of a theater," Bogdanow said in a 2005 interview shortly after renovations finished and the tastefully designed IFC at last opened in the Waverly's place. Where the Waverly, once a respected cinema, fell from grace in its final years, IFC offered a carefully curated selection of art films on seats imported from France, elevated popcorn options and such endearing built-in quirks as the peepholes.

IFC has since become a New York institution in its own right, and the peepholes an enduring secret – like clockwork, every few years, there's another set of social media users who post videos and images of them, having just found out about their charming existence. "We do see these, sort of, waves of people, finding out about it," said Dew, adding that every time someone new discovers them "they think that they're the first person to ever realize it. But, you know, we don't disabuse people of that notion."

ANGEL IN ADORATION
AT JUDSON MEMORIAL CHURCH

The artist's mistress

55 Washington Square South
212-477-0351
judson.org
Call to arrange a visit, or come after 11am Sunday service; the window, in the arch directly above the entrance, is also visible from the street
A, C, E, B, D, F and M trains/West 4th St; N and R trains/8th St – NYU

The Judson Memorial Church offers a superior collection of stained glass by painter and decorator John LaFarge: 15-foot lancet windows depicting evangelists, saints and other religious figures in the artist's innovative "opalescent glass" style. One side window, an isolated tondo only 35 inches across, provides a view into LaFarge's private life. Called *Angel in Adoration*, the lovely figure there – wings, halo, hands crossed over her heart – has the face of Mary Whitney, LaFarge's mistress.

The artist and his mistress: LaFarge didn't invent it. You don't even have to go outside of Judson Memorial Church to strike on the theme: Augustus Saint-Gaudens, who drew the marble relief of the baptistery, took his sculpture models to bed, and Stanford White, one of the church's architects, was so fond of vulnerable young girls he's remembered by history as a kind of priapic demon. In fact if LaFarge stands out it's not for casual romance, but caring too much. When Whitney joined his atelier in 1880, the artist lost his head. "He was definitely goofy about her," says consultant Julie Sloan, overseer of the Judson Memorial stained-glass restoration in the 1990s. "He didn't go to Stanford White's girlie parties, he didn't have a lot of women on the side. His relationship with Whitney seems to be unique."

The two were lovers by 1892; LaFarge became increasingly estranged from his wife, with whom he had seven children. At the same time, Whitney's face starts appearing on LaFarge's angels. James Yarnall, the foremost LaFarge scholar, called the irony of using a mistress as the model for angels "colossal." In one image the artist even painted Whitney's face on a figure representing Chastity.

LaFarge was respected as an artist and art historian, but poor judgment largely defined his life. He destroyed his professional relationship with Louis Comfort Tiffany, colleagues took him to court for grand larceny, his own children refused to work for him, and he died with $13 in the bank. "He lacked the business sense," his son, who lacked the redundancy sense, later said.

> For the largest display of Mary Whitney-inspired faces and figures, see LaFarge's mural at the Church of the Ascension on 10th Street. "She's most of the angels," says Julie Sloan.

TRACKING MINETTA BROOK

An underground river flows through the Village

Around Washington Square Park
Steve Duncan's site: undercity.org
A, B, C, D, E, F and M trains/W 4 St; N and R trains/8 St – NYU

One of the most suggestive, eerie, and seemingly fictitious features of the Village is Minetta Brook, a river that flows secretly underground. There are tales of flooded restaurants, and men with fishing poles gathered around holes in the concrete floors of basements, and garden fountains tapping the black water deep below. But Minetta exists. It was once a creek full of trout; sometime in the early 1800s it got entombed by a blanket of humming metropolis.

Today you can follow the course of the buried stream as it flows from about Fifth Avenue and out to the Hudson River. With an ordinary flashlight you can even see it, but you'll need the tour plan of Steve Duncan, Internet personage and expert on all things subterranean. "From the tops of bridges to the depths of sewer tunnels," according to Duncan, "these explorations of the urban environment help me puzzle together the interconnected, multidimensional history and complexity of the great metropolises of the world." The hidden stream is the subject of his doctoral thesis. It's also very clearly his obsession: when he talks about it – gesturing with scuffed hands, a rolled cigarette wagging from his lip – you know you've found an authority. Here are the highlights of his recent tour of the Village's own hidden river.

45 West 12th Street

This house is a relic of the old stream course. It overlaps its neighbor oddly, and actually has a wedge-shaped floor plan. The creek used to cut a diagonal across the lot, and the structure was built to skirt it.

60 West 9th Street

The address doesn't interest us: what does is the manhole cover in the street out front. It's a DPW (Department of Public Works) type, with large holes. Look in one hole and shine a flashlight down another. The water you see, according to Duncan, is a combination of "natural water flow and water used by residents in the area." Minetta, in other words, has been channeled into the city's infrastructure.

Minetta Street

Here, as the name indicates, is deep in Brook territory. The kinked shape of this street (unique in Manhattan) is said to follow the path of the old water. If you hunt out the manhole cover – a DPW "hexagon" model like the one above – you'll see a steady flow, and be as close to the original stream as you can get without a crowbar and hip waders.

WASHINGTON'S MOTTO ON THE MEMORIAL ARCH

The ends justify the means?

Washington Square Park
nycgovparks.org/parks/washingtonsquarepark
A, C, E, B, D, F and M trains/West 4th St; N and R trains/8th St – NYU

The Memorial Arch in Washington Square is full of symbols. Some you'll find in other places in the city, for example the beavers and flour barrels on the shield of the New York City seal (see page 16) and the rising sun from the seal of New York State. On the north side of the arch, above the statues of Washington himself – one at war, the other at peace – appear the seal of the United States, and the coat of arms of the Washington family. Above both statues is carved the first president's motto: EXITUS ACTA PROBAT.

The meaning of this Latin phrase is routinely given as "The ends justify the means." In terms of moral clarity, it's roughly on par with "Kill 'em all and let God sort 'em out." The Washington family coat of arms dates back to the 1100s, but the motto was added by George Washington himself. What did he mean?

A Latinist at the Columbia University Classics Department offers some insight. Part of the problem is the modern notion of the word "justify." "When you say 'justify' in English," he says, "it immediately jumps in people's minds that the acts are bad but the outcome is good, whereas in Latin – when I think of how 'probo' is used – it doesn't necessarily have that connotation. It's more in the sense of 'commend' or 'approve of.'"

The phrase first appears in Ovid's *Heroides* (2.85), and in that context means something like "the outcome proved the wisdom of the action." As a motto it has been attributed to Machiavelli, and the Inquisition, and has been seen as an ethics briar patch since at least the 17th century. By the time it reached Washington, it had become a stock phrase, and in its best light likely had the meaning: "The goodness of the deed is reflected in the outcome." If you prefer a bloodier Washington, you'll like the alternative suggestion that the general actually embraced the quote's dark side, and by adopting it meant to say that the Revolution was a noble enough cause to justify the heap of corpses it would leave behind. That's the way with translations: sometimes what they translate is you.

Washington's coat of arms has another striking detail, one of national resonance. You can't see it in stone, but the three stars over two stripes are meant to be red and white. The motif is a primary candidate for the inspiration behind the American flag.

DE FOREST HOUSE

Unique in New York

7 East 10th Street
L, 4, 5 and 6 trains/Union Sq – 14th St; N and R trains/8th St – NYU

Even those who generally resent the word "picturesque" will allow that 10th Street in Greenwich Village has the quality, and lots of it. Variety, too. The authoritative *American Institute of Architects Guide to New York (AIA)* assigns half a dozen influences to the street: Neoclassical, Italianate, Gothic Revival, Venetian Gothic, Bavarian, Victorian. But this is just a warm-up for the alien excesses of the five-story house just east of Fifth Avenue. "Unique in New York," reads the AIA, "is the exotic, unpainted, and intricately carved teakwood bay window which adorns No. 7."

"Unique" is not easy to pull off in this town. If you're familiar with East Indian architecture, you'll know what you're looking at; if not, the house might as well have dropped from space. The balcony is made entirely of wood, and every surface is carved in delicate filigree. The decoration starts at the front door and swarms all over the jutting oriel, and continues further up, and even spreads as if through some animating charm to the adjacent building: vines and leaves and scales; moons, birds, elephants, flowers.

Lockwood de Forest, the man behind this marvel, was one of the founders of the prominent decorative arts firm Associated Artists (see page 278). His interest in East Indian carving was professional and personal. After a wedding trip to the subcontinent in 1873, the designer was so impressed with the arresting style, he set up a woodworking facility at Ahmedabad to create hand-carved pieces for the export market. In 1887, after buying Nos. 7 and 9 on 10th Street, he ordered simple brick architecture and outfitted it with this one-of-a-kind adornment. The building has since been divided into separate units, but when de Forest lived here, the inside matched the outside: wooden panels and screens, exotic furniture, colorful trim in red Agra sandstone and blue Damascus tile. The bronze patterned ceiling flickered with reflections.

One of the balcony's most impressive features has nothing to do with virtuoso artisans or the Orientalizing trends in late 1800s decorative arts – it's just something nature came up with. Although the balcony was carved well over a hundred years ago, the details are still crisp. Teakwood, incredibly tough, is also imbued with oils that protect it from pests and preserve it from the elements.

18 WEST 11TH STREET

The bomb factory of the Weather Underground

L train/6th Av; N, Q, R, L, 4, 5 and 6 trains/Union Sq

The townhouses on 11th Street from Nos. 14 to 24 resemble the other stately homes on the block, and are virtually identical to each other – with one conspicuous exception. No. 18 has a jutting wedge angling from its face, as if some force neatly spun part of the house clockwise. You might be thinking there's a tale here somewhere. There is.

In the spring of 1970, No. 18's owner James Wilkerson left on vacation to St. Kitts, unaware that his daughter Cathlyn would use the subbasement as a meeting house for the Weather Underground, a radical leftist organization born from student opposition to the Vietnam War. On March 6, Wilkerson and four other Weathermen were making bombs from nails and dynamite. Just before noon the bomb factory became a bomb, period. No. 18 blew up.

Wilkerson stumbled out of the flaming house naked: the blast had ripped her clothes clean off. Three other bomb makers were killed with such violence that a neighbor summoned later to identify them (Dustin Hoffman, strange to say) had trouble telling what body part he was looking at. The intended target of the bomb was probably Columbia University. When James Wilkerson was later asked if he ever talked to his daughter about her involvement, he reportedly said, "Never." He added: "And she never offered."

What do you do with a blown-up historic townhouse? Whatever you can get away with. The angular design that sets the house apart was drawn up by architect Hugh Hardy, who soon afterward sold the property to Norma and David Langworthy. The Langworthys had to fight the stuffy Landmarks Commission to let them go through with construction. "Hugh wanted to make a statement," says Norma, "that this was a new building, not an old building redone, and that's the way it was." No. 18 stands out for another reason: for the last thirty-two years, Norma has kept a Paddington bear doll in the front window and changes its costume according to the season and the weather. "It has nothing to do with the Weathermen," she says. "My husband is dead, bless his heart. But he loved bears. We have all kinds in the house."

After the explosion Cathlyn Wilkerson and fellow bomb maker Kathy Boudin disappeared for ten years. Wilkerson served a short prison term in 1980; Boudin, also found guilty of other crimes, wasn't released until 2003.

THE LAST GASLIGHT LAMPPOST (19)

A relic from the age of flame

Patchin Place
Off 10th Street, between Greenwich and 6th Avenues
A, C, E, B, D, F and M trains/West 4th St; 1, 2 and 3 trains/14th St;
L train/6th Av

Patchin Place, a tiny gated cul-de-sac off West 10th Street, has been forgotten by the forces of development. It looks more or less like it did 150 years ago. At the street's end, before a painted brick wall, you can find a living fossil: a black cast iron lamppost, complete with crossbar (for propping a ladder) and luminaire, and topped by a decorative eagle. It's an old gaslight lamp. There used to be tens of thousands just like it in New York City – now there's only one.

The evolution of street lighting in New York nicely mirrors the evolution of lighting technology. At the beginning the city's streets flickered with flame. In 1697, fed up with "the great Inconveniency" in the "Darke time of ye moon," the city council ordered residents on busy streets to put lamps in their windows. Oil-burning lamps on wooden posts were used from just before the Revolution, and gaslight followed half a century later. The cast-iron post of the sort you can see in Patchin Place – fluted 8-foot-tall base, octagonal luminaire – was introduced in the 1860s, and soon spread everywhere.

The reign of fire ended in 1880. Electricity has come to define the night: for us, it's the anemic orange of high-pressure sodium lamps. We have to reach back to contemporary accounts to relive the effect of electricity on those accustomed to flame. In 1883, British journalist W.E. Adams compared electric light on Broadway to the moon, to fairy light, to hoar frost. He noted the novelty of stark shadows of tree branches printed on the sidewalk. "The effect of the light in the square of the Empire City can scarcely be described," he wrote, "so weird and so beautiful it is."

Today the lone gaslight lamppost in Patchin Place is fitted with a fluorescent bulb: a cross of old and new. Modern replica lampposts of the same sort – also using electric bulbs – were planted in nearby Washington Square during the recent renovation. "It's so charming," one detractor sitting on the back of a bench said, pausing from rolling his cigarette to twiddle the scornful quotes in the air. "I'm here since I was born, and this place used to have character. Now look."

MARIE'S CRISIS

Piano bar for a Patriot

59 Grove Street
212-243-9323 – mariescrisiscafe.com
Piano bar open daily 5:30pm–3am
1 train/Christopher St – Sheridan Sq

There are no monuments to Thomas Paine in New York City, only a portion of Foley Square that no one calls, and likely never will, Thomas Paine Park. But you can visit where the great man lived his final days, and where he died. Take the 1 train to Christopher Street, turn on Grove, and follow the sound of singing.

Marie's Crisis is a small, ancient bar, where stage types, and anyone else who appreciates the proximity of booze and a piano, can holler along to Broadway and classic pop standards. The bar used to skew gay; now it has settled comfortably into the (considerable) overlap shared by the gay and musical theater scenes. Paine is not forgotten here: the bar's name nods to his Revolutionary War pamphlets (*The Crisis*; "Marie" comes from the original owner, Marie Dupont), and a bronze plaque on the wall outside bears his portrait and a quote: "The world is my country, all mankind are my brethren, and to do good is my religion." These are fine words to consider while friends and strangers sway in unison around a piano, shaking the floorboards with the chorus to "The Age of Aquarius."

Paine was born in England. He failed at several jobs, nearly went to debtor's prison, moved to America in his late thirties – and the light of destiny shined full. His *Common Sense* (1776) is generally considered the most influential pamphlet in the nation's history. Paine wrote that the principal goal was "to rescue man from tyranny and false systems." He was unafraid to group the clergy in the second category, as shown in a later work *The Age of Reason*, a damning analysis of the contradictions and illogic in the Bible. America wasn't ready to hear it. After being hailed as the voice of the people, Paine ended up begging around New York City: drunk, penniless, mistrusted by the government and abandoned by his friends. With the help of charity he moved to Greenwich Village – which really was a village at the time – and died there in 1809 at the age of 72. Only six people attended his funeral.

"Hey, Joe," says the waiter, shouting to be heard over Queen's "Bohemian Rhapsody," "do we know the spot where Thomas Paine actually died?" Joe, the bartender, glances up from his sudoku puzzle, and points both thumbs at his feet as if to say: "Right here." According to bar tradition, the area next to the cash register corresponds to the location of Paine's old rented room.

THE HESS SPITE TRIANGLE

New York City's smallest piece of private property

110 7th Avenue S

In the sidewalk on the corner of Seventh Avenue and Christopher Street is a 300-square-inch mosaic parcel widely considered to be New York City's smallest piece of private property, and also arguably its most slyly vindictive. The Hess Triangle elevates spite to an art form: The tiny, three-sided spit of sidewalk exists solely for the purpose of vengeance.

The origin story of this strange pavement plaque starts in the early 20th century, when the City of New York used eminent domain to claim and clear dozens of area buildings to make way for an extension of Seventh Avenue and the subway below it. Getting to Midtown from lower Manhattan is now significantly easier as a result, but building owners at the time were incensed that their private property was being ripped from their possession for the sake of a private IRT line.

Perhaps no one was as upset by this as the heirs of David Hess, owners of a five-story apartment house called "the Voorhis", which was located in the center of the land slated for destruction – they fought the city tooth and nail to save the address from demolition. Despite their attempts, City Hall was the victor, and by 1914 the Voorhis had been condemned – except for the plot's easternmost portion which, due to sloppy surveyor error, technically remained the property of the Hess estate. The city asked that the incensed heirs donate the uselessly tiny tract and allow it to become public sidewalk, but they refused. Instead, in July 1922, the heirs cemented the corner into local legend with the installation of a mosaic which reads "Property of the Hess Estate which has never been dedicated for public purposes."

Just over a decade later, in 1938, the Hess estate sold their triangle for $100 to the next-door cigar shop, which was purchased (along with the triangle) by Yeshiva University, and then 70 Christopher Realty Corporation. The triangle still lives on in the pavement, its tile now cracked but its message still clear; an old emblem of downtown's prevailing refusal to conform to either societal norms or the street grid. "The 100-year-old Hess Triangle could be said to represent everything about the Village's iconoclasm," says a Village Preservation executive director, calling it a "nearly century-old tribute to one quixotic effort to resist the march of time, and to the idiosyncratic street pattern which defines the Village."

PALAZZO CHUPI

A palazzo atop a former horse stable

360 West 11th Street
palazzochupi.com
1 and 2 trains/Christopher St – Sheridan Sq

Ask the average New Yorker to design their own apartment on a limitless budget, chances are they would come up with something a tenth as fantastic as Julian Schnabel's real digs in the West Village. People love it or hate it, but the Palazzo Chupi blazes with what hardly exists anywhere in the city: real, balls-out whimsy.

Schnabel, most recently famous for his Oscar-nominated direction of *The Diving Bell and the Butterfly*, and famous well before that for his painting and sculpture, can hardly be blamed for knowing what he likes. At the Palazzo Chupi he perched an oversized Venetian palazzo atop a former horse stable in the West Village and painted it radioactive scarlet. Then he filled the place with beautiful things: sculpted fireplaces, Moroccan tile, timbered ceilings, dozens of works of art, and a 40-foot basement pool. The singleness of aesthetic purpose has become a selling point. "Every element and detail in this extraordinary new building [was] created and designed by Mr. Schnabel," claims the realtor's promotional video. It's not just a place to live. It's a "residential work of art."

For many neighbors, it's something of a graphic nightmare. They hate the color, they hate the incongruity, they hate the name. "I have no idea what 'chupi' means," said Andrew Berman to the *Villager*, "unless it means 'big, ugly building that never should have been built.'" Berman is the director of the Greenwich Village Society for Historic Preservation, and his beef with Schnabel goes beyond personal: it's a matter of taste. "He's obviously trying to pretend that this looks somehow Florentine or Venetian, when, really, it looks like a Malibu Barbie house that exploded or something." If Berman strikes you as a man unaccustomed to getting exactly what he wants from life, he's one voice in a chorus: after construction began in 2005, demonstrators gathered outside the building site to protest. Schnabel, who currently lives in the palazzo, met the uproar with ego intact. "In principle, the protesters are right," he's quoted saying in *Vanity Fair*, "but they're wrong about me and this building."

WESTBETH RESIDENCE AT
THE OLD BELL LABORATORIES

A hive of artists in the West Village

55 Bethune Street
212-691-1500
westbeth.org
1 and 2 trains/Christopher St – Sheridan Sq; A, C, E and L trains/8th Av

Anyone who enjoys the romance of elevated trains should make a point of visiting the Westbeth Residence, where you get the startling sight of tracks going right through a building. This behemoth, occupying the entire block between West, Washington, Bank, and Bethune Streets, is actually a dozen interconnected structures; the offices that once quivered with every passing train belonged to Bell Laboratories, founded here in 1898. The lab had its fingers on every aspect of information and communications technology well into the 1960s, breaking ground in vacuum tubes, radio, both black and white and color television, the binary computer, radar – countless innovations.

When it closed shop as the largest industrial research facility in the world, Westbeth became the world's largest artists' residence. With funding from the J.M. Kaplan Fund and the National Endowment for the Arts, low- and middle-income artists and often their families moved into the hundreds of loft apartments at a rent that still remains a fraction of the market price for the neighborhood. In those early days, the West Village was a rough area. "It was hard to have your children out and feel safe," says Susan Binet, who has been here since the beginning. "It was full of derelicts, hookers … you know." Binet, a woman with grey hair and smart green eyes, brought up three children here. Originally an actor and dancer, she also got a nursing degree as a backup. Now she's on the Westbeth board of directors. "The thing about it is, we were all supposed to become successful and move on. And we didn't. We stayed." If you have ideas about staying here too, forget it: the waiting list, which was ten years long, officially closed in 2007.

Binet's daughter Lauren talks about Westbeth like an eccentric family member everyone loves. "People joke that it's an insane asylum because it's so easy to get lost. There's a dance studio on the roof, there's galleries where people show their art, music studios in the basement, pottery studios, printmaking studios – it's amazing."

Meanwhile, on street level, the Westbeth gallery is preparing one of its regular openings. Hanging on the walls are dozens of colorful still lifes of flowers, rendered with the genteel realism of yesteryear. The elderly painter inches her walker across the floor, nodding and smiling at well-wishers.

The Boss underground

14th St/8th Av subway station, stairway leading down to the L train platform

The "Moneybags" statue in the 14th Street-Eighth Avenue subway station is one part of a vast public art project, *Life Underground*, on permanent exhibition here since 2001. "Moneybags" caps the railing of a landing on the stair between the A-C-E and L lines, and if there's any foundation to local lore, rubbing the statue as you pass will make you lucky with money. Or at least put you in a frame of mind to make sound decisions about money. Or spice your poverty with ironic wish fulfillment. Or just embarrass you in front of your date. Whatever the reason, people do it: "Moneybags" is always buffed to a high shine.

Experiencing *Life Underground* for the first time can be the right kind of confusing. One minute you're scurrying along, just another subway rider with somewhere better to be, and the next you're surrounded by surreal, pudgy characters of bronze purposefully going about *their* business. Tom Otterness, the work's creator, has said that his subject is "the impossibility of life in New York." Impossible, but going on, day after day. There are dozens of vignettes: cops, cleaning ladies, families, businessmen, gentlemen, rogues, as well as inscrutable animals and mystery objects (top prize: a howling bell with a tongue for a clapper). Most compelling about the work is how unwanted the human viewer's attention seems to be here. The bronze figures don't try to teach us any lessons: they are far too absorbed in their own dramas of power, authority, and work to bother with us at all.

The exception is "Moneybags." He stands with his hands clasped behind his back, and appears to maintain a dreamy surveillance of the hustling throng. He's at once smug, menacing, vulnerable, lofty, and weirdly adorable. He also has an antecedent: the character is based on caricatures of corrupt Tammany leader William "Boss" Tweed by the brilliant cartoonist Thomas Nast. Tweed embezzled tens of millions of dollars in taxpayer money, and his public feud with Nast, who largely invented the American political cartoon, made for good copy in the 1870s.

THE "BRAINS"

From 14th to 42nd

7000 OAKS

The transformation of all life, on 22nd Street

22nd Street between 10th and 11th Avenues
A, C and E trains/23rd St

7000 Oaks by German artist Joseph Beuys is a collection of basalt pillars, each installed next to its own tree, lining a whole block of 22nd Street. The work is deliberately quiet, almost secretive. Beuys's goal in art, as far as it can be summarized, was to trigger a spiritual response in people, to remake the world as a great forest. He also took the long view: the trees were planted as saplings, but the artist thought they would create "a very strong visible result in 300 years."

The trees and their stones line both sides of the street. They weren't put there by Beuys himself: *7000 Oaks*, installed after his death, is an extension of a much more ambitious project of the same name in the town of Kassel, Germany. The first tree was planted there by the artist in 1982, the seven-thousandth by his son Wenzel five years later. Most of the trees are oaks, to which Beuys was particularly attracted ("it has always been a form of sculpture, a symbol for this planet") but there are also chestnut, gingko, ash, maple, walnut. Each tree received an enigmatic marker: a basalt column around 4 feet high. Basalt is born in volcanoes, and can spontaneously create columnar forms, sometimes with uncanny regularity like, Beuys said, "perfect, beautiful organ pipes." Each planting is an event that marks the transformational connections between ecology, society, and life in general. The tree grows; the stone, if it changes at all, can only grow smaller through weathering. The relationship between tree and marker is thus continually evolving, and it's the change that is the real subject of the work.

This is not necessarily a pitch that the Chelsea crowd finds readily audible. One of the more engaging aspects of *7000 Oaks* is how unframeable, how uncollectible, how unsellable it is. Dia Art Foundation, which financed the original project in Kassel, started installing this extension in 1988 on 22nd Street, where it keeps its main offices. Now the work is very much a part of the neighborhood. "You mean it's ... a thing?" says a smoking man in a delivery uniform, and he shrugs himself off the basalt marker as though it has become suddenly electric.

THE OLD NABISCO FACTORY

Birthplace of the Oreo cookie

75 Ninth Avenue
A, C and E trains/14th St; L train/8th Av

The large industrial building on Ninth Avenue that houses the Chelsea Market was once a factory. A hint to what kind of factory: in 2002, 15th Street at Ninth Avenue was officially named Oreo Way. The occasion was the 90th anniversary of the invention of America's most popular cookie.

The building was erected in 1898 to house the industrial bakeries of a conglomerate that went by the name National Biscuit Company – Nabisco for short. Their first hit was Barnum's Animal Crackers, but Oreos, invented in 1912, would practically take over the universe. Their unmatched success – over 490 billion cookies devoured so far – has been attributed to the "interactive food" feature. Everyone has their eating style, from the dunkers to the soakers, to the twisters, to the snappers, to those poorly understood freaks who rake the cream filling out with their teeth and throw the chocolate away. If you're curious, 490+ billion individual Oreos make for around 35 trillion calories, and many more if you figure in Double Stuff. It's enough to feed everyone in Norway for ten years, minus the vitamins.

Today Oreos are made all over the world, but until 1958, Ninth Avenue was the place. With a massive population and an unbeatable combination of manufacturing and distribution, New York City bred food innovations. Here are a few more.

Tootsie Roll

Poor Austrian native Leo Hirshfield began producing handmade candy in Brooklyn in the 1890s. He struck on the simple formula: chewy + chocolate = a lot of money, and named the candy after his daughter Clara, a.k.a. "Tootsie."

Häagen-Dazs ice cream

The thicker-than-average ice cream, dreamed up in the Bronx by Polish immigrants Reuben and Rose Mattus, is a masterpiece of branding. The name isn't Polish, or Danish, or Hungarian, or anything. It's gibberish: Reuben thought it up at the kitchen table.

Graham crackers

The recipe was perfected in New Jersey, but these "digestive biscuits" didn't take off until their inventor, Reverend Sylvester Graham, started serving them to residents of his Greenwich Street boarding house in Manhattan.

Jujubes

This candy, with a texture like cold tar, has been a boon to dentists since German immigrant Henry Heide began making it in New York in 1920. Heide also produced Jujyfruits, Red Hot Dollars, and 11 children.

THE REMAINS OF PIER 54

The would-be destination of the Titanic

Under Little Island at Pier 55 between 13th and 14th Street in Hudson River Park

Over 112 years after the most famous shipwreck in history, all that remains of the vessel's intended destination is tens of rotting wooden posts in the Meatpacking District.

On 10 April 1912, the RMS *Titanic* set sail from Southampton, England on its maiden voyage, bound for New York City's Pier 59. But of course, the purportedly "unsinkable" ship never did arrive, and only her lifeboats ever made it to Pier 59, dropped off there days late by the rescue vessel RMS *Carpathia*, which subsequently went south, bringing those spared the Atlantic's icy waters to Pier 54, where thousands warily waited to learn if their loved ones were among the living.

Once one of the numerous Chelsea Piers which lined Manhattan's west side, Pier 54 experienced more than its fair share of prominent wrecks: Three years after hosting the *Titanic* survivors' grievous homecoming, the ocean liner RMS *Lusitania* – briefly the biggest passenger ship on Earth – launched from Pier 54 on what would be her final trans-Atlantic crossing. From the pier, the *Lusitania* with almost 2,000 passengers sailed north to Liverpool, never getting past Ireland: On 7 May 1915, a German submarine torpedoed the vessel, sinking it, killing 1,195 of its passengers and becoming the cause of such public outcry that the incident was considered a significant reason the US entered World War I two years later.

Then, in the small hours of 6 May 1932, catastrophe came for the pier itself when a trash fire beneath it grew into a roaring inferno. It took 800 firemen to control the blaze, and by the time it was out, Pier 54 was no more. In time, it was rebuilt, and the decades passed. Then, decay set in. In 1991, Pier 54's crumbling superstructure was demolished; in 2015, its concrete slab went too, to make way for the public park Little Island.

Today, all that remains of the once grand pier is its steel archway, still emblazoned with the faded words "Cunard White Star," and, on the park's southern side, an array of mostly submerged wooden pilings, left to create a habitat for aquatic life. For those who happen to look down near the arch, a small round plaque offers a glimpse into the site's history, telling the story of the *Titanic* in brief beneath the words "The Unsinkable Ship."

THE PLAYERS

Where Hamlet lived and died

16 Gramercy Park South
theplayersnyc.org
Call ahead to schedule a tour: 212-475-6116
4, 6, N and R trains/23rd St; 4, 5, 6, N, Q, R and L trains/Union Sq

In Gramercy Park stands a bronze statue of Edwin Booth, New York's most famous Shakespearean. To see it, you have to know someone who has a key, or peer through the iron fence, or climb over – Gramercy is Manhattan's only private park. But there's a better way to get to know the actor: arrange a tour of The Players, the nearby gentlemen's club that Booth founded.

"In the 19th century if you thought Hamlet you thought Edwin Booth," says Players librarian Ray Wemmlinger, "and if you thought Edwin Booth you thought Hamlet." Today, of course, if you think Edwin Booth you think the brother of John Wilkes Booth, the man who murdered Abraham Lincoln (see page 110). This theatrical connection is one of the strangest aspects of the tragedy. John Wilkes was an actor, as were his brothers Junius and Edwin. The assassination took place in a theater, and after shooting the president John Wilkes jumped onto the stage and delivered what can only be called a line: "*Sic semper tyrannis!*" ("Thus always with tyrants.")

It's a mark of Edwin's fame that his career survived the crime of his crazed brother. Edwin was so respected, in fact, he raised the station of actors in general. "In 1888 Booth brought together a group of gentlemen," says Wemmlinger, "who were prominent not just in the theater but in a number of different professions. These fellows became the founders and the incorporators of The Players." So Booth helped lift the "rogues and vagabonds" stigma against actors, creating at the same time something like America's only museum of the theater. Downstairs at The Players are elegant drawing rooms; upstairs is the nation's best collection of 19th-century plays, journals, letters, prompt books, and cabinet photos. There is also the virtually untouched bedroom where Edwin Booth lived (and died). It's a trove of memorabilia: a sword used in *Macbeth*, a leather pouch from *The Merchant of Venice* – even the real human skull the actor used for Hamlet. "Anyone who's involved with the theater is extremely impressed by this room," Wemmlinger says, with understatement.

Booth had three Hamlet skulls, all real. The one at The Players once belonged – in the closest sense – to a convicted horse thief.

The Booth brothers only appeared on stage together once, in *Julius Caesar*. The performance was a fundraiser for the statue of Shakespeare in Central Park (see page 248).

APPELLATE COURT HOLOCAUST MEMORIAL

The gates of hell on Madison Square

Manhattan Appellate Courthouse
27 Madison Avenue
N and R trains/23rd St

Although it's 38 feet high and incised with sweeping flames, this memorial to the Holocaust on the west side of the Appellate Courthouse generally goes unnoticed. In many respects the camouflage is intentional; Harriet Feigenbaum, the memorial's creator, carefully chose a marble that would blend well with the architecture. Also, she thought her stark subject matter called not for broad symbolism, but hard, simple facts. This is a sculpture you need to get close to and read to understand.

The focus of the work is what Feigenbaum calls "a photograph interpreted in stone." While hunting in the photo collection in the main branch of the New York Public Library, she came across an aerial view of Auschwitz taken during an Allied bombing raid on August 25, 1944 – a full five months before Auschwitz was finally liberated. "I saw that photo," she says, "and immediately knew it was the one." She was struck by the cold precision there, the detached bird's-eye view of atrocity. The inscription to appear along with the sculpture had already been determined by the memorial committee: *Indifference to Injustice Is the Gate to Hell*. The photo stresses not so much the implicit injustice against the 11 million human beings killed in Nazi concentration camps as the consequences of failing to stop it. Feigenbaum spent six months in Italy refining her carving and selecting marble for the stone photograph and the tall column that rises above it. The theme is reinforced by the column's flames, which drift toward the courthouse – the seat of justice – threatening to engulf it.

The memorial was unveiled in May, 1990. It's interesting to note that a dozen years later former senator and 1972 presidential candidate George McGovern made a public statement about American failure to bomb the railroads and gas chambers of Auschwitz, the horrors of which the Allies had learned from escapees. The failure affected McGovern personally: he was an Air Force pilot during the war, and bombed targets only 5 miles from the camp. "God forgive us," he said, "for that tragic miscalculation."

METROPOLITAN LIFE TOWER

The Venice connection

1 Madison Avenue
N and R trains/23rd St

There is a persistent but overlooked connection between Manhattan and Venice, Italy. Both are island cities, where the streets are corridors and the tightly packed buildings expand upward rather than outward. Both Venice and Manhattan have a Guggenheim Museum and a Harry's Bar (called Harry Cipriani here, it is, according to the owner of both establishments, "almost an exact duplicate of the original"). Gondolas, piloted by gondoliers wearing straw hats and stripes, have always floated among the rowboats on the Lake of Central Park. Recently artist Julian Schnabel reinforced the theme when he suspended his bright pink palazzo in the middle of Greenwich Village (see page 146).

The most visible nod to Venice in New York City is the elegant Metropolitan Life Tower. Rising fifty stories above Madison Square, the tower was completed in 1909, when it became the tallest building in the world. This was still the dawn of skyscrapers; a *Times* article announcing the tower plan uses language that wobbles like a newborn fawn. "It will go more than 500 feet into the air," the writer promises, and have "offices in it, and elevators running up to the top."

Architects Napoleon Le Brun & Son sought design tips and inspiration in the world's existing towers; the one eventually chosen as the MetLife model was Venice's Campanile in St. Mark's Square. Also that city's tallest building, the Campanile lorded over the Venetian lagoon for hundreds of years before a spectacular collapse in 1902. Rebuilt over the next decade to exactly match the original, the Campanile now lords again. Here the twinning of New York and Venice becomes something more than symbolic: not only are the outline and proportions the same, construction of Venice's Campanile and its New York mimic took place at the same time.

But why reach into the musty past for engineering tips at all, especially from towers prone to collapse? "The problem for the architects in a building of this sort is harder than the engineering problem," the old *Times* article points out. "It is hard to make such a building, particularly if the base is square, look like anything but a big box on end." You can say that again. And again. And again.

THE ROSCOE CONKLING MONUMENT

The Great Blizzard of 1888

Madison Square Park, south end
nycgovparks.org
N and R trains/23rd St

The southernmost monument in Madison Square Park is the model of simplicity: a bronze gentleman, making a vague gesture with his right arm, and ROSCOE CONKLING chiseled in the stone under him. The name might be unfamiliar. U.S. congressman and senator Conkling led the Republican Party during the Grant presidency, but today he's less often remembered for his accomplishments in life than the freak circumstances of his death. Conkling battled the Great Blizzard of 1888, and lost.

The blizzard is the most famous in American history. During the night of Sunday, March 11, a cold front swept over the rainy city; the rain became sleet and then gales of snow that shook buildings and shattered windows. By Monday morning all trains in and out of New York had stopped. Roscoe Conkling left his home on 29th Street and, like on any other weekday, headed downtown to his Wall Street office. The weather went from fierce to berserk: "It seemed as if a million devils were loose in the air," reported the *Herald*. Pedestrians were blown down flat and tossed against buildings; the wind, according to the *Sun*, "rose and fell and corkscrewed and zigzagged and played merry havoc with everything it could swing or batter or bang or carry away." In some places the snowdrifts were 30 feet deep.

These were the conditions when 58-year-old Conkling, who had sat alone in his office all day, finally buttoned his coat and headed back uptown. His goal was the New York Club on 25th Street; the politician trudged the howling streets to Union Square, where he became suddenly blinded and disoriented. It took him an hour to locate north and forge a path through the snow, finally arriving at the threshold of the club – where he promptly fell flat. Conkling never recovered, and died of pneumonia a month later.

Friends put up the money for this statue by John Quincy Adams Ward. The proposed site was Union Square, but park commissioners thought Madison was more appropriate. The simple monument has stood here since 1893.

NEARBY

Worth Square, the wedge between Broadway and Fifth Avenue, is marked by an obelisk to General William J. Worth. It's a rare case of a New York monument that also serves as a gravestone: Worth is not only memorialized here: he is here.

GRAND LODGE
OF THE FREEMASONS

A very open secret society

71 West 23rd Street
212-337-6647
nymasons.org
Free public tours Monday to Saturday 10:30am–2:15pm
F and M trains/23rd St; N and R trains/East 23rd St – Broadway

The Grand Lodge of New York was once the largest Freemason lodge in the world. Founded in 1782 (although Freemasonry in colonial America goes back further), its current location is, very surprisingly, a nineteen-story building on busy 23rd Street.

So many important figures have been Freemasons, the group has a hazy and sinister reputation for world domination. This makes them inclined to be more accommodating than most institutions. On the 14th floor there's the Masonic library. Along with a maquette of King Solomon's Temple (central to lodge ceremonies) and busts and portraits of prominent Masons (fourteen U.S. presidents, including George Washington), the library features an elaborate facsimile of the *Processus Contra Templarios*, a record of the fourteenth-century Vatican trial against the Knights Templar. There's no proof of a connection between these Knights and the Freemasons but, says director Thomas Savini, "We have the trial here because so many people think there is." It's like an exhibit on the finger of god in a museum of natural history. Savini is smart enough not to let the crazies bug him. "We get all kinds," he says. "We get people who think we're trying to take over the world and want to know where the treasure is. As long as they're careful with the books and respectful of our house rules, they're welcome to come in." The library is a powerful resource: over 60,000 books, one of the largest collections of Freemasonry material in the world.

To form an even more complete idea of New York Masons, visit the lodges on the lower floors. The tour is very – some might say suspiciously – open to the public. Within minutes of escaping the rush of 23rd Street you can be in one of the high-ceilinged, plush ceremonial halls – the Ionic Room, the Renaissance Room – listening to the guide's corny jokes. The halls, redecorated in the 1980s, emit a sumptuousness that is a little generic, but partly because except for the period details they're all exactly the same. The underlying theme seems to be "Freemasons Are Not Threatening In Any Way!" Most of the doors are open to you, but this will do less to reassure a certain type of visitor than convince him that the closed ones conceal darker halls stained with sacrificial blood.

STONE FOXES
AND THE FUR TRADE

Guards, off duty

242 West 30th Street
1 train to 28th Street

July 27, 1933: three men entered 242 West 30th Street, took the passenger elevator to the tenth floor, made their way to the offices, and pulled out guns. They herded the bookkeeper and owners into a large factory space, where a dozen workers were cutting fox pelts. Two of the men tied the employees up while a third, who "appeared to understand fur values," crammed the choicest pieces into cardboard boxes. The thieves took the freight elevator down and made off with $15,000 worth of furs.

November 21, 1935: two loan sharks, Samuel Mintz and Maxwell "Kitty" Nathan, were convicted of operating a lending business without a license. They targeted the fur trade and they were good at it, depositing up to $100,000 a month. The two proved difficult to prosecute because Mintz was popular among furriers. One, Joseph Fund, admitted to taking out three $100 loans at 5 per cent interest; he worked at the Knickerbocker Fur Company, located at 242 West 30th Street.

February 22 1936: a woman walking down West 30th Street was passing number 242 when she was nearly killed by a large object smashing next to her on the curb. The object was Andrew Turkchensky, 39, who "either fell or jumped six stories to his death." He was a fur cutter and worked in the building.

December 31, 1936: the offices of furriers Cutler & Ostrowsky on the sixth floor of 242 were having a New Year's Eve party. Four bandits broke in, locked the celebrating workers in a stockroom before ransacking the show floor for "mink coats and a large number of Persian lamb skins" valued at more than $10,000.

You're becoming aware of a theme. In the span of a couple of years, all these dramatic stories occurred at the same building; all were reported in the *New York Times*. Bandits, tragedies, accidents, mobsters, gunmen: it's just a glimpse of the roaring fur trade that defined the neighborhood in the 1920s and 1930s.

Constructed in 1927, 242 West 30th is decorated by two very serious and emblematic stone foxes, a tribute to the countless animals that were exploited here for their skins. The foxes made, as you may have noticed, lousy guards.

For another, weirder architectural relic of the fur trade, try one block south at 214 West 29th, where stone gnomes fondle squirrels and pelts with a longing that borders on pornographic.

THE EAGLES OF OLD PENN STATION

One entered the city like a god

7th Avenue at West 33rd and West 31st Streets
1, 2 and 3 trains/34th St – Penn Station

Two stone eagles stand on Seventh Avenue in front of Penn Station, one at 33rd Street and the other at 31st. Nearly 6,000 pounds of solid marble each, they claw their granite plinths with chest out and wings up, staring puzzledly at the passing traffic. If the eagles seem a little off, it's because although they're in roughly the right place, they're in the wrong time. Once part of the imperial façade of the beloved old Penn Station, the birds are now grounded in front of the despised new one, and their presence feels more like an insult than a tribute.

Architects and historians talk about the original Penn Station like they would about a murdered relative. "How tragic, how sad," said historian David McCullough in the documentary *New York*, "that so many Americans will never know what it was like to arrive in New York for the first time in your life at Penn Station." The waiting hall was the largest indoor space in the city, with coffered vaults and Corinthian columns modeled after the Caracalla baths of ancient Rome. Outside rose a perimeter colonnade 35 feet high; there were entrances on all four sides – a first for railway stations – and above each hung a great clock wreathed in stone and flanked by allegorical figures of Night and Day. When it was finished in 1910, architects McKim Mead & White thought they'd built a metropolitan temple for the ages.

The old Penn stood for only fifty-three years. Jets and highways spelled the end of the train era; in 1962 the Pennsylvania Railroad, weary of operating costs, announced plans to raze the Beaux-Arts treasure and replace it with Madison Square Garden, which on its best day looks like a Soviet uranium enrichment facility. The rail system was damned to a subterranean maze at the same location. Yale University professor Vincent Scully summed it up: "One entered the city like a god; one scuttles in now like a rat."

It took workmen more than three years to smash up the acres of carved granite and travertine. Sculptor Adolph Weinman's stonework – capitals, angels, allegories – was piled into a swamp in New Jersey. The eagles that stare at Seventh Avenue today bear no plaque to explain their past, and canvassing the Penn Station area reveals that practically none of the security guards, hotel clerks, office workers, friendly drunks, ticket sellers or ticket scalpers have ever noticed them.

HERALD SQUARE CLOCK ⑪

Minerva, goddess of wisdom, presides

Intersection of 6th Avenue, 34th Street and Broadway
B, D, F and M trains/34th St – Herald Sq; 1, 2 and 3 trains/34th St – Penn Station

For decades triangular Herald Square has been one of the most swarming intersections in Manhattan. Saks and Macy's ("The World's Largest Store") made it the city's richest retail center; today few shoppers or tourists ever stand still long enough to appreciate a reminder of its earlier days as a newspaper headquarters: the ringing of the mechanical clock. Clocks that entertain are rare in New York City; mechanical clocks at street level are rare anywhere. And with reason: when the bronze hammers swing at the bell, pigeons scatter and conversations stop.

The clock was never meant to be so low: it once commanded the square from atop the *New York Herald* newspaper building. The muscular bronze blacksmiths (just theater: the bell is clapped by a separate mechanism) have names: Stuff and Guff. Behind them stands the goddess Minerva, outfitted with a shield and spear as though gearing up for a bloody run on Macy's; her pet owl Glaucus (see page 298) perches on the bell's apex. Minerva generally symbolizes wisdom, but that's not the first quality historians generally apply to the *Herald*. "Cunning" is a better fit. The paper, founded by James Gordon Bennett in 1835, was low-brow and vivid: Bennett claimed a newspaper's job is to "startle" the reader. If success is measured in sales, he was right: in the mid-1800s the *Herald* was the most-read rag in the United States and perhaps the world.

The Herald Square clock rang from the newspaper building from 1895 to 1921. In 1940 it was situated where it stands today as part of a beautification effort following the demolition of the elevated train. "Sixth Avenue has been redeemed from the blackening and rumbling bondage of the elevated," reads a triumphal *Times* article announcing the new arrangement. "Minerva, goddess of wisdom, who presides over the clock, is to return to Herald Square."

You'll find more owls perched around the square. Two, on either side of the clock top-piece, have eyes that spook and surprise passers-by: at seemingly random moments, they glow bright green.

The clock is also a memorial to James Gordon Bennett himself. His more principled rival, *Tribune* editor Horace Greeley, has done better: there are two Greeley statues in the city, one in Greeley Square just south of the clock and another at City Hall.

URBAN FOSSILS

Ancient beasts in the walls

New York City is a prime spot for fossils. The Museum of Natural History has one of the largest collections on the planet. If the wild calls, you can pick up your own fossil in the hurricane debris of the city's beaches. There is a third, perfectly metropolitan way to connect with the deepest kind of history: hunting for the long-dead animals frozen in

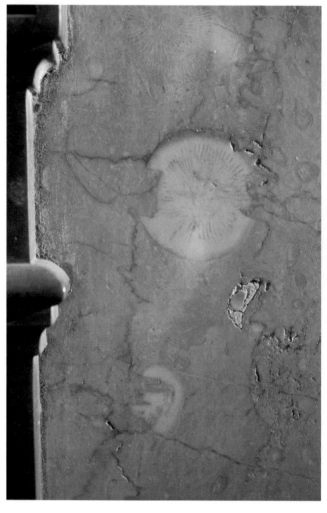

the quarried stone of buildings. Nobody had these accidental exhibits in mind during construction. It gives architectural fossils a special appeal: the building is just a public surface until you arrive, with your squint and your curiosity, and make it a museum.

Macy's

The pillars of the lower floor are dressed with a stone similar to the one opposite; the best fossils are in the handbag department. The impressionable lady next to you is thinking about dropping a thousand perfectly good dollars on a Louis Vuitton; you are examining sea creatures that lived before the earth had land animals, or leaves, or insects.

Tiffany's

The red limestone that surrounds the display windows is full of ancient sea lilies, plant-like animals related to the starfish. Studying architectural rock brings home how the city has collected material from all over the globe: this stone formed around 100 million years ago, in what would become Spain.

Saks Fifth Avenue

The stone of the cornices has the toothsome name "Ste. Genevieve golden vein marble" but it comes from Missouri. It's dotted with Devonian corals (pictured) that lived 360 million years ago.

Rockefeller Center

Perhaps the most surprising display of fossils. The dun Indiana limestone that faces the entire surface of the towering G.E. Building, as well as every other building in the complex, has been kept appealingly rough: you can still see the drag and blade marks from the quarry. At two paces, it's just rock. Lean in and you'll discover a fine tapestry composed of the remains of tiny creatures: hundreds of different species that settled at the bottom of a tropical sea that once covered the Midwest. (The same rock faces the Empire State Building and the Metropolitan Museum of Art.)

Base of Cleopatra's Needle, Central Park

American Museum of Natural History geologist Sidney Horenstein, whose fascinating work is the basis of this entry, has called the white limestone under the Egyptian obelisk "solid fossil." Every bit of it is shot through with the disk shells of nummulites (the name comes from the Latin for "coin"). There's a thematic connection: it's the same stuff the pyramids at Giza are made from.

DAILY NEWS BUILDING LOBBY

A 4,000-pound globe at the center of the world

220 East 42nd Street
4, 5, 6, 7 and S trains/Grand Central – 42nd St

The great Art Deco buildings in the city have a heroic quality that's been missing ever since. Rockefeller Center, the Empire State, the Chrysler. They have what you might call unembarrassed grandeur. Add to this list a structure that is less visited, but features an attraction that resonates with the 1930's mindset: the Daily News Building and the titanic 4,000-pound globe in its lobby.

The globe is sunk into the floor, and lit dramatically from below through tiers of frosted glass. The impression is one of quiet, unstrained power: if the glowing sphere turned out to provide a mysterious energy that permeates the entire building, you would not find this totally surprising. On the polished brass and terrazzo floor around it spread dark jags, like the wind bearings on an ancient compass rose; above rises a recessed canopy of angular black glass. The *Daily News* used this address as headquarters from 1929 to 1995, and counterbalancing the idealism is a sense of the hustle and nerve of a major international newspaper. In case the message was lost on anyone, set into the floor in brass are place names followed by a number: Johannesburg: 7988, Bermuda: 768 – the distances in miles from New York City, the center of the world. But also in the floor are facts meant to expand the mind: "If the Sun were the SIZE of this GLOBE," reads one, "the EARTH would be the Size of a WALNUT and Located at the Main Entrance to Grand Central Terminal."

In the same spirit of cosmic precision, the gigantic planet has been mounted, at untold extra hassle, to the proper tilt of the Earth. And it moves. Regularly, like a ticking clock, the whole ball revolves a few degrees on its axis. Vernon, the man behind the lobby desk, has worked next to the globe for decades but still seems a little in awe of it. "If you go all the way in, you'll see: that's hand-painted. They didn't fool around with all this other crazy stuff," waving his hand to impugn modernity in general. "Somebody actually *painted* that."

Superman's newspaper

Fans of Superman will recognize the Daily News Building as the setting for the Daily Planet, the newspaper of Clark Kent and Lois Lane in the Richard Donner film of 1978. The Daily Planet Building first appears in animations of the DC Comic in 1942; the inspiration may have been the globe-topped Paramount Building in Times Square.

MANHATTAN SOLSTICE

When the Solar System aligns with the grid

Visible on any cross street in the grid above 14th Street, usually on May 28 and July 12

When the Commissioners' Plan of 1811 laid the city grid system, the streets were made to follow Manhattan's natural axis. The island is tilted 29 degrees from plumb, a fact that often puzzles New Yorkers when, after a daily life of subway and city plans oriented to the geometry of the grid, they see Manhattan on a map where New York is no longer the center of the universe. It's one of the city's ironies that a street plan so rigidly defined by the cardinal directions is actually more than just a little off.

Twenty-two days on either side of the summer solstice (usually June 21), New Yorkers get an awesome reminder that Manhattan is just a spot on a spinning globe locked into orbit around a star. On these days the sun sets directly in line with the cross streets. The event has been given the name Manhattanhenge, hinting at ancient mysteries, but part of the beauty is a lack of design – or better, how neatly the Solar System seems to have annexed a design conceived for a different purpose. Every town on Earth has a sunset, and streets, but only New York is an island city made up of measured canyons and titanic buildings.

You can observe the event on any cross street, but it's most spectacular where the buildings are huge – 42nd Street has become the favorite. And you have to go to the extreme east side of the island to get the full effect of the sun threading the needle. Because it spans 42nd, the Tudor City Bridge is the only place you can get a clear view without dodging traffic.

By 8 o'clock, a small but dedicated crowd has gathered. "Here it goes," someone says, as the sun tracks from the left into the gleaming corridor, and the chink of sky ahead, already washed in orange, suddenly flames gold. The bridge chitters with the sound of cameras while the sun, strangely magnified, inches down the gap. Then it's gone: the sky fades to peach, grading into violet where it meets the airy silhouette of New Jersey. Down below a police car squawks at a ragged group squinting into the last flush of color: "Get out of the middle of the street!"

In winter Manhattanhenge occurs again, but flipped: evenly spaced on either side of the winter solstice (usually December 21), the sun rises at the eastern end of cross streets.

BRISTOL BASIN

While men love freedom

Waterside Plaza, Waterside
FDR Drive at 25th Street
Cross the pedestrian bridge over the drive then go up (left) to access the plaza
within the apartment complex
N, Q, R, W trains to 23rd St; 4 and 6 trains to 28th St; L train to 1st Av

There are spaces in the city that have a strong affinity with somewhere far away. A full wooden cottage built in Sweden has stood in Central Park since 1877. The Islamic Cultural Center on the Upper East Side is set at an angle to Manhattan's grid in order to face Mecca. In the Battery, the Irish Hunger Memorial (see page 28) has literally brought Ireland over – Irish plants and Irish rocks – to create a little patch of Eire in the Metropolis. On the other side of FDR Drive at 25th Street there's a whole apartment complex that sits on foreign land. The American Institute of Architects guide describes the place like this: "Brown towers of a cut and carved cubism mounted on a platform tucked in a notch of the East River." They don't say what the platform rests on. The answer: Bristol, England.

How this came about is a sad but impressive story. This part of the waterfront was in development during World War II. The ships going out, bursting with food and materiel to supply the British, were too light on the return voyage, so they were filled in England with the rubble of bombed cities for ballast. You can't see this rubble (the point of the Waterside Plaza was to perch a terrace right on the river), but there is a plaque dating from 1942, difficult to read, that tells the story with white-hot defiance.

"Beneath this East River Drive of the City of New York lie stones bricks and rubble from the bombed city of Bristol in England. Brought here in ballast from overseas, these fragments that once were homes shall testify while men love freedom to the resolution and fortitude of the people of Britain. They saw their homes struck down without warning. It was not their walls but their valor that kept them free."

From 42nd to 59th

ACTORS' CHAPEL, ST. MALACHY'S ①

Broadway's church

239 West 49th Street
212-489-1340
actorschapel.org
A, C, E, 1 and 2 trains/50th St; N, Q and R trains/49th St; B, D and E trains/
7th Av

Actors praying to make it on Broadway, or praying in general, might be glad to learn that New York has a place designed for that very thing. St. Malachy's on 49th Street – just a skip from half a dozen big-production theaters – has long been billed as the "Actors' Chapel."

St. Malachy wasn't an actor himself – or wasn't any more than your average 12th-century archbishop. The chapel dedicated to theater arts has its own space: interwoven wooden arches that frame a brightly lit recess, creating a kind of miniature stage. Five painted portraits hang there. On the left is Dina Bélanger, patron of concert pianists; before she became a nun, Bélanger was a student at New York's Conservatory of Music. Next to her hangs St. Cecilia, patron saint of music. To the right are St. Vitus, patron saint of dance, and Fra Angelico, an early-Renaissance painter with a special gift for religious themes. In the center of the chapel, looking rather small in his blocky gilt frame, hangs the star of the show: St. Genesius, patron saint of actors.

The story of Genesius is just weird enough to be true. He was a popular pagan actor during the reign of Roman Emperor Diocletian, who delighted in slaughtering Christians. The actor got to know early Christianity when he went undercover to research a role for a play mocking Christ and his followers. In the middle of a performance, as Diocletian himself sat in the audience, Genesius took method acting to its extreme when he made a spontaneous conversion. "As the words of baptism were spoken," according to the *National Catholic Register*, "and the water fell upon his head, the actor realized his faith." For this he received the harshest review of all time: torture and beheading.

This is all interesting, but what really makes St. Malachy's an actor's place is the schedule. Currently the church offers several masses on weekends to fit the odd work lives of Broadway people, including an 11 pm "Post-Theater" Saturday service for actors and stage hands coming out after curtain.

THE BRILL BUILDING

Tragic reversal in Times Square

1619 Broadway at 49th Street
1, 2, A and C trains/50th St; N, Q and R trains/49th St

The area of Times Square steeps in a constant, twitching bath of colorful light: that there might be fascinating buildings behind all that glow is at best an afterthought. In the relative dark of the area's upper end at Broadway and 49th, one unique structure deserves your attention: the Brill Building. It has the only Art Deco façade in the neighborhood, and an odd addition: over the entrance, and again even more imposingly ten stories above the street, you'll find large, lifelike portraits of a young man with a dead gaze. Anyone who's ever wondered why more buildings don't include monumental portraiture, here's your answer: it looks a little strange.

The young man is Alan E. Lefcourt, son of the building's developer. In fact it should be called the Alan E. Lefcourt Building, and the reason it isn't is a tale of tragic reversal. Alan's father Abraham Lefcourt started out as a shoeshine boy and worked his way up, in true metropolis fashion, to the top of a realty empire. He was devoted to his only son; on the boy's 13th birthday he gave him a Midtown skyscraper, and named this building on 49th after him. That name was soon going to be known throughout the world: drawn up in 1929 when Lefcourt was worth around $100 million, the Times Square building was, on paper, the tallest anywhere. Then in the space of a couple of years Lefcourt's boy died of anemia, the stock market crashed, the building got downscaled, investors filed lawsuits, the empire crumbled, and Lefcourt himself died, perhaps by his own hand. The brothers who leased the property foreclosed, and put their own name on it. The Brill Building would go on to be a pillar of the American music industry.

NEARBY
Big Apple Corner

Five blocks up Broadway on 54th Street, you can see perhaps the only memorial to a nickname. The intersection is officially called Big Apple Corner. The origin of the term "the Big Apple" as slang for New York City is a bit foggy, but it seems to be a product of 1930's black culture. Big Apple was the name of a popular Harlem jazz club; playing there meant being at the top of your game. The term was also used by African-American stable boys at the racetrack, where it was heard by sports columnist John FitzGerald, who then popularized it in the press. Big Apple Corner is near the hotel where FitzGerald lived and eventually died.

TIMES SQUARE SOUND SCULPTURE

"People are not that observant"

Southwest corner of 46th Street and Seventh Avenue, on the traffic island east of Broadway
1, 2, 3, 7, N, R, Q, S, W trains/42nd Street – Times Square; 1 train/50th Street; N, R and W trains/49th Street

It sounds like some kind of extraterrestrial," smiles John, gazing at his feet in puzzlement. John is from Ghana and he wears the red jacket of the street crew who sell tickets to the tour buses. Times Square is his beat and he works the same corner "every day, all day long." He cocks his head to lower his ear a little through the din of one of the world's most visited places. From the surrounding streets rumble cars and trucks, the ventilation ducts of the building on the other side of Broadway moans, and a thousand languages babble from the high tide of tourists. But at this moment only John is aware for the first time that from underfoot, at this precise point, a distinct but unearthly hum swells endlessly.

This sound sculpture – titled simply *Times Square* – is the work of artist Max Neuman, and it has sung here since 1977. Just what is singing is unclear. If you get on the ground and put your eye to the metal grate, all you see are dirty girders and the urban dandruff you'd expect: bits of paper, bottle caps, the odd coin. It seems the street itself is singing. The effect is something like a huge bell a few seconds after being struck. And while it doesn't change much, the sound is busy with layered tones; it has a vroom in it, like it's continually heading off somewhere.

"It sounds like chimes," says Guy, who a moment before was hustling over the traffic island with his head down, like any New Yorker obliged to cross Times Square. "It's cool that you could live in the city for a long time and still discover new parts of it. Like a treasure map." What is the sound saying? "Maybe that people are not that observant."

Or that everywhere is somewhere. This artwork plants a curious flag on a nondescript corner that teems with distraction. Noticing it reminds you, strikingly, of the presence of your own self, right here and now.

CHURCH OF ST. MARY THE VIRGIN

Impossible in Times Square

145 West 46th Street
212.869.5830
stmvirgin.org
N, Q, R, 7 and S trains/Times Sq

At some point you're going to find yourself in Times Square. It's inevitable. Before despairing at its unholy blend of human chaos, visual bullying, and the corporate leer, hop down 46th Street to the most surprising church in the city. Later, when you show the place to friends, amazement is nearly guaranteed. St. Mary the Virgin is a 19th-century Gothic church that, while handsome on the outside, is unbelievable within. How this dark cavern of architecture, lanced with amber light through the stained glass, can fit in the middle of the block is a riddle. "You got Rockefeller on one side," says Stefan, the custodian, "and you got Times Square on another, and all the theater around us. When they walk by here they go, 'Huh?'" aping a dumbfounded local. "Everybody's just amazed that there's this gem in the middle of everything."

For the full effect, enter from 47th Street, where the back door is just a limestone surround in a wall of yellow brick. Around you are a coffee shop, 24-hour parking, a diner, a Mediterranean restaurant, and the dull Mordor of the looming News Corporation headquarters building on Sixth Avenue. From the sidewalk you can feel the darkened church's currents of cool air and incense. Duck through the door, and within a dozen paces you're in front of a great pillar at the apse. If you marvel at how the tall nave can fit in here, continue on to the side chapels where the church pushes out further, and then further still to a degree that screws with most of what you know about physics.

There's an added attraction here. The building is, aside from surprising, also a pioneer (and a true New Yorker): St. Mary the Virgin is the first steel-frame church in the world. With luck, you might get a tour of the basement with friendly archivist Dick Leitsch. "They'd never built a church like this before, so they didn't know what kind of bracing they needed. Totally overkill," he chuckles, flipping a light switch to reveal a maze of supporting steel trusses. "No way this is ever going to fall down."

CHRISTIE'S AUCTIONS

The collector's world, open to the public

Christie's New York
20 Rockefeller Plaza
212.636.2000
christies.com/en/locations/new-york
B, D, F and M trains/47 – 50 Streets – Rockefeller Cntr

Christie's New York is a name familiar to most as a marketplace for everything fine and rare; the secret here is that the auctions are open to the public. Whether you're a high-rolling collector or not, there are good reasons to go. For one, the items on offer, which are generally interesting in themselves. For another, the people who hunt them, who desire and obsess over them – and ultimately fight to own them. Because Christie's is also a brush-up on the cold truths of how art and commerce are two sides of the same coin: here "priceless" gets defined by a convenient dollar value. What's destined for the block is first displayed in viewing rooms, with the projected worth on the title card. But you never know what something really costs until the dust clears. Check the calendar, choose an area that interests you – rare wines, Chinese ceramics, post-Impressionists – and enjoy the spectacle for what it is: part gallery, part boxing ring.

"Seventy-five thousand," says the auctioneer. "A rather incredible painting, to say the least! Seventy-five thousand," he repeats, "And now seventy-eight thousand – thank you sir! Eighty thousand?" The salesroom is plain: gray walls, rows of chairs with an aisle in the middle. Large monitors display on one side an image of the lot up for bid, and on the other the rising number in dollars, with the rest of the world's major currencies ticking up below. These numbers have a mesmerizing power: they're the province of human chaos, but gently intensified by the auctioneer, whose expert performance is an attraction of its own. He holds a pen in one hand and a small gavel in the other, and when the bids have stalled he leans out eagerly, peering over his glasses: it's at the same time chummy and authoritative. His hands come together in a formation that looks like prayer. "Are you sure?" he asks. "Sebastian?" he says to one of the telephone bidders standing along the walls. "Bidder online," he says, glancing into the ceiling where a camera has connected the salesroom to the entire globe, "are you sure? Fair warning!" Then the hands drop: the gavel raps down, and all the contingencies evaporate. The final number on the screen has become fate.

Later, asked what it's like to be up there, regular Christie's auctioneer James Hastie says, "It's very rewarding and enjoyable, actually. But never forget: they're throwing money at you! And if you like people and you get into the action, and you get a full crowd, it just makes for a very fun experience."

THE PIG OF SAINT PATRICK'S

Comical and unterrifying

Lady Chapel of Saint Patrick's Cathedral (exterior)
Corner of Madison Avenue and 51st Street
212-753-2261
saintpatrickscathedral.org
E and M trains/5th Av – 53rd St; B, D, F and M trains/Rockefeller Ctr; 4 and 6
trains/51st St

Asked if the cathedral has any interesting secrets to tell, the good ladies at the welcome desk of St. Patrick's shake their heads. "No," says Eileen. "No," says Marianne – but then she points a thumb to the rear of the church. "Unless you want to see the pig?"

The "pig" is a stone demon that crawls up the outer wall of the Lady Chapel at the cathedral's back end. For years the sculpture has been an inside joke among St. Patrick's priests, who have a good view of it from their second-story apartments in the rectory a few feet away. It's the first thing they see when they look out in the morning, and nobody knows what it is.

Five minutes later Marianne nods at the sculpture while the traffic blares by on Madison Avenue. The creature doesn't look very much like a pig. It doesn't look like any earthly thing: it's a stubby-armed monster grappling on the arched windows, with three-toed feet, a bulbous abdomen, and a cockscombed neck that disappears into a gap in the stonework.

"Someone thought it was a hippopotamus," says Monsignor Ritchie. He and Father Joe have come to stand at the open rectory window above the sidewalk, their feet about eye-level. The two live upstairs. "Bishop Sullivan thought it looks like it has a duck foot." They say the pig plays no role in the priestly schedule other than obscure fun. "But," says Father Joe, "when I show somebody the cathedral, I tell them to look up there. Nobody's ever seen it, it's one of those little oddities."

Monsters are longstanding companions of churches; some are visitors from Hell. Did it ever occur to the priests that the original intent might not be so playful, that the pig might have some darker business up there? "Playful," Father Joe and Monsignor Ritchie say in smiling unison, nodding their heads.

They're right. The Lady's Chapel is a later addition, built not by chief architect James Renwick but Charles T. Mathews. According to an old cathedral guide book, Mathews lived for a period in France, and acquired "a taste for gargoyles." His original plan called for hideous grotesques, but the trustees made him settle for something more "comical and unterrifying." The gargoyles were removed in the 1940s when they became unstable; the "pig" tucked away in its snug corner was left alone.

AUSTRIAN CULTURAL FORUM ⑦

24 stories high, just 25 feet wide

11 East 52nd Street
212-319-5300
acfny.org
Tours can be booked at new-york-kf@bmeia.gv.at
E and M trains/5th Av – 53rd St

The Manhattan grid creates all sorts of design opportunities and challenges; one of the city's pleasures is seeing how clever people have turned that inevitable division of streets and blocks into art. The Austrian Cultural Forum on 52nd Street has pulled off a noteworthy trick: cramming a 24-story tower into a mid-block footprint only 25 feet wide. There are brownstones wider than that – in fact the institution's former headquarters were in a townhouse at the same site. The solution made a star of Raimund Abraham, the building's Austrian-born architect, and led critic and historian Kenneth Frampton to proclaim the Forum "the most significant modern piece of architecture to be realized in Manhattan since the Seagram Building and the Guggenheim Museum." It's curious that virtually no one who isn't either Austrian or in the architecture profession knows about it.

"We get a lot of students of Raimund Abraham," says the man behind the desk. "Not a lot of walk-ins." But by all means walk in, because inside is where the magic is. From the street the building's façade – glass, steel, aluminum – suggests a mask or a machine (the architect called it "a cross between *Blade Runner* and an Easter Island sculpture") but the inside is comfortable, even airy, with a lot of pale wood and clean angles. Some of Abraham's greatest ideas remain hidden away in the guts. A large part of the footprint was sacrificed to fit in an emergency stair (required by code) that runs the entire vertical length, but is confined to the rear of the structure, leaving the front entirely open. During the tour, the guide lingers in the concert hall (there are over 150 film and music events a year), giving you an opportunity to appreciate how well the acoustical panels echo the blond wood of the chairs, and how the size – it seats about seventy-five – sets a record for high-culture intimacy. "The Bösendorfer piano," the guide says, "is made in Austria. They normally use gold detail, but made a special piano for us with silver, to go with the room." Piano? "A moment," she says, and hits a button on the wall: immediately a warning buzz goes off as a rectangle of ceiling detaches and begins a slow descent toward the floor. It's a built-in hidden piano compartment. "People like this part," she smiles.

LEVER HOUSE PLAZA

Big art for working stiffs

390 Park Avenue
212-421-7027
Monday to Friday 7am–7pm; Saturday 7am–1pm
E and M trains/5th Av – 53rd St

The Lever House has always been an icon: it's the first "curtain wall" skyscraper, where the outer shell is hung on a load-bearing structure within. Recently the building has come to notice for a different reason: as an unexpected contemporary art museum.

Constructed in 1950-52, the building was initially the headquarters of British soap manufacturers Lever Brothers. The crystalline slab, 24 stories high, sparked a rage for curtain walls: within ten years, the mile of Park Avenue from Grand Central to 59th Street shimmered with glass. Landmarked in 1982 and restored by real estate company RHR Holding, today the Lever House looks like it did half a century ago. With one compelling difference: the outdoor plaza now features large, even monumental sculptures and installations by prominent artists.

This is thanks to Richard Marshall, a friend of the owners and for twenty years a curator at the Whitney Museum. Originally RHR Holding mulled a commercial application for the spot, but the building's landmark status limited the options. Marshall pushed the idea of an ever-changing exhibition space, where artists would present large sculptural works in the plaza, supplemented by other work in various media in the glass-encased lobby. Now the project is Lever House policy.

Major sculptures by (among many others) Damien Hirst, Keith Haring, and Jeff Koons have been shown here. Artists are attracted by the chance to install their work in a part of town that no one would think to call edgy, and RHR Holding makes gains in the nebulous area of cachet. But it's basically a public service. "Galleries have shows to sell something, and museums ask admissions," notes Marshall. "We don't do either. We don't sell anything. We don't charge anything. And it's open every day." Asked if the art isn't maybe a bit much for the office crowd (for instance, Hirst's 35-foot bronze sculpture *Virgin Mother* is a pregnant woman with half her skin peeled off), Marshall says, "I hear complaints and I hear compliments."

Cross the street to 375 Park Avenue to visit another icon of functionalist architecture: Mies van der Rohe's 38-story Seagram Building, erected five years after the Lever House.

THE CITIGROUP CENTER'S HIDDEN FLAW

The skyscraper that might have fallen

601 Lexington Avenue
E and M trains/53rd Av – Lexington; 4 and 6 trains/51st St

The Citigroup tower kept an engineering secret for nearly two decades. Instead of relying on the cage system that is usual among skyscrapers, the fifty-nine-story building stays upright thanks to four enormous supports that connect at the center of each face rather than at the corners. The impact on the eye is uncanny: the skyscraper seems to float. That's not the secret. After construction in 1977, it was found that a hard wind could send the whole thing crashing into the street. The story still has the power to chill anyone who lives or works in the area.

The danger dawned on the tower's brilliant structural engineer, William LeMessurier, when he was asked by a curious university student about the integrity of the just-finished Citigroup Center in strong diagonal or "quartering" winds. LeMessurier thought the question was interesting enough to make it the special focus of an engineering class. Slowly an inherent flaw began to creep out of the math: the design was compatible with welded joints, not the bolted joints the tower relied on. LeMessurier determined that in rare but very possible hurricane conditions, a 70-mile-an-hour wind could result in epic catastrophe.

Retrofitting was hastily conducted – at night. For two months the building flickered with the glow of welding; the fires were bright enough for LeMessurier to see from an airplane window as he flew into La Guardia. "Nobody knows what's going on," he said to his wife, "but we know and can see it light up the sky." The intervention remained a secret until a 1995 *New Yorker* article, which compliments everyone involved. "The crisis at the Citigroup Center," it reads, "[...] produced heroes, but no villains." When the alternative might be an entire neighborhood flattened under a horizontal skyscraper, it's the least you could hope for.

Some office workers in the building know the story, and while they feel safe enough they're more attentive than usual to the wind, which tugs on the structure in ominous ways. "When it's really strong," says a man who works on the 52nd floor, "you can feel the elevator scrape against the moving building. You just kind of get used to it. But there's one thing ..." The door to his office sometimes swings open when a gust blows outside. It's not a draft (the windows are sealed): it's the whole building tipping gently over.

THEOSOPHICAL SOCIETY LIBRARY

The occult capital of New York City

240 East 53rd Street
library@theosophical.org
theosophical.org/library
Library open Tuesday, Wednesday, Thursday and Saturday 1pm-5pm
E and M trains/Lexington – 53rd St; 4 and 6 trains/51st St

The stretch of 53rd Street between Third and Second Avenues is a little dingy. You'll find several downscale restaurants (Thai, Italian, Spanish, Chinese, Indian), a frame shop, a hair salon, an X-rated DVD emporium. Hidden among all this on the south side is a beige townhouse – library above, bookshop below – that is something like the occult capital of New York City. It's the headquarters of the Theosophical Society.

The Society's stated goal is to preserve and realize "ageless wisdom." It was founded in 1875 by one of the oddest personalities in the city's history. Helena Blavatsky – writer, traveler, musician, mystic – circled the world on a spiritualist quest a century before anyone uttered the term New Age. She heard voices and was driven by visions, and would likely have been locked up if she weren't a wealthy aristocrat. While still in her teens, she made a scandal in England by sitting astride her horse Cossack-style, and again during her marriage to a Russian general: when the vows got to the word "obey" she reportedly flushed and murmured "Surely I shall not." Instead she disappeared, trading the drawing room for the whole globe, surviving the explosion of a passenger ship en route to Egypt, fighting in Italy's unification wars, crossing the American Rockies in a covered wagon. She lived in New York, where she led a spiritualist salon on West 47th Street that came to be known as "The Lamasery." She later settled in India.

At the townhouse on 53rd, a poster of Blavatsky hangs in the small stair that leads from the incense-misted bookstore up to the Theosophical Society Library. It's the image you often see of her: chin resting on her open hand, a gaze so deep it's practically fifth-dimensional. The library is only one room, but its contents disregard notions of "space:" you'll find sections on Philosophy, Reincarnation, Death, Consciousness, Hermetics, Meditation, Mysticism. Anyone is free to read there, and on the first page of every volume is a printed notice that should encourage mystics and skeptics alike: "The Theosophical Society has no dogma ...We urge the reader to decide for himself what is realistic, scientific, and impersonal."

GREENACRE PARK

Manhattan, distilled

217 East 51st Street
greenacrepark.org
Daily 8am–8pm (closed in winter)
E and M trains/53rd St; 4 and 6 trains/51st St

New York is dotted with oases: spots where a person can step off the amusement ride of the city for a moment and breathe an air of peace. Many of them occur naturally and are highly personal: a stairwell or a couple of trees might do it. Others are wholly engineered, and of these Greenacre Park on 51st Street is the champion.

The most striking feature is the total rejection of nature. Greenacre makes no effort at *rus in urbe*, the facsimile of countryside. You don't feel like you've left Manhattan so much as entered a space where Manhattan's characteristics have been distilled to the very essence. There is geometry here, and public life, and incessant noise, and the peace on offer is a Manhattan-flavored peace: it's busy and self-aware. The centerpiece is a 25-foot cascade that mimics the tiers of the cityscape: thousands of gallons of water roar continuously over climbing blocks of granite, and on either side the ivy wraps around the underlying stone at right angles. The roar is a calculated effect. Sit in the fine mist of the lower terrace with a book, and the street only a few paces away becomes muted: the constant waterfall static amounts to a kind of silence. The air in the small park even has a pleasant and unnatural scent: a hint of chlorine.

The need for urban oases was officially recognized under Mayor Lindsay with his Vest Pocket park initiative (see page 229). Sound is a feature of more than one; the use of roaring water to mask the honks and growls of the city has the compelling name "grey noise." Constructed in 1971, Greenacre was paid for by a private institution, and its rules are many and specific: no moving the chairs between terrace levels, no exercising, no touching the plants, no pets. The security guard, who might otherwise pass his time staring at the rushing water in a hypnotic sway, won't hesitate to enforce.

Paley Park

Greenacre has a conceptual sister three avenues away: Paley Park on 53rd Street. Paley offers a minimalism that also serves to distill an aspect of Manhattan: with a plain, solid wall of water, and symmetrical files of slender honey locust trees, it's chic. See it in the evening when the cascade is lit from behind with sodium light, and the water blurs and gleams like brushed gold.

MARILYN MONROE SUBWAY GRATE

Where The Girl became The Legend

Southwest corner of Lexington Avenue and East 52nd Street
4 and 6 trains/51st St

The subway goes by, and air billows through the sidewalk grate, blowing up Marilyn Monroe's skirt. If it's not the most famous moment in American cinema, it's not far down the list. It happened on the corner of Lexington and East 52nd.

Marilyn Monroe was always slated to star in *The Seven Year Itch*. In the film (and the Broadway hit it's based on) Monroe's character appears in the script as simply "The Girl." The story is straightforward: trusted husband is home alone, Girl tempts him into a frenzy. Director Billy Wilder thought the film might never make it past Hollywood's prudish production code. Eventually he conceded a crucial point: in the play the two eventually wind up in bed together, while in the film the tension is never resolved. Monroe comes out even more desirable for it.

The iconic "subway scene" seems practically wholesome today, but its notoriety endures. Trusted husband (Tom Ewell) and Monroe stroll out of the cinema on a hot summer night. "Oh, here comes the breeze from the subway!" Monroe sings, "Isn't it delicious?" New Yorkers already know the answer to this ("No"), but who cares? We're in Movieland. The shooting took place on September 9, 1954, and was widely publicized: by the time Monroe arrived in her pleated halter dress, a thousand spectators had gathered, along with a jostling pack of press photographers.

In the same way the husband's upstairs neighbor is simplified as The Girl, so has Monroe's entire film career – her entire person – been compressed into this one moment: bare legs revealed as the subway passes underground. Subway Marilyn posters, Subway Marilyn coffee mugs, tee shirts, key chains, mouse pads, piggy banks: you can find all this in Fifth Avenue trinket shops. But few people make the pilgrimage to Lexington and East 52nd Street. The manager of the restaurant fronted by the legendary grate says that those who do are a little let down. "There's no plaque or sign or anything." Steve McClendon, a sanitation worker who sweeps the grate "twenty or thirty times a day" doesn't know the film, and seems shaky on just who Marilyn Monroe was. After suffering an imitation of the iconic pose, he smiles. "Oh, that," he says, "Yeah, I've seen that."

THE COLE PORTER PIANO

There's no love song finer, but how strange the change from major to minor

Waldorf Astoria
301 Park Avenue
212-355-3000
hilton.com/fr/hotels/nycwawa-waldorf-astoria-new-york
4 and 6 trains/51st St

O n the Park Avenue mezzanine of the Waldorf Astoria stands a Steinway piano. The top is cracked, the finish is worn, the instrument is silent: a fallboard is locked over the keys. But the piano emanates, like an antenna tuned to nostalgia, the elegance of old New York: dinner jackets, evening dresses, cigarette cases, cocktail parties. It used to belong to Cole Porter.

Porter moved into the Waldorf Towers in 1934, but he began defining New York through his music long before that. Some of his songs draw directly from the city – "Washington Square," "Take Me Back to Manhattan," "I Happen to Like New York" – but there is a general quality in his compositions that seems to express what is romantic and smart and fashionable about urban life. It's the idea of New York without all the details.

The piano was built in 1907. It's a midsize mahogany grand the color of dark honey, with double Empire-style legs and hand-painted garlands and court figures. Porter gave it to the hotel in 1939, but it stayed with him in his apartment suite, arranged curve-to-curve with another piano, until he died in 1964. In a way, the instrument maps the fate of piano song. Putting clever words to chords made Porter a social lion. After his death the piano was moved to the Royal Suite, a baronial luxury apartment that runs the full length of the 50th Street block on the hotel's top floor. Later it filled the Waldorf Astoria central lobby with a kind of classic luxury soundtrack in the Peacock Alley lounge, until finally settling into its spot on the mezzanine directly over the hotel's main entrance on Park Avenue. At some point during this trajectory the piano became the "Cole Porter piano" – that is, a piece of museum furniture. On the mezzanine it was played for fifteen years by Daryl Sherman, one of the best performers of the dying song form. "This is not me playing," she would say before a rendition of "Night and Day" – "This is Cole Porter's spirit playing by Ouija board." When the Waldorf Astoria was bought by the Blackstone Group in 2007, operations were streamlined and Sherman was shown the door. Now the piano mostly stays locked.

Steinway & Sons offers a replica of the Cole Porter grand. It's called the "High Society."

Porter's Waldorf Towers suite, 33A, went on the market in 2010. The rate: $140,000/month.

THE FRED F. FRENCH BUILDING

Babylon on Fifth Avenue

551 Fifth Avenue at 45th Street
7 train/5th Av; S train/Grand Central – 42nd St

Many of New York's Art Deco buildings are beautifully suggestive of Mesopotamia. The design trend has been traced to D.W. Griffith's 1916 film *Intolerance* and its seductive sets, but some taller New York buildings – the "setback" giants that climb the sky in diminishing tiers – look like Bronze Age step pyramids because of an early zoning law. To see the forces of design and regulation at work on a masterpiece of modern Babylon, visit the Fred F. French Building on Fifth Avenue.

The Manhattan setback zoning law was America's first. It ordered that once a structure reached a certain height, it had to step inward from the street. The earliest tall buildings used this model as a matter of structural necessity, but with the metal frame folks worried – with good reason – that sunlight would disappear from the metropolitan sidewalk forever. The French Building illustrates the law: it begins to step back a dozen floors up, until the tower gradually shrinks to 25% of the area of the footprint, at which point it was allowed to go as high as the very vault of heaven. The temple-like profile is in part accidental, but the cladding is Babylonian Art Deco at its purest. The French is flushed with ochre masonry, trimmed in black, and the tower is topped by a vivid frieze in colored faience: griffins flanking a stylized sun.

But to get the full flavor of yore, enter the lobby. The entrance is a glowing bronze tribute to the Ishtar Gate, with decoration that is "a most literal evocation of Manhattan as the New Babylon, of the skyscraper as Nebuchadnezzar's hanging garden in the desert" (*New York* 1930; Stern, Gilmartin and Mellins). The lobby itself is vaulted with gilt mythical animals, leading down to the most stupefying elevator bank in the city. On either side, the polished bronze doors gleam with stylized allegories, as if lifted directly from the throne room of a god-king.

The setback zoning law was in effect in New York from 1916 to 1961.

Sloan & Robertson consulted when the French Building went up in 1926; for another example of their Babylon-enriched architecture from the same period, see page 216.

FORD FOUNDATION ATRIUM

A box of forest on 42nd Street

320 East 43rd Street (atrium access on 42nd Street)
212-573-5000
fordfoundation.org
Tuesday to Sunday 9:30am–5:15pm (March to October); 9:30am–4:45pm
(November to February)
Admission free
4, 5, 6 trains and 7 train/Grand Central – 42nd St

There's no other building in New York City that pulls off a green trick like the one on display at the Ford Foundation. The back entrance is an atrium as tall as the structure itself: twelve stories of open air enclosed on two sides by glass. On the ground – it would be strange to call it the floor – are terraced levels of jungle flora. As you open the door you're aware of a rush of oxygen and the aroma of damp wood, and a whisper in your head: *This is not what I expected to find on 42nd Street.*

To be precise, not all of the plants are of the jungle sort. Lal, a gardener here, says that they are "a mix of tropical and temperate." For an example of temperate he points to a pine; the tropical is most everything else: Lal recognizes many of the types of vegetation that he can see in his native Guyana. The atrium does indeed have the feeling of a parcel of earth quarried from some distant, humid forest. At the same time it's pleasantly neat: swept tile paths cut through the plants, converging at the bottom on a wishing fountain. "We give the coins to UNICEF," says Eddie, a guard who has been at the Foundation thirty years. He says the best time to come – and he should know – is around 10 o'clock in the morning, when the sun slants through the windows from the east.

The atrium is impressive to the eye, but the motive behind the design is deeper than beauty. The Ford Foundation, a legacy of automaker Henry Ford and his son Edsel, is a private charitable corporation; focus issues include poverty, education, and social justice. Architects Kevin Roche and John Dinkeloo recognized that the moral lifeblood of such an organization is transparency. Roche imagined Foundation workers peering out across the open atrium and feeling more aware of their colleagues, everyone connected by a communal sense of responsibility. If the idea sounds oppressive, the reality isn't – or at least not visibly so. The offices with their lighted windows, divided into floors by weathered iron beams, seem to share a purpose with each other, and with the fragrant plant life below.

THE GRAYBAR BUILDING RATS

Art deco pests

Lexington Avenue between 43rd and 44th Streets
4, 5, 6, 7 and S trains/Grand Central – 42nd St

Often mistaken for an eastern extension of Grand Central Terminal, the Graybar Building on Lexington Avenue has its own identity, and a pioneering one. After completion in 1927, the brick and limestone headquarters of the Graybar Electric Company became the largest office tower in the world. The façade is aligned to the Assyrian geometries that informed 1920s Art Deco (see page 212), and while the titanic curly-bearded allegories of Transportation and Communication on the east face set a distinctive tone, the building's uniqueness is best expressed lower down, on the struts that hold up the awning. There you'll find New York's only architectural rats.

The rats are easy to miss; it wasn't until 1933 that they came to the attention of the *New Yorker*. "When plans for the building were being developed," The Talk of the Town reads, "the architects thought they ought to strike the maritime note somewhere in its decorations." This note is found in the bas-relief albatrosses that decorate the façade, but the architects Sloan & Robertson also brilliantly marked a parallel between the awning struts and the hawser lines used for mooring or towing ships. It goes beyond rats: the ones scampering up the front of the Graybar are frustrated by "bafflers" – the funnels that guard real rats from stowing away on ships in harbor.

Made of cast iron, and segmented into angular planes that would appear modern to the Jazz Age passerby but robotic to the modern one, the rats look like they're up to no good. And there are more: each of the iron struts connects to the building at a rosette composed of rat heads.

The Graybar was an A-rated building in its early life, with offices of publishing giants Condé Nast, Vogue, and Vanity Fair, as well as those of Remington typewriters. Over the years the address slipped in status, and one by one the cast-iron varmints disappeared. When the building was restored in 2000, among the special instructions on the technical drawings was the irregular phrase: "Replace missing rats."

THE WHISPERING GALLERY IN GRAND CENTRAL

Telegraph by Guastavino tile

Grand Central Terminal, 87 East 42nd Street; dining concourse directly in front of the Oyster Bar & Restaurant
Open 24 hours

Grand Central Terminal has an unmarked spot with otherworldly properties: a handsome vaulted ceiling where you can speak softly into one corner and be plainly heard by someone in the opposite corner 40 feet away. The effect is truly uncanny, and cuts through the surrounding din of echoes, whistles and roars of the biggest train station in the world.

There are several buildings in the States and abroad with the architectural quirk that produces the whispering gallery effect; what you need is an unbroken ellipsoid and points of focus directly opposite one another. Grand Central's whispering gallery is just in front of the Oyster Bar & Restaurant, and the pattern of tiled vaults continues inside where staff and patrons still find new sweet spots of particular clarity. For best results, speak facing the corner, as close to the stone as possible. Make sure your cohort is in the diagonally opposite corner, not one next to you. The sound is said to "telegraph" along the vault, and the term is apt: the voice you hear has a spectral, disembodied quality, as though transmitted through some antiquated technology.

Another feature of whispering galleries: they're generally flukes. Perfectly ellipsoidal tile ceilings are certainly not, however – those we owe to the hard work of Spanish-born builder Rafael Guastavino. The architect came to New York from Barcelona with his son in 1881 and soon after patented his "Tile Arch System" of standard-size, interlocking terracotta tiles. The tiles had distinct structural advantages: they were fireproof, and could be applied directly into mortar over long arches and vaults without the need for temporary supports. Although employed in Catalonia for years, the technique was hardly known in the United States. Guastavino and his son eventually filed over twenty patents, and the demand for the arch system became so fierce, tile makers couldn't work fast enough to meet it.

Guastavino tile is a prominent feature of Beaux-Arts New York architecture and can be found in dozens of notable buildings, including the Cathedral Church of St. John the Divine, the Registry Room at Ellis Island, and the Federal Reserve Bank.

U THANT ISLAND

Manhattan's smallest island, and former sovereign nation

East River at 42nd Street

In the middle of the East River at about the level of 42nd Street rises a scrubby hump of land with a metal navigation tower. Less than an acre in area, U Thant is Manhattan's smallest island, but it has seen some interesting history.

The island began as a granite outcrop called Man o'War Reef. It was once the scene of a perfectly New York City adventure: in the 1930s, a group of teens trying to swim across the river from Manhattan were forced by the current onto the reef, which then began to disappear as the tide came in. A playwright who was watching the fiasco unfold through binoculars from a tower apartment called the authorities and all the boys – who were by then standing in a foot of water – were saved. When the first Manhattan-Queens tunnel was dug beneath the river for a tram service to the company town of Steinway & Sons (see page 390), excavated rock from Manhattan was piled onto the reef to make it a permanent island, and a hundred-foot shaft was sunk straight down to branch the dig from the center of the river out to either shore. The finished tunnel is the closest most people ever get to U Thant Island: the 7 train passes through it directly underneath.

When the shaft was filled in, the island was forgotten by all but cormorants, which nest there. In 1977 a UN group called the Peace Meditation at the United Nations leased the hump from the city, planted shrubs, and named it after the Burmese former Secretary General. For years, the only people allowed to set foot here was this group of UN employees.

Now it's totally off limits. Probably the most curious event in the island's history turns on this point. In the summer of 2004, during the Republican National Convention, local artist Duke Riley rowed out to U Thant in the early morning dark. He then hoisted a banner bearing a personal emblem of electric eels and claimed the island a sovereign nation. "I'm drawn to those environments," Riley says of New York's islands. "You're in one of the most hyper-developed cities in the world, and here are these tiny untouched secret places." While the Coast Guard was chasing him, they failed to notice Riley's banner, which flew from the navigation tower for days. When asked what he planned to call his miniature island nation, the artist pauses, then laughs. "Really, I don't even know if I got that far."

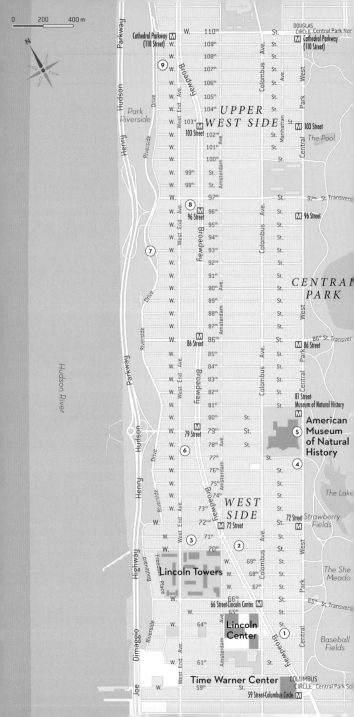

Upper West Side (59th–110th)

33 WEST 63 RD STREET

A stranded tenement

*1 and 2 trains/66 St – Lincoln Center; 1, A, C, B and D trains/
59 St – Columbus Circle*

On the Upper West Side, at the bottom of a canyon of glass and brick residential towers, one small building stands out – or more accurately, has forced neighboring giants to stand awkwardly around it. 33 West 63rd Street is just five stories tall, bordered in rough-cut stone, with the full complement of black iron fire escapes zigzagging across the face. A tenement, in other words. It used to be one in a row – the walls on either side are windowless where adjacent buildings were shorn off – and the row used to be one in a large crop of tenements that sprang up in this neighborhood in the late 1800s and gradually broadened with the arrival of the IRT subway line in 1904.

How did No. 33 become so isolated? Spite, mostly. The owner, Jehiel R. Elyachar, was described by a former tenant of the lonely tenement as "a tiny, skinny, bent over little gnome of a man." He had made so much money in real estate and construction – a fortune of over $100 million, by one reckoning – he could indulge in the rich curmudgeon's preferred sport: mad stinginess. While giving generously to various Jewish-American and Israeli causes before he died in 1989, including schools and homes for the aged, Elyachar was the kind of guy who ends up getting sued by his own children. When developer Paul Milstein began buying several properties on the corner of Broadway and 63rd to build a retail and apartment tower, Elyachar agreed on a price, and then played out a series of bait-and-switch deals that were so fiendish, Milstein gradually understood that he was caught not in a business fiasco but some kind of sinister game. He finally threw up his hands and built his tower with an L-shaped footprint, leaving the stranded tenement where it was. And still is.

San Juan Hill

Buildings come and go on a practically daily basis in New York, but to the west of the lonely tenement you can find the site where an entire neighborhood was swept from the map. The Upper West Side between 65th and 59th Streets at Amsterdam Avenue was once one of New York's largest African-American communities. Called San Juan Hill, a 1940 Housing Authority report deemed it "the worst slum in New York City." 1,500 families were displaced when the tenements were torn down to build the Lincoln Center, but demolition was delayed to film the gritty street scenes of West Side Story.

THE PYTHIAN

The fantastical lodge of a forgotten order

135 West 70th Street
212-496-1334
1, 2 and 3 trains/72nd St

IF FRATERNAL LOVE
HELD ALL MEN BOUND
HOW BEAUTIFUL
THIS WORLD WOULD B...

The Pythian

The inscription above the entrance to The Pythian reads: "If fraternal love held all men bound, how beautiful this world would be." The message is hard to argue with; what deadpan pharaohs and the monsters of Babylon have to do with it is open to question. This weird building is the work of architect Thomas W. Lamb, who made his name designing outrageous movie palaces in the 1920s (see page 328). He brought the same anything-goes attitude to The Pythian, looting along the way a hodgepodge of antiquity: snarling griffins, bull teams bearing gigantic urns, double-headed capitals and gilt hieroglyphs. Constructed in 1926, the building served as the central meeting place for New York's lodges of the Knights of Pythias.

Mostly unknown today, the Knights of Pythias was the first American fraternal organization chartered by an Act of Congress. Promoting charity and "universal peace," the Knights can boast three U.S. Presidents, including FDR, and at the time of The Pythian's construction fraternity was booming: over 100 lodges in New York City alone. The order's founder was inspired by the Greek legend of ancient travelers Damon and Pythias. Pythias was sentenced to death by the tyrant of Syracuse; Damon gallantly agreed to stand in for his friend while the latter went home to put his affairs in order, with the understanding that if Pythias skipped, Damon would be executed in his place. Panting Pythias showed up just as the axe was about to fall, and the tyrant was so impressed he freed both men. The two have symbolized selfless friendship ever since.

The Pythian is decorated with some of the strangest and most striking colored terracotta in the city, but you can scarcely find a New Yorker who knows it. Long gone is a chance to visit the polished stone lobby, the theater, or any one of the several lodge halls: The Pythian was chopped into condominiums in 1983. Asked if such a bizarre structure attracts bizarre residents, the doorman shakes his head. "Nice people," he says. "Normal people. If I could afford it, I'd live here." At last check, a one-bedroom runs about $1 million.

Although they're gone from this address, the Knights still exist: over 2,000 lodges worldwide.

When membership in the order fell off, the Knights of Pythias leased part of the building to Decca Records, where in 1954 Bill Haley and His Comets recorded their Top 40 juggernaut "Rock Around the Clock".

SEPTUAGESIMO UNO PARK ③

The smallest park in the five boroughs

256 West 71st Street
nycgovparks.org/parks/M282
Dawn to dusk
1, 2 and 3 trains/72nd St

Central Park is Manhattan's largest park, of course. To give some idea of the vastness, just a dozen years ago researchers discovered buried under the leaves a genus of centipede totally unknown to science. If your taste in green goes in a cozier direction, head three blocks west on 71st Street to Septuagesimo Uno. It takes less time to walk past this park than pronounce the name (it means "seventy-one"). At 0.04 acres it's New York City's smallest.

The story of this curious nook cuts right to the core of Manhattan urban planning. At a time when uptown was still dotted with farmhouses, Mayor DeWitt Clinton implemented his far-sighted Commissioners' Plan of 1811, dividing the island above 14th Street into the grid system of north-south avenues and east-west cross streets we take for granted today. Although public parks were figured in (at 53rd, 66th, 77th, and 120th Streets), by the 1960s the growing population and crush of buildings had outpaced the average New Yorker's ability not to go insane.

This situation was eased somewhat by Mayor John Lindsay's Vest Pocket park initiative. Since everywhere was already crammed with buildings, the initiative specialized in sprucing up the vacant lots between them. Septuagesimo Uno is just brownstone-width. It may be the only park in New York City with a street address: 256 West 71st Street – the address of a house that was condemned in 1969 and whose narrow footprint the park now occupies. The City of New York Parks & Recreation signs block most of the view when the gates are closed, and the standard list of prohibitions becomes comedy: "Performing or rallying, except by permit" (where?); "Obstructing entrances to the park" (there's only one, and if you're reading the sign, you're obstructing). With its wooden benches, slender plant beds, and single tree, what Septuagesimo Uno is big enough for is you and a friend, or just you and a book. It may be all you need.

For other Vest Pocket parks in Manhattan, see page 206.

LORD CORNBURY

Only in New York, circa 1720

New-York Historical Society
170 Central Park West
212-873-3400 – nyhistory.org
Tuesday to Thursday, Saturday and Sunday 11am–5pm, Friday 11am–8pm
B and C trains/81st St; 1 train/79th St

T he New-York Historical Society is the oldest museum in the city: the name even has an early 1800s hyphen. Restored in 2011, the lobby now contains a wall that splashes a number of impressive artifacts: the pistols from the Burr-Hamilton duel, an early New York State seal, a painted wooden carving of a Sauk Indian chief, and, in a corner hanging below busts and portraits, a painting of a strikingly unattractive lady in blue silk. According to the tag on the wall, the subject is a mystery. "Unidentified artist;" "Unidentified woman, ca 1700-1725." But historians have long known who it *probably* is: Viscount Cornbury, Royal governor of the British colonies of New York, and noted transvestite.

It's written on the gilt frame: "Among other apish tricks, Lord Cornbury, the half-witted son of Henry Earl of Clarendon, is said to have held his state levees at New York, and received the principal Colonists dressed up in complete female court costume." This is from British writer Agnes Strickland's *Lives of the Queens of England* from about 1850, but the painting had been amusing people since well before that. It would be a different matter if Cornbury were less than the highest-ranking man in the New World, or if his reason for dressing in women's clothing weren't such a transparent pretense: "It was necessary for him," wrote a German diplomat in 1714, "in order to represent her Majesty [Queen Anne], to dress himself as a woman." Perhaps Cornbury also felt the necessity to flounce at the windows of his home, or skip in silk dresses along the battlements of the fort, or hide behind trees "to pounce, shrieking with laughter, on his victims" – some of the other apish tricks he was known for.

Patricia Bonomi, the viscount's biographer, has tried to change this perception. She writes that "the transvestism charge was in all likelihood a slander," a tale concocted by Cornbury's political opponents. No British officials mentioned the habit. But many colonists did, and there remains of course the portrait. It was bought by the Historical Society from a British family, and had been identified as Cornbury as early as 1796.

ID DAY AT THE MUSEUM OF NATURAL HISTORY

Whatever you've got, they'll explain it

American Museum of Natural History
Central Park West at 79th Street
212-769-5100
amnh.org; check for ID Day schedule
B and C trains/81st St – Museum of Natural History;
1 train/79th St

Once a year in early summer, the American Museum of Natural History puts its matchless expertise at the service of the New York public. "ID Day" (ID for "identification") fills the Grand Gallery of the museum's first floor. Around the perimeter are stations where visitors bring whatever bizarre natural objects they've bought, found, or always wondered about for a swift professional analysis. The experts come from the fields of Earth and Planetary Science, Botany and Ecology, Anthropology, Entomology, Herpetology, Mammalogy, Paleontology, Ichthyology, and Ornithology – whatever you've got, there's someone on hand who can explain it to you.

If you're empty-handed, come anyway. The stations are littered with artifacts, fossils, feathers, shells, minerals – an entire survey of natural history that you're invited to handle and learn from. And watching people unpack their unidentified treasures is its own entertainment. "Basically there are three types," says an expert at the Paleontology table. "There's people who've actually found something, and they're curious. Those are my favorite because they're here to learn. Then there are people who've bought or found things that they know everything about, and I tell them what they already know. And then there's the crazies." One year a man brought what he'd determined was a "straight-shelled nautiloid" that swam the Paleozoic coast of what is now New York. The expert identified it as the solidified contents of a caulking gun. When one woman asked for verification of a 150-million-year-old primitive bird, the expert had to break the news that her "fossil" was a blown glass sculpture of a rooster. They're not all wrong: one bone turned out to be a fossilized walrus skull. The paleontologists were so excited, the owner donated it to the museum's permanent collection.

At the Earth and Planetary Science station a man unwraps a lump of metal found in the Bronx; he suspects it is a meteorite. The expert weighs the lump in his hand and, as the owner's eyes tick avidly along, buffs a corner with sandpaper and drags it over a piece of ceramic to examine the residue. He frowns. "Meteorites are very magnetic," the expert says, and applies a magnet – which falls off. "That pretty much tells the whole story." The lump's owner takes the news pretty well for somebody who thought he'd brought a chunk of outer space.

MILLSTONES OF THE COLLEGIATE REFORMED PROTESTANT DUTCH CHURCH

The oldest pieces of colonial New York

368 West End Avenue
212-787-1566
westendchurch.org
Church office open weekdays 9am–5pm, Sunday service at 11am
1 and 2 trains/79th St

On West End Avenue at 77th Street there's a brick Flemish-style church. Inside, at the entrance to the main chapel, are stacked three large circular stones girt in iron with holes in the middle. They look like they would be more comfortable in a barn, but for history they're unbeatable. The stones are millstones, and they're likely the oldest pieces we have of colonial New York.

The West End Collegiate does little to publicize the stones because as an institution it has very little to prove. Established by British royal charter in 1696, the church is the single oldest corporation in the United States. But the millstones aren't just part of an eccentric collection of old colonial hardware: they speak to the very essence of the early church. Dutch settlers came to New York (they called it New Amsterdam) in 1624. There is a record, just two years later, of a François Molemaecker "employed in building a horse-mill, with spacious room above, to serve for a congregation." The location of this mill became Mill Lane; there's still a block-long snippet of it left between Stone and William Streets. Amused Indians used to come to service and fill the loft with pipe smoke while they laughed, as if to deliberately goad fussy Jonas Michaelius, the pastor. "As to the natives of this country," he wrote, "I find them entirely savage and wild, strangers to all decency, yea, uncivil and stupid as garden poles, proficient in all wickedness and godlessness." But like all earlier chroniclers, he is awestruck by the beauty and natural abundance of primeval Manhattan.

The millstones are actually older than New York – or any other American city. They were quarried in Belgium and brought here with the earliest settlers. The church met at the mill until 1633, when it moved to a plain building on Broad Street (now long gone). The mill address was taken over by Shearith Israel, New York's earliest Jewish congregation. When Shearith Israel moved uptown to 70th Street, they dug up the old stones, kept two (you can see them in the synagogue), and gave four to the Collegiate Church. One is now embedded in the alley wall of next-door Collegiate School. Three stayed in the church narthex.

JOAN OF ARC ISLAND

Stones from Joan's prison tower in Rouen, and fragments from the cathedral at Reims

Riverside Drive at 93rd Street
1, 2 and 3 trains/96th St

There is indeed a place in New York City with the winsome name "Joan of Arc Island." But far from a wooded sanctuary where teenage girls with swords roam free, it's an island only in the sense of traffic island – that is, an enclosed urban area bordered by a curb. The main event is an equestrian statue at the center, lined up directly with 93rd Street. Saint Joan, staring straight into the sky.

There are plenty of women in New York City statues but they're mostly mythological or allegorical: the Joan of Arc was the first based on an actual woman. It's also the city's only statue – and wherever there are statues of Joan of Arc this tends to be true – of a woman seated on a horse. The artist, Anna Hyatt Huntington, was the daughter of a professor of zoology and an accomplished animal artist who, after moving to Paris to refine her technique, became captivated by the maiden warrior. Determined to create a work honoring Joan's consecration, Huntington visited the French sites associated with key events in her personal history. At that time in Reims there was a Paul DuBois statue of Joan of Arc (and a copy of it in Paris) that closely resembles Huntington's in having the gaze fixed on the sky, but the American sculptress puts the heaviest emphasis on the sword. "When [Joan] went into battle," Huntington said, "she unconsciously raised it to heaven to ask the blessing of the Lord on it...That was the idea of the statue."

In 1910, Huntington submitted a life-size plaster model of Joan to the Paris Salon, where it received honorable mention and some sexist amazement. More important, the work completely won over members of a New York monument committee dedicated to commemorating the 500th anniversary of the saint's birth. The statue was unveiled on 93rd Street three years late (1915), but the lag provided a detail that makes this work truly unique. The base includes stones from a tower in Rouen where Joan was imprisoned, and fragments from the cathedral at Reims where, thanks to her, Charles VII was crowned. Stone from France's great historical buildings was depressingly available in 1915: the Germans had started bombing a year earlier.

Other fragments of the bombed Reims Cathedral

Corpus Christi Church on West 121st Street and Broadway also has fragments of the bombed Reims Cathedral: stained glass in the apse windows.

THE LOTUS GARDEN

Suspended above 97th Street

On top of the parking garage, south side of 97th Street between Broadway and
West End Avenue
Entrance stair on east side of garage
Sundays 1pm–4pm, April through November
Admission free; members ($20/year) get a key and unlimited daylight use
during the week
1, 2 and 3 trains/96th St

n the middle of 97th Street there's an oil-stained and gasoline-scented parking garage, with a narrow stair on the left; climb it and you'll come upon a hidden extravaganza of green. Fruit trees, shrubs, herbs, flowers, fish ponds, winding paths. The place is called the Lotus Garden, and it's New York City's only elevated community garden. "Totally a secret," says head gardener Pamela Wagner. "It's so easy to walk by and not see us."

The garden has soil three and a half feet deep (the minimum required for the root systems of the trees) with private plots carved out like puzzle pieces. The plot holders pay yearly dues, but on Sunday afternoons anyone can visit, and sit, and enjoy the oddity of suspended nature. Although it attracts regular visitors ("We've had people write entire novels up here," Wagner says) the place feels like a private hideout, the plants creating an effect of healthy solitude.

The tranquility is sweeter for being hard-won: this spot was once a green war zone. When two movie theaters here burned down in the 60s, neighbors decided to reclaim the property for nature. With authorization from no one, they cleaned the plot up and began planting. The key figures in this transformation were Carrie Maher and Mark Greenwald, who lived in a small penthouse ("We called it a pent-hovel," says Maher) that looked down directly on the vacant lot. This was a time of ecological activism that required more involvement than, say, shopping at an organic supermarket. "There was one group called the Green Guerillas," Maher recalls. "They used to fill Christmas bulbs with sunflower seeds and then grenade them into vacant lots."

While the municipal forces wrangled over the future of the property, it gradually filled with shrubs and blossoms. Soon block associations joined the cause, and then city planners, and finally a committee led by Maher and Greenwald was formed to convince real estate developer William Zeckendorf Jr. that, whatever building he planned for the site, a space set aside for the garden could only enhance it. Zeckendorf agreed. The space he offered was one-sixth of an acre, and happened to be in mid-air. For once, everybody's happy.

Townhouse for a mystic

319 West 107th Street
212-864-7752
roerich.org
Tuesday to Friday 12pm-4pm, Saturday and Sunday 12pm-5pm
Admission free, contribution suggested
1 train/110th St

The brownstone at 319 West 107th is a three-story tribute to the mystical Russian painter Nicholas Roerich. At the door there's a modest plaque and a bell. When you enter, there might be no one in the vestibule to meet you. You might hear someone practicing on the piano on the second floor, or pass a silent visitor on the wooden stair – but most likely, you'll have the house to yourself.

Intimacy is the special feature of this small museum, following the motto of the late director Daniel Entin ("Do whatever you want. Spend as long as you like."). Entin was an unassuming white-bearded gentleman with a gleam in his eye that hinted at hidden resources. He used to live on the ground floor of the museum he had directed for three decades. If you wanted to chat, he would sit you at the kitchen table and tell you what he knew about Nicholas Roerich, which was pretty much everything. What you wouldn't hear: why you came in the first place. "Roerich's painting is just the kind of art that touches a certain kind of person," Entin would say. "There's something that grabs the people whom it grabs. Others couldn't care less." The director seemed OK with either type.

There are over 200 Roerich works here, but his greatness as a painter is beside the point: the museum is less art collection than spiritual center. Nicholas Roerich became interested in Eastern philosophy in 1910, when he helped design the first-ever Tibetan temple outside Asia in St. Petersburg. His life thereafter was structured by two overlapping interests: Buddhism, and the unity of mankind through the arts. He'd already gathered a following in Russia when the Revolution forced him to move to the States; after outgrowing several buildings, he had a large complex erected on the corner of Riverside and West 103rd, with schools for every branch of the arts, teacher and student residences, and exhibition spaces. The building is still there, but the school didn't survive the Depression. Shortly after the painter's death in 1947, the Nicholas Roerich Museum was founded on nearby West 107th Street.

The paintings, vividly colored allegories and landscapes reflecting Roerich's expeditions in Tibet, cover the walls of the elegant brownstone. Admirers come from distant countries, seeking a spiritual connection, but Entin was most touched by the walk-ins. "A lot of them are in and out in 3 minutes. Then somebody will come in and burst into tears."

Street deaths

So much of New York life is public, it's expected that the city has seen its share of public death, too. Here are four cases of people passing their last and most private moment right on the street.

John Lennon

Main entrance to the Dakota Building, 72nd Street and Central Park West

In a 1980 interview, John Lennon described life in New York: "I can go out of this door now and go to a restaurant. You want to know how great that is? Or go to the movies? I mean, people come up and ask for autographs or say 'hi' but they won't bug you." On December 8 of the same year, Lennon and Yoko Ono had just stepped out of a limousine and were crossing the sidewalk into the Dakota Building where they lived, when Lennon was shot four times in the back. His killer Mark Chapman had asked the musician for an autograph at the same spot only hours before.

Max Beckmann

61st Street and Central Park West

Nazi Germany declared painter Max Beckmann a "degenerate artist," and so made him a nomad. He fled to St. Louis, then Amsterdam, and in 1949 moved to his last home, New York. His health was bad. "My time ran out long ago," he wrote in his diary while on the train. Beckmann held on for more than a year, poor and famous: he taught classes at the Brooklyn Museum Art School to pay the bills at the same time he had recent paintings in exhibition at the Met. He had just left his apartment to cross Central Park to see one of them, *Self-Portrait in Blue Jacket*, when a heart attack snuffed him out, right on the sidewalk.

Eli Black

Northbound Park Avenue ramp at the MetLife Building (formerly the Pan Am)

At 8 am on February 3, 1975, Eli Black, chairman of the two-billion-dollar conglomerate United Brands Company (later named Chiquita Brands International), used his briefcase to smash a hole in the sealed window of his forty-four-story office in the Pan Am Building and, after removing the shards because, investigators said, "he apparently didn't want to cut himself," leapt out of the hole and plunged straight down onto the northbound ramp of Park Avenue below. Later it was surmised that Black, depressed and overworked, had opted for suicide rather than face prosecution for paying a $2.5 million bribe to the president of Honduras for lower tariffs on banana exports. Chiquita's crooked political maneuvering was so pervasive in banana-growing countries they called the company *El Pulpo* –"The Octopus."

The first victim of Billy the Kid

Roughly the corner of Pearl and Madison Streets

Headline from the Times, September 10, 1876: "TWO COMPANIONS QUARREL AND ONE STABS AND KILLS THE OTHER." The victim was a brush maker named Thomas Moore, just 19 years old. His killer was a 17-year-old named William McCarty. The two were drinking at a liquor store on the corner of Pearl and Hague Streets (about where Murray Bergtraum High School is today). They began arguing, then punching, and eventually McCarty drew "a large-bladed pocket-knife, and made a lunge at his antagonist. The point of the blade struck Moore under the left eye, and glancing downward, the blade imbedded itself in his throat, inflicting a ghastly wound from which the blood poured copiously." It's a description of the first murder of career outlaw Billy the Kid, as McCarty would later be known.

Upper East Side and Central Park

GLACIAL ERRATICS

Geological wanderers in Central Park

Central Park
Glacial erratics are found throughout the park; the stone pictured is 50 yards
south of the carousel (mid-park at about 64th Street)
From dawn to 1am

The natural charm of Central Park is all the more impressive for being mostly artificial. The trees are planted and carefully tended, the hills are sculpted, the creek that flows through the Ramble can be turned on and off like a faucet. In the area of bedrock, however, the park is the real deal. Geologists love this place. Glaciers slowly scraped and polished the earth down to the schist – the bones of Manhattan – and then melted back, leaving scars that tell the story of the deep past. Also left behind are curious boulders that were lifted by the ice and tumbled and transported from miles away. They're called glacial erratics.

The term "erratic" takes from the sense of its Latin root meaning "wander." A glance is enough to determine that the glacial erratics in the park are travelers from afar: they look completely different from the stone they rest on. The south side of the Sheep Meadow has a line of the alien boulders; stuck in layers of topsoil, many probably haven't moved since the ice muscled them into place thousands of years ago. Near the Heckscher playing fields stand the starkest erratics, particularly one 8-foot hulk perched directly on the bedrock just south of the carousel.

"You can tell that one is Yonkers gneiss," says Dr. Charles Merguerian, chair of the Department of Geology at Hofstra University and the foremost expert on the rocky past of Central Park. Erratics, he explains, are precision tools: by matching the boulder's composition to distant bedrock, you can determine where it got plucked up by the roving glacier. "You put two dots on the map: where they ended up and where they came from," says Merguerian. "Make a line, and that's the direction the glacier moved in."

Glacier movement is visible also in the scour marks, or striae, left in bedrock. These you'll find throughout the park; notice that they're all oriented roughly north-south. Where erratics have come to rest directly on the scarred bedrock you get the full picture: deposition and erosion, the two effects of glaciation. Merguerian notes that some of the erratics may have been moved slightly during the park's history, but it's tempting to imagine the moment, say 12,000 years ago, when after an eternity suspended in glacier, the boulder sank through the last sliver of melting ice and hit bottom with a modest *clunk*.

PHRENOLOGY IN CENTRAL PARK ②

Highbrow, lowbrow: Shakespeare vs. the Indian

Central Park
Shakespeare is located at the head of the Mall (where East Drive connects with Center Drive at about 66th Street), Indian Hunter 100 yards west (toward Sheep Meadow)
From dawn to 1am

Two statues at the entrance to the Central Park Mall – Shakespeare, and an Indian – offer a tidy illustration of one of history's more harebrained notions. Phrenology, the "science" of determining character and personality traits by the shape of the skull, was a hot ticket in New York in the mid-19th century. Two enterprising quacks, the Fowler brothers, got rich off the idea at their Nassau Street office, where they made consultations, gave lectures, and published books and journals. Edgar Allan Poe was a devotee, as was Walt Whitman (perhaps because the Fowlers told him his bumpy skull indicated "a tendency to the pleasures of voluptuousness"). The most influential New Yorker of the time, William Cullen Bryant, had such respect for phrenology he made it central to a speech he gave in the spring of 1872 to celebrate the unveiling of the John Quincy Adams Ward statue of Shakespeare.

"Come down to the phrenologists of the present day," Bryant said as the crowd admired the new bronze, "and they tell you of the visible indications of his boundless invention, his universal sympathy, his lofty idealism, his wit, his humor..." Visible indications. Bryant, the namesake of Bryant Park, was a poet, editor, publisher, and general advocate of public welfare. That this decent, educated man also believed that Shakespeare's genius was written wholesale in his "noble countenance" shows how entrenched the pseudoscience was.

While Bryant was delivering his speech, another statue – by the same sculptor, no less – crouched stealthily only a hundred paces to the west. Ward's Indian Hunter was modeled on sketches the artist made in the Dakotas, and praised as a true model of "aboriginal physiogonomical types." The difference to Shakespeare's smooth, egg-like head couldn't be starker. The Indian's hairline starts so low, it looks like he's wearing some sort of bushy headgear.

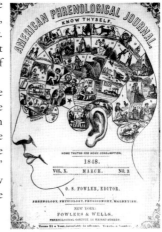

Today we're less likely to scrutinize foreheads for signs of talent, but the stain of pseudoscience persists in the language. If you consider these two statues, you are witnessing the origins of the term "high brow," meaning sophisticated, and "low brow," meaning the opposite. It's the legacy of yesterday's crackpot fad.

THE ELM TREES OF CENTRAL PARK ③

The best-tended trees in the world

Central Park
The Mall (beginning where East Drive connects with Center Drive at about
66th Street, ending at Bethesda Terrace)
From dawn to 1am

Central Park has over 25,000 individual trees, of about 150 different species. Those that line the Mall – the wide, straight path that leads to Bethesda Terrace – are American elms (Ulmus americana). The tunnel of foliage they create is one of the favorite images of New York, and seems as fixed as the Empire State Building or the Brooklyn Bridge. But these elms require constant, fretful attention: a pall of death hangs over them, and always has.

The Mall was intended to be Central Park's answer to the allées of France's geometric gardens. The straightaway is the exception in park designers Frederick Law Olmsted and Calvert Vaux's plan, otherwise based on interwoven loops and curves. The preference for the Mall's trees was from the very beginning the American elm – the choice, according to the Parks Department, of "almost every Main Street and college campus in the country in the 19th century." The soil was judged unfit for the large transplants; the contractor, in a gesture that resonates like an omen today, vowed that if the trees failed to survive for three years he would forfeit his fee. A year later nearly all of them were dead. A second group of smaller trees followed, and survived into the early 1900s – when gradually they, too, began to die.

Most of the elms we see in the Mall today date from around 1920. At the same time a biologist in Holland identified a fungus, spread by beetles, that came to be called Dutch elm disease. It soon crossed the Atlantic, and began to ravage the shade trees on those countless Main Streets and campuses. Most of New York's American elms have died; many consider those on the Central Park Mall to be the greatest collection anywhere.

Nobody feels the weight of this more than Neil Calvanese, Operations Vice-President of the Central Park Conservancy. "Beetles you can deal with," he says. "Fungus you can deal with. But fungus carried by beetles? It's an elm-killing machine." When the Conservancy started managing the park in 1998, the elms became a special priority. They are scrutinized for any sign of the disease, branches are fastidiously tested, whole trees are uprooted to prevent spreading. Calvanese figures the cost of protecting the elms has amounted to "millions of dollars." They may be the best-tended trees in the world.

THE WITCH OF BETHESDA TERRACE

The life of the night

Central Park
Located at the top of Bethesda Terrace at the head of the central stair
From dawn to 1am

The larger impact of Bethesda – fountain, lake, boats, forest – is so visually gratifying, it's perhaps natural that the fine details go unnoticed. The stone of the entire terrace is textured with sculptures, each unique, comprising what Central Park's first critics judged the richest public carving in America. The work is abstract in places, and figurative in others, and often a skillful collision of the two. The weirdest detail is the wicked tableau on one of the two large stone posts at the top of the stair passage: a flying witch, a jack-o'-lantern, a crescent moon.

The designer of the stonework was Jacob Wrey Mould, an English immigrant and something of a mad wizard. In 1868, when the park was nearly finished, the British magazine *The Builder* called him "brilliant, accomplished, ingenious, erratic." This sounds like a fair description of someone who, after designing the eye-watering arabesques and teeming birds lower down the terrace, would top it off with a witch. There's a calculated method at work, however. "He has delight in his art," cooed Clarence Cook in one of the first descriptions of the park, "that it is far easier for him to make every fresh design an entirely new one, than to copy something he has made before." Examine the pendant motifs of the posts and the medallions on the balustrade and you'll see what Cook meant. The interwoven patterns are an effect that Mould picked up from Islamic design, of which he was an expert; the balustrades, with their swirling birds and plants, represent the four seasons. Up above, on the other side of the carriage path (renamed Olmsted & Vaux Way after the park's designers) you'll find two stone posts: the witch flies on the western face of the western one.

West because: it's the direction of the setting sun. The carved scenes represent the different times of day: the witch's thematic opposite (eastern face of the eastern post) features a sunrise over the ocean. It's been suggested that the witch and the jack-o'-lantern, as symbols of Halloween, were Mould's way of either slighting or honoring the Irish, who brought the tradition to the city. But it's as likely that he was simply having clever fun. How to express the dead of night, a time that is effectively invisible? D.H. Lawrence said that birds are the life of the skies; well, the witch is the life of the night.

KENTUCKY COFFEE TREES

Mastodon food in Central Park

Central Park
In the Ramble at about 76th Street; walk uphill on East Drive from Loeb
Boathouse, turn left at the bronze panther and go fifty paces due west
From dawn to 1am

There is a small stand of very odd trees in Central Park. They're highly poisonous: even insects stay away. Tough seed pods hang uneaten on the bare branches far into winter. The fallen seeds are ignored by pretty much every living thing except paleontologists. For instance Carl Mehling of the American Museum of Natural History: "I mean, what would bother with this?" he asks, plucking what looks like a blob of dark glass from the soil. He knows the answer: a mastodon.

Seed dispersal is a vital trick in every plant's adaptive skill set. Some seeds fly on fibrous wings, some exploit the forgetfulness of hoarding squirrels, many are happiest in manure. In a 1982 paper, biologist Daniel Janzen and geoscientist Paul Martin addressed an ecological puzzle: why the fruits of some trees rot untouched, and why their husk is too tough or seeds too big for critters to eat. It was thought that plants with ineffectual "dispersal syndromes" were poorly evolved; Janzen and Martin suggested that they are in fact beautifully, exquisitely evolved, but the creatures they were tailored to attract – mastodons, giant sloths – went extinct 12,000 years ago.

A book on the theory, *The Ghosts of Evolution* (Connie Barlow), places the Kentucky coffee tree in the tiny category of "extreme anachronisms" – plants that make little sense in their present ecology. Since the end of the Pleistocene they've relied on floods and chance to keep the species going; meanwhile they're haunted by what once ate them. In the grass Mehling spies a fallen pod and cracks it open. Inside, seeds glisten in energy-rich goop like green rubber cement. "So good," he says, breathing deep. "Like chocolate and bananas." Now you know what mastodons like. To make the glassy seeds germinate, Mehling explains that you have to "scar" them, as the teeth and gastric juices of gobbling Pleistocene megafauna would. Otherwise they'll remain marbles forever.

But just because decorative mastodon food grows in Central Park doesn't mean that the beasts really lived on Manhattan? "Corner of Broadway and Dyckman," Mehling says back in the museum's fossil room; he points at a brown lower jawbone the size of a dinner platter. Fossils from a dozen mastodons have turned up in New York City, two of them in Manhattan. "Look at those teeth," Mehling nods. Each one is deeply ridged, and bigger than your fist.

ROCK TUNNEL TRANSVERSE

Fresh eyes on a marvel

Central Park
79th Street Transverse, midway at Belvedere Castle
Park open from dawn to 1am; transverse always open to cross traffic

Much has been made of Central Park's illusory "naturalness." One aspect of this feat of planning is seldom remarked today: the flow of foot and vehicle (and horse) traffic within and through the park. How to work an 840-acre block of green into the guts of a growing metropolis? It was a problem, and the area at Belvedere Castle, a schist outcrop called Vista Rock, was a particularly sticky part of it. Central Park designers Frederick Law Olmsted and Calvert Vaux likely owed the success of their proposal to striking on an inspired solution: sinking transverses below ground level. You can walk the whole length of the park (recommended) and never realize that major city arteries flow under your feet. The first visitors in the 1860s were amazed by the multi-level character of the paths and transverses: the experience of seeing cross-traffic in any form passing directly below or directly above was totally novel.

Today our experience with cars, and the freeways and onramps of major cities, make multi-level traffic seem mundane. But there's one spot in the park where you can witness this engineering challenge of the 1850s with fresh eyes. The footpath down Vista Rock branches off to the right about fifty yards east of the castle, leading seemingly nowhere. Take it. Go down the stone stairs. Emerge onto the 79th Street transverse, with more or less constant east-west car and bus traffic. Olmsted and Vaux foresaw this congestion, but imagined the transverse choked with "coal carts and butcher's carts, dust carts and dung carts." Believe it or not, standing here below the promontory to appreciate the tunnel blasted through the schist was a favorite thing for early park visitors to do. In 1869 Clarence Cook described the tunnel with a lingering distrust in its newfangledness. "After careful examination," he wrote, "the roof was found to be sound and firm." Going to see the blasted rock was so popular, this nice stone staircase was added some years after the park's completion.

> The tunnel was created with gunpowder. Dynamite hadn't been invented yet.

EQUESTRIAN STATUE OF KING JAGIEŁŁO

A medieval king uprooted by World War II

Central Park
Southeast corner of the Great Lawn at roughly 80th Street
From dawn to 1am

The statues of Central Park have little to do with the city. Nobody minds. There are poets, explorers, a heroic dog, a Beethoven. New York thrives on the motley jumble: there's a place for everybody.

Impossible, though, to whistle along the east side of the park and not find the sudden appearance of this bloodthirsty Pole a little jarring. Astride a pawing warhorse, with two naked swords crossed above his crown (and yet a third on his belt), King Władysław Jagiełło glowers at the Great Lawn. The monument is strange. But history reveals that the king makes perfect sense, right where he is. This Central Park statue has a more personal tie to the city than any other.

You have to go back to the New York World's Fair of 1939, often considered the last flourish of innocence before the planet went to hell. The first commercial TVs promised a new era of communication, the League of Nations promoted the unity of man, and crowds lined up to see a robot that smoked cigarettes. The organizers of the Polish pavilion must have turned heads when they wheeled King Jagiełło into place (*three* swords?). The statue commemorates the Battle of Grunwald, where, in 1410, Jagiełło led Lithuania and Poland against the invading Teutonic Knights of Germany. According to tradition, the evening before the fight the German commander delivered Jagiełło two unsheathed swords with the message that if he were a man, he would know what they were for. The next day the Germans got their asses handed to them.

The battle remains Poland's greatest military victory. Sculptor Stanisław Ostrowski worked on the monument over a period of years, but the decision to make it the centerpiece of the Polish pavilion in 1939, when Nazi Germany was looking for any excuse to attack, was a masterpiece of chutzpah. The Fair officially opened in the spring; on September 1, the Nazis launched a coordinated offensive that literally wiped Poland off the map. The statue raised its symbolic middle finger for just four months. Then the legendary king, along with the Polish pavilion workers and organizers, became suddenly homeless.

So most of them settled in New York. Ostrowski too. Big-hearted Mayor Fiorello LaGuardia lobbied to keep the statue, and in 1945 it was presented to the City of New York by the Polish Government in exile. The king's been here, frozen in victory, ever since.

GRANITE STATUE OF ALEXANDER HAMILTON ⑧

A reminder of the Great Fire

Central Park
nycgovparks.org/parks/centralpark/highlights/11942
On the west side of East Drive at about 83rd Street, behind the Metropolitan Museum of Art
From dawn to 1am

Fires have always been a mortal threat to New York, and especially so before the city installed its first major water distribution system in 1842 (see page 66). There are no monuments to the great blazes of the past, only absences. The last traces of the Dutch period were erased from downtown in successive fires in the 19th century, and one disaster, the so-called Great Fire of 1835, destroyed more property than any other event in the city's history. The statue of Alexander Hamilton that stands in Central Park, while not exactly a fire memorial, is a curious reminder.

The Great Fire began with a gas explosion in a dry goods store on today's Beaver Street. It was a frigid December night: roaring winds soon spread the flames to the surrounding buildings while bucket brigades and volunteer firemen tried to chip through the iced-over wells to water, which then froze in the hoses or blew back in sprays of cutting ice. The blaze soon spread to the Merchants' Exchange on Wall Street. Inside was the first marble work ever carved in the United States: a 14-foot-tall Alexander Hamilton by sculptor Robert Ball Hughes. The monument, celebrated as the country's finest statue, depicted Hamilton in classical robes and stood tall in the Exchange's Grand Rotunda.

Dodging flames, a group of sailors dashed in to save the statue; they managed to lift it from the base and were wrestling it toward the exit when the roof collapsed and they fled for their lives. According to a later account: "The artist stood gazing on the scene with listless despair; and when his favourite production of his genius, on which he had bestowed the labour of two long years fell beneath the ruins he sobbed and wept like a child."

A model of the work can be found at the Museum of the City of New York. The statue standing today in Central Park, by Carl Conrad, was commissioned by Alexander Hamilton's youngest son John Church Hamilton. It's carved from a material you don't see in many portrait statues: granite. John Church is said to have chosen the durable stone so that whatever future disaster the city had in store, this time his father's monument would survive.

SENECA

A vanished village

Central Park
Footprint of the village was between 81st and 89th Streets and between old Seventh and Eighth Avenues; foundation stones are 50 yards east of the children's playground at the 85th Street entrance
From dawn to 1am

n a page from the *Times* dated July 9, 1856, we learn the following: John Humphries was arrested for assault (two stabs with a sheath-knife); a new fire engine was given a trial run on Franklin Street; Mr. George Armstrong drowned on a fishing excursion; and by the end of the month, a whole community would have to vacate the area west of the old reservoir. "Within the limits of the Central Park," reads the article, "lies a neat little settlement, known as 'Nigger Village.' [...] It is to be hoped that their removal will be effected with as much gentleness as possible."

The village had a proper name: Seneca. There's only one physical trace of it left, the corner of a stone foundation at about 85th Street across the path from the children's playground. By all accounts, Seneca was exceptional. Even the *Times* article is careful to note the "pleasing contrast" it made to the miserable shanties of the Irish ("in common with hogs and goats") further south. Founded in 1825, the village had three churches, wood houses on assigned lots, a natural spring, basement schools, and a population of over 260, mostly African-American. Far from a ghetto, it was a rural refuge from the chaos, disease, and bigotry of downtown. It also gave black residents what they needed by law in order to vote: their own land.

In 1853, the city passed a bill authorizing the takeover of the swath of Manhattan destined to become Central Park. Seneca plot owners were paid off and the settlement was erased. In the summer of 2011, a team of Columbia archeologists dug in the area and found the minutiae of village life: crockery, cooking pans, a child's shoe. Ashley Anderson, an educator who assisted with the digs, found a belt buckle. "There were other primarily African-American villages," she says, "but a progressive community, and middle class? It was monumental." She also reveals a detail that is not covered in the Conservancy tour: the corner of foundation, supposedly the only physical trace of Seneca, is not that of a church, as was generally believed, but actually a later construction built exactly on top of it. In other words all that's left of Seneca is a kind of architectural echo, and what still lies hidden underground. When asked where these pioneering African Americans went, Anderson only shakes her head. No one has been able to find out.

ANDREW HASWELL GREEN MEMORIAL BENCH

The Father of Greater New York

Central Park
nycgovparks.org/parks/central-park/monuments/638
After turning onto Central Park Driveway (at about 104th St) from East Drive, take the first northbound path and continue about 60 yards
From dawn to 1am

On January 1, 1898, New Yorkers woke up to a city that had nearly doubled in size from the previous day to 3.5 million, making it the second largest in the world after London. The reason was the consolidation of the boroughs – Manhattan, Bronx, Queens, Brooklyn, and Staten Island – and the man behind the plan was one Andrew Haswell Green. In the far north of Central Park, at the edge of a small clearing on top of a hill, there is a large marble bench. It's the only monument to Green in New York City.

Creating the metropolis boundaries earned Green the nickname "Father of Greater New York" and is more than enough reason to memorialize him. But the man's influence goes further. In 1895, generations before the city would finally confront its own self-destructive forces in the 1960s, Green founded the American Scenic and Historic Preservation Society, dedicated to protecting city green spaces. He served on the Board of Commissioners during Central Park's construction, and is largely responsible for keeping the plans in line with the masterpiece that designers Frederick Law Olmsted and Calvert Vaux originally conceived. Green was also crucial to the formation of the New York Public Library, which without him would have had no book circulation.

And here's this marble bench. It's in the unvisited northern end of the park, and accessed by a narrow trail that even those who know the place are lucky to find twice. In the summer the grass is yellow; in winter the snow goes unshoveled. There is litter all around. A roomy, smooth stone bench in a secluded spot surrounded by trees: it might as well have a sign that says VAGRANTS WELCOME.

If you think Green deserved better, how the man is remembered is rather sweet compared to how he died. "Andrew H. Green Murdered," reads the *Times* headline from November 14, 1903. A man named Cornelius Williams stalked Green as he was returning from work and, just as the 83-year-old approached the iron gate of his home on 40th Street, shot him five times with a pistol. "He deserved it!" Williams stated in testimony. "He forced me to do it!" It later turned out that not only was Green innocent of any wrongdoing, he and his killer had never even met. Cornelius Williams was insane.

PAINTINGS IN THE STETTHEIMER DOLLHOUSE

A small but distinguished collection

Museum of the City of New York
1220 Fifth Avenue
mcny.org
212-534-1672
Monday, Thursday and Friday 10am-5pm, Saturday and Sunday 10am-6pm
4 and 6 trains/103rd St

A rare version of Marcel Duchamp's *Nude Descending a Staircase* hangs in the Stettheimer ballroom. Drawn in ink, wash, and graphite, and signed by Duchamp on the lower left, the work captures all the energy and daring of one of modernism's great masterpieces. To get the full benefit, enter the ballroom through the north door and then work gradually right. Also, be 5 inches tall.

The painting is one of many you'll find in New York's most improbable art collection, the Stettheimer dollhouse, where the paintings and drawings, generally not much bigger than postage stamps, are not facsimiles but *real* – bona fide works of art from the hand of celebrated artists. The Stettheimers – Carrie, who made the dollhouse, and her sisters Ettie and Florine – were daughters of a wealthy German banker who deserted them when they were children. After years touring Europe, the sisters and their mother settled in New York at the ritzy Alwyn Court on West 58th Street. The Stettheimers were defiantly "modern:" they smoked cigarettes, rejected romance, marriage, and children, and had a theatrical penchant for bright wigs, diamond collars, and Venetian costumes. Their apartment became a popular salon among the artists and intellectuals of New York's avant-garde. Florine, a painter, was the driving force; Ettie, a writer, was the wit and conversationalist; Carrie was the hostess and miniaturist. She was nearly 50 when she began the dollhouse, fashioning many of the finely detailed furnishings by hand. The tiny paintings were presented by artists who frequented the salon; the ballroom contains works by renowned modernists Duchamp, Albert Gleizes, and Alexander Archipenko, among others, as well as a pair of drawings and a 6-inch alabaster statue by Gaston Lachaise.

Ettie offered the dollhouse to the museum after Carrie's death in 1945. Florine Stettheimer surmised that Carrie doted on the house (thirty years in all) as a way of sublimating a frustrated ambition to be a set designer. The reader might surmise that the Stettheimer's bohemian salon was a collective sublimation of three women trapped in a kind of permanent childhood. Whatever the case, *Nude Descending a Staircase* alone is worth a visit.

GARBAGE MUSEUM

Why would somebody throw that away?

343 East 99th Street
Not technically open to the public: try your luck
6 train/96 St

That Billy Joel's *Greatest Hits* album you threw away in 1995, for a perfectly good reason, exists somewhere. It might be floating in the ocean, or under 40 feet of rot in a landfill, or ash on the wind. Or, if it's lucky, sitting in a clean crate with other undesirables in a Sanitation Department depot on East 99th Street as one of thousands of "exhibits" in the Garbage Museum.

The museum isn't in any way official, and you won't find it in any guide to the city. What it offers isn't even really intended for your amusement. It's a vast collection of objects that, for whatever reason, prompted a trash collector on his rounds to pause and ask the question: Why would somebody throw that away? Sanitation workers are the ultimate arbiters of value in New York City, and from time to time they grant reprieves. As powers go, this one is pretty great. Unloved toys, frumpy technology, posters in cheap frames, paintings by artists with no discernible talent, silent cuckoo clocks, second-place bowling trophies. Many of the objects fall into the flexible "perfectly good" category: old books and albums, kitchenware and sports equipment. Others are freakish riddles: a real dog, enormous, muscled, stuffed like a hunter's memento.

As with most great things, the Garbage Museum owes its existence to the quirks of one man. Nelson Molina first started bringing in objects off the street in 1981 to decorate his own area of the locker room. Slowly, the exhibit expanded as co-workers added their own rescued items. "It doesn't matter what it is," Molina told the *Times*. "As long as it's cool, I can hang it up and I've got a place for it."

What the Garbage Museum makes a place for isn't what you would choose to make a place for, and this is the better part of what's good about it. While you probably won't be chased out ("It's not for me to tell you where you can go and can't go," says one worker on the sidewalk out front), you won't be pandered to. These guys have made a display of our collective sense of value. It's about us, but not for us.

SQUADRON A ARMORY

The castle on Madison Avenue

Madison Avenue between 94th and 95th Streets
Only the Madison Avenue façade is original; the Park Avenue side is a recent addition in similar style
4 and 6 trains/96th St

First-time visitors to the Upper East Side are often pleased to discover that there's what appears to be an entire medieval castle on Madison Avenue. Two towers of red brick look down on the street, with arrow slits and turrets, and even crenellated tops. Today the walls enclose a school: look through, about where you'd expect the drawbridge to be, onto a playground full of yelling kids.

The castle was once home to Squadron A, the "New-York Hussars," an elite social club that used the yard inside for mounted drills. The building was started in 1894; the Hussars, originally strictly for show and sport, became a unit of the New York State National Guard in 1889 and went on to fight in the Spanish-American War and in both World Wars. On the wall you see a bronze plaque with their motto: *BOUTEZ EN AVANT* ("Charge").

The style of the brick building has been reported as "ancient Norman castellated," but it might as well be Camelot. Periodically, you can even see tendrils of ivy crawling up the rounded corners, as though arranged there by a fastidious backdrop artist. If you enjoy the incongruity of castles above taxicabs, you might appreciate it more to learn that the turrets, the towers and everything else were nearly knocked to rubble. When the Squadron A Armory became a school, plans were made to replace the towers with sixteen-story modernist replacements. But the city, still reeling from the destruction of Penn Station (see page 172) landmarked the building in 1966.

NEARBY
Islamic Cultural Center

Three blocks to the east of the Squadron A Armory is an interesting case of a building that occupies the pitiless grid on its own terms. Most New York mosques interpret the direction of Mecca to be simply "east." But, as mentioned elsewhere (see pages 108, 180 and 182) Manhattan's grid is tilted to fit the island. The designers of the Islamic Cultural Center of New York at 1711 Third Avenue dispelled any doubt about the true direction of the holiest site in Islam by orienting their mosque to the exact geodesic – the shortest possible line between two points on a sphere – with Mecca. What looks crooked on the map is Islamically perfect.

THE ZIEGFELD HEAD

The last piece of a legendary theater

52 East 80th Street
4, 5 and 6 trains/77th St or 86 St

Perhaps because we most associate statuary with antiquity, when buildings become unwanted it pains us to see the decoration tossed in the trash. New York has offered more of that kind of pain than most American cities. The landmarks conservation movement was in part sparked when a photographer discovered a stone angel from the recently demolished Penn Station (see page 172) leaning among rubble in a New Jersey dump. When the legendary Ziegfeld Theatre was sold a couple of years later and slated for razing, New Yorkers cried out but the newly-formed Landmarks Commission was powerless to stop the destruction. Today the Ziegfeld is dust, but one piece still survives. It sits on East 80th Street, behind a gate, near the basement entrance of a townhouse and – as if to make a point – next to the trashcans.

Designed by Viennese set designer and architect Joseph Urban, the Ziegfeld Theatre was created to be less a building than an otherworldly experience. "Unlike most of us, who see art in the flat terms of our environment," reads a *Times* article on the theater's 1927 opening, "Mr. Urban is a creator who paints nothing more tangible than dreams." Inside, the theater was shaped like an egg with the walls curving toward the stage; outside was a modernist proscenium arch in limestone with colossal engaged columns on either side, the fluting like the folds of a drawn curtain. Bright floodlights raked the white building at night, creating dodging patterns of shadow and glow on West 54th Street. High above the entrance perched stylized masks of comedy and tragedy, curved and ribbed like ram's horns; draped over them were 12-foot-tall protectoresses with mesmerizing eyes.

The Depression ruined the theater's Broadway business. After becoming a movie venue, and then a television studio, it finally folded in 1966 and was sold to make room for a soulless glass and steel tower. Shortly after the deal theatrical producer Jerry Hammer was riding in a limousine with the property's developer. When they passed the old stone theater, the developer said he was about to demolish it; as a joke, Hammer said if that was the case he wanted one of the giant staring guardians. Four months later he heard noises outside his townhouse on East 80th Street. "It's a truck with a crane," Hammer told the *Times*, "and a head, and they ask me where I want it." The head has been here ever since.

THE MURALS OF BEMELMANS BAR ⑮

Murals for rent

Carlyle Hotel, 35 East 76th Street
thecarlyle.com
212-744-1600
Sunday–Monday 12pm–12am, Tuesday–Thursday 12pm–12:30 am, Friday–
Saturday 12pm–1am
4 and 6 trains/77th St

Bemelmans Bar in the Carlyle Hotel is mellow and warm, as if the whole room is encased in 1930s amber. The bar itself is polished granite bordered in leather, the tables are topped with black glass, the gold leaf ceiling casts powdery reflections. But eventually in the dim light you'll start to notice the walls – or the odd characters painted on them. A leggy kangaroo, for example, sitting at a café table with a joey in its pouch. A giraffe with pinstriped trousers and lace-up shoes (four of them), doffing its hat to a passer-by. A rabbit smoking a cigar. Since 1947, the bar has carried off a design triumph unique in New York City: the meeting of liquor and children's illustration.

The author of the paintings and bar namesake is Ludwig Bemelmans, an Austrian writer and artist who moved to New York while still in his teens. For years young Bemelmans was a busboy at the Ritz-Carlton Hotel; he used to hide behind the palm trees in the dining room and sketch people on the backs of menus. In 1939 he published the first in a series of books about a mischievous French girl named Madeline who lives in a Parisian boarding school. They made him famous.

"The mural," says Tommy the barman, nodding to the characters on the walls, "shows the four seasons in Central Park." Tommy has worked at the Carlyle for half a century and has the gift of rapid, respectful small talk. While he tells the story he squeaks out cork after cork from wine bottles without even looking down. "But it's the four seasons in Central Park with *animals* instead of people. And *years* ago." Certain landmarks you'll recognize: Belvedere Castle, Cleopatra's Needle. But these exist in an unhinged dimension where dachshunds wear Panama hats and bunnies build giant snowrabbits. Why it works is a pleasant riddle. Bemelmans' hand isn't cute: it's loose and classy at the same time, and makes its own kind of sense.

Bemelmans liked travel, and hotel life. Instead of taking money for the mural he opted for eighteen months rent-free at the Carlyle for him and his family. There's a story that they were actually already living in the hotel and Bemelmans offered to paint the mural because he was broke. "You know," says Tommy, "I'm here fifty-three years, and that's all I ever heard. So I don't know what to tell you."

DWELLINGS ON MADISON AVENUE

Ruins for the Little People

942 Madison Avenue
4 and 6 trains/77th St

On a second-story window ledge of the old Mortgage and Trust Company building, you can spy what looks like a nest of clay: a red mound topped by a mysterious structure. A telephoto lens reveals that the structure is made from miniscule bricks and, very oddly, has the unmistakable stamp of human settlement. It could be an abandoned home for Southwest Indians – Hopi or Zuni – but Indians only an inch tall.

The miniature ruins are the work of artist Charles Simonds. "For the past three years I've been going around the streets of New York," he says in a 1972 film about his structures, "building dwelling places for an imaginary group of Little People who are migrating through the city. Each dwelling tells part of the story of the life of these people." The dwelling visible from Madison Avenue is one of three in the same area; another can be seen tucked under the pyramidal roof of a chimney rising behind the Mortgage and Trust and the third is exhibited inside the Whitney Museum directly across the street. The attention of the museum anoints Simonds as a major American artist, but the project, begun downtown, really belongs on the street: the questions it raises – of security, community, change – are street questions. Embedding the clay structures in corners or on curbstones was how Simonds connected with New York: outside, under the eyes of neighborhood people. In the film we see him silently tweezering bricks the size of grains of rice to form tiny walls on a cement foundation in the Lower East Side, while onlookers try to figure him out. "Does he get paid for that?" asks one.

Simonds built each ruin with the idea that the action of the city would eventually wear them down to nothing: one less refuge for the Little People. The piece on Madison, called *Dwellings*, is naturally protected by elevation: the ledge and chimney structures have been here since 1981. The Mortgage and Trust is now tenanted by David Webb jewelers; employees can see the ruin in perfect detail – rough brick walls fortified by sticks – just outside the window of their small kitchen space. Saleswoman Alma Continanzi relishes the secret. "In this big city," she says, "here's this little corner that nobody would know."

VETERANS ROOM IN THE SEVENTH REGIMENT ARMORY

Interior decorating for old warriors

643 Park Avenue
armoryonpark.org
See online calendar for events; for tours call 212-616-3930
4 and 6 trains/68th St – Hunter College; F train/Lexington Av – 63rd St

Built in 1880, Seventh Regiment Armory is the only armory in the United States that was privately funded. Every detail reflects the taste of the members: scions of New York's great Dutch and English families who were in general so well-off, the Seventh's nickname was the Silk Stocking Regiment. "It's the wealth of New York," says Kirsten Reoch. "This is it."

Reoch is project director at Park Avenue Armory, the nonprofit that is laboriously restoring the building and reinventing it as a cultural arts center. Today the best way to see the inside is to attend an event – for example a concert of the New York Philharmonic – and then wander through the ground floor until you come upon the remarkable Veterans Room. Here you'll see how well a limitless budget agrees with the military.

"At that time the decorative arts weren't considered womanly," says Reoch. "It was part of fine art, in a way. Men were very involved." To say that the decoration is manly falls short: the room might as well be lacquered in testosterone. Studded timber beams, wrought iron, polished woods; dragons, eagles, jousting knights, gladiators. The painted frieze around the ceiling cornice tells, in individual panels, the entire history of warfare. Even more remarkable: it all hangs together. The Veterans Room is an early effort by the decorators who would soon conquer the city as the design collaborative Associated Artists: Lockwood de Forest, Samuel Colman, Candace Wheeler, and Louis Comfort Tiffany. Tiffany was the guiding hand, and the Veterans Room is considered his most complete interior anywhere.

One detail summarizes the whole spirit of the place: the large pillars wrapped in tightly coiled iron chains. The effect is handsome, tactile, martial. During the Civil War, a regiment officer had the idea that a long chain attached between two cannonballs would skim across the field and, as Reoch tells it, "chop all the men on the other side in half." It might have worked, except field cannons are impossible to sync. The only time the man-chopping chain system was tried, the first ball shot out and whipped around behind the line. The chains here are a Seventh Regiment inside joke.

> The metallic touches embedded in the design were meant to be seen under 19th-century gas lighting. In the constant flicker of flames, the Veterans Room would have glittered like treasure.

MOUNT VERNON HOTEL MUSEUM

A last gasp of pastoral Manhattan

421 East 61st Street
mvhm.org
212-838-6878
See opening and tours hours on the website
N, R, 4, 5 or 6 trains/59th Street – Lexington Av; F train/Lexington Av

There are a handful of 18th- and 19th-century houses in Manhattan that create an illusion of stalled history: Dyckman Farmhouse, Morris-Jumel Mansion, Merchant's House. They all have creaking floors, a scent that is somewhere between polish and dust, and tables laden with wax food. The Mount Vernon Hotel is of this kind, with a difference. "After architectural historians came here," says Carol, a guide, "they determined that we are the only building still standing that operated as a day hotel."

If you don't know what a day hotel was, Carol says: "Think country club today." "Country" is exactly correct: although it now faces the humming Queensboro Bridge and is shadowed by the vaguely evil One Sutton Place North (a forty-story slab of black glass, it's been called the "2001 Monolith"), at the time of operation Mount Vernon was 4 miles into the boondocks. Urban New York City stopped at about 14th Street; those who could afford it would make the trip up the Boston Post Road in a carriage, or up the East River in a boat, to relax at this well-appointed stone carriage house. Upstairs the ladies sewed and sang; downstairs the men drank and played cards. The museum reveals curious aspects of the period. Novels are exclusive to the ladies' parlor, the men preferring newspapers. Water, generally foul at the time, is absent from the dinner table. The hotel was more than a place to take the air: it was a refuge from the cholera and yellow fever that burned through downtown.

Because the shift is frozen along with the history, Mount Vernon is the best site in the city to see the change, which hit Manhattan hard and fast, between traditional and modern city life. The dining room chairs are just beginning to show the uniformity of mass production. In the kitchen is a traditional hearth, but in front of it stands a more modern reflector oven. The parlor contains a harp, a pianoforte, and a flute, while in the corner squats a barrel organ, a machine that could play a short list of popular songs (No. 7: "Yankee Doodle"). In the 1820s, East 61st Street was a small and special dirt road. A generation later it would begin to lock with the grid.

The carriage house was built in 1799 and operated as a day hotel from 1827 to 1833. The land originally belonged to Col. William Smith and his wife Abigail Adams Smith, daughter of Founding Father John Adams.

Upper Manhattan

THE PORTALS OF PARADISE

New York: The Big Apocalypse

Cathedral Church of St. John the Divine
Amsterdam Avenue and 112th Street
stjohndivine.org
212-316-7540
Monday to Saturday 9:30am-5pm, Sunday 12pm–5pm
1 train/110th St – Cathedral Pkwy

The Cathedral Church of St. John the Divine is unfinished, but it's already the biggest cathedral in the world. "Actually," says humble Al Blanco, a volunteer greeter, "I like to say that it's *more or less* the biggest in the world." Cologne Cathedral is higher, and the one in Seville is wider, and St. Paul's in Rome, while more massive, is not a cathedral at all but a basilica. It doesn't matter: St. John the Divine is awesomely huge, and pacing its insides is one of the most transporting architectural experiences New York has to offer. "People are just taken away by the size," Blanco says, "and the feeling that size gives." You have to wonder what feelings the designers wanted to give with the frightening carvings that decorate the front door.

The Portals of Paradise, the array of limestone sculptures that frame the cathedral entrance, were completed in 1997. Of the many biblical figures portrayed, seven – Isaiah, Jeremiah, Ezekiel and Daniel; Amos, Hosea and Jonah – are prophets. If prophets share one thing, it's a sweet tooth for carnage. Ezekiel stands on grimacing skulls, a nod to his Dream in the Valley of Dry Bones and representing, according to the cathedral brochure, "total destruction." The capital under Amos and Hosea shows a bus full of unlucky commuters hurtling off a broken Brooklyn Bridge. But it's the stonework between these two that many find most chilling. "New York City," reads the brochure, "including the Twin Towers, is portrayed under a mushroom cloud." The Towers are pitched for a fall, and couched in roiling flame.

Scaring folks into church is as old as God, of course. And it's worth noting that the whole cathedral is named after the author of the nutty Book of Revelation. Still, many have deciphered sinister intent in St. John the Divine. It's been called Masonic, pagan, Satanic – if you squint hard enough, you'll find it here. But if the building makes some uncomfortable, it's less due to a wicked cabal than the clash that naturally results when a medieval colossus, complete with medieval stagecraft, is constructed in the 20th century – and on into the 21st.

BLESSING OF THE BICYCLES

You are performing a good work

Cathedral Church of St. John the Divine
Amsterdam Avenue and 112th Street
stjohndivine.org
Blessing given in early spring, check for schedule: blessingofthebikes.com
212-316-7540
Monday to Saturday 9:30am–5pm, Sunday 12pm–5pm
1 train/110th St – Cathedral Pkwy

Throughout the year St. John the Divine hosts events that some have complained are unchurchly. The criticism is less an indictment than a signal that where special programs are concerned, the cathedral gets New York. It gets the zombie-lovers who attend the Procession of the Ghouls every Halloween, and the pet owners who bring their dogs, cats, birds, ferrets, llamas, elephants, etc. to the yearly Blessing of the Animals, and the cyclists who roll their bikes into the church every spring for the Blessing of the Bicycles.

There are thousands of brave cyclists in the Death Race of New York City streets, and not all of them escape unscathed. In 1998, Glen Goldstein, the organizer of the Blessing of the Bicycles, approached St. John the Divine's leadership to see if some ceremony might be held in the interest of bicycle safety. The church gladly offered to allow bikes in the cathedral for a blessing with holy water. It's the kind of arrangement that would grate on the less tolerant: the cathedral is Episcopal, Goldstein is Jewish, and attendees are what-have-you (the event website: "Regardless of your religious beliefs – or lack thereof – you are welcome").

More come every year. Led by a trio of bagpipers (one of them in Lycra), hundreds of cyclists wheel their rides through the cathedral's sculpted portico to the polished stone central aisle, forming orderly rows. The atmosphere is more comradely than solemn or even reverent. And though it's likely more bikes than you've ever seen under any roof, let alone a church roof, the Gothic enormity of the cathedral sweeps awesomely all around with room to spare, and the words of Reverend Tom at his podium rebound with echoes. "Whether you cycle for recreation or sport," hums the reverend, "whether you commute to work, or for whatever reason you cycle...or roll in any way that does not involve internal combustion ...you are performing a good work." When the speech is over, a shimmering chorus wells up as the cyclists, following an unspoken cue, ring their bells in unison.

The first recorded traffic accident in American history happened in New York, and involved a bicycle. Henry Wells lost control of his horseless "wagon" on upper Broadway, "going in a zig-zag fashion" until he knocked Evylyn Thomas off her bike. She survived.

THE PEACE FOUNTAIN

A puzzling battle of good versus evil

Cathedral Church of Saint John the Divine
112th Street and Amsterdam Avenue
stjohndivine.org
212-316-7540
1 train/110th St

No surprise that the Cathedral of Saint John the Divine – peculiar in its own right – plays host to the weirdest public statue in New York City. The 40-foot-high *Peace Fountain* is a heap of wild imagery: twisting flames, giant crustaceans, a DNA helix, a smirking moon, the severed head and nervous system of Satan, lovesick giraffes. Rising from the center is a gaunt Archangel Michael with a broadsword.

Two tourists take a stab at interpreting it:

"It's basically a guy with wings making out with a giraffe. And somehow Lucifer got his head ripped off by that ... whatever that is."

"Some kind of lobster. But that other part looks like shark teeth. I guess if you put it in a public fountain, it's just art."

"It's all art, dude."

Coded messages are nothing new in Christian statuary, and churches in medieval France, where St. John the Divine takes many of its cues, used demons and the damned for decoration. *The Peace Fountain* has been criticized for its vaguely pagan flavor, but Christianity is full of second-hand paganism, and anyway the gibe "Pagan!" has never had much impact in New York. So while the sculpture may not please everybody, it's definitely in the right place. But what does it mean?

For those who take the time to look, there's a convenient bronze plaque that explains everything – perhaps a little too explicitly. The fountain traces the continuity of life in the cosmos along a theme of good triumphing over evil. Giraffes, "among the most peaceable of animals," are good. The crab "reminds us of life's origins in the sea," and DNA is life's "key molecule." Greg Wyatt, the sculptor-in-residence of St. John the Divine, created *The Peace Fountain* in the cathedral's crypt. It was installed in 1985 and has been inspiring, offending, and baffling people ever since.

In counterbalance, the fountain is ringed by dozens of smaller bronze sculptures with inspiring messages from across the whole spectrum of spirituality: Aesop, Gandhi, John Lennon. These smaller works were created by local schoolchildren. It might take more than that, though. While the tourists debate aesthetics, a group of first-graders troop down Amsterdam. One boy freezes, and fixes a leery eye on the fountain until his schoolmate tugs him back into line.

CHURCH OF NOTRE DAME

A French cave, plus benefits

405 West 114th Street
ccnd-nyc.org
212-666-9350
1 train/Cathedral Pkwy or 116 St – Columbia University; A, B and C trains/
Cathedral Pkwy or 116 St

If you like a touch of theme park with your religious architecture, Notre Dame near Morningside Park has an unexpected attraction: the entire wall behind the altar has been sculpted to look like the interior of a cave. Not just any cave, but the famous grotto of Lourdes in southern France, complete with stone face, crawling ivy, and a niche for a statue of the Virgin.

It's natural for this church to have a marked French influence: Notre Dame was built as a chapel for the Fathers of Mercy, a community of French Catholic missionaries. The link to the grotto of Lourdes is owed to Estelle Livingston Redmond, a prominent Catholic from one of New York's oldest families, who purchased the land and financed the church's construction with the provision that it promote devotion to Our Lady of Lourdes, a manifestation of the Virgin Mary that was first reported at the French cave in 1858. Redmond believed that the natural spring water at Lourdes had healed her own son. The parish was officially affiliated with the French shrine in 1913, enabling worshippers – according to a process that the Roman Catholic Church presumably understands – "to obtain the same spiritual benefits as pilgrims who travel to Lourdes, France."

This affiliation stretches further than you think – all the way to the afterlife, in fact. In 2008, on the 150th anniversary of Mary's appearance, Pope Benedict XVI decreed that a pilgrimage to Lourdes on its jubilee year was worth a plenary indulgence – a kind of get-into-Heaven-free card. During the week corresponding to the Virgin's first apparition (February 2–10), faithful Catholics could visit "in any church, grotto or decorous place, the blessed image of that same Virgin of Lourdes, solemnly exposed for public veneration" and have their stay in Purgatory reduced to zero. During that week, you could catch a Knicks game, see *The Lion King*, and save your immortal soul all in the same town.

Today, the Church of Notre Dame continues its spiritual link to the grotto in France: it's an outlet for Lourdes water. "I would like __ bottles of Lourdes water" reads an order stub attached to the visitor pamphlet. "(I enclose an offering of $ __ to cover the cost of shipping.)" According to a worker at the chapel: "It comes from France in containers, and then we put it in these little bottles."

HARLEM FIRE WATCHTOWER

The last of the first skyscrapers

Marcus Garvey Park
From dawn to 1am
2 and 3 trains/125th St

On the top of a hill at the highest point of Marcus Garvey Park stands an old iron structure. If you ask around the neighborhood, you'll hear varying theories on what it was for. Slave market. Military fort. Lighthouse. "I know there's a big-ass bell up there," says one man. "That's about it." The big-ass bell weighs 10,000 pounds, and to understand its original purpose, you have to imagine a Manhattan where the buildings are at most five stories tall, and made of wood.

The Harlem Fire Watchtower on Mount Morris Hill, one of several iron watchtowers built during the same period, once commanded an uninterrupted view of the land around it. Until the mid-1800s when the Croton Aqueduct began feeding fresh water into Manhattan (see page 66), fires were frequent and catastrophic. Older watchtowers were built of wood, and sometimes had an unfunny knack for catching fire along with everything else. In the 1840s an alternative was found, and with it the architectural key that would soon set the Manhattan skyline soaring. While on a trip to Italy, the engineer and inventor John Bogardus had the idea that the richness of ancient architecture could be reprised in cast iron. Structural iron had been used sparsely in small bridges and lower structures, but the cost remained prohibitively high. Bogardus took advantage of cheaper and more readily available iron, and the strength of interlocking cast beams. The system he conceived for the watchtower distributed weight throughout a metal skeleton – the same system that makes modern skyscrapers possible.

When Bogardus built his first tower on 33rd Street and Ninth Avenue in 1851, it became the only freestanding iron-frame structure in America. Another tower on Spring Street soon followed. Bogardus bid on the Mount Morris tower, but was beaten out by a rival who had the good sense to follow his innovative design. In all, nearly a dozen iron watchtowers were eventually built throughout Manhattan. As the city rose around them, these structures, which drew the blueprint for height, became obsolete. The Harlem Fire Watchtower is the only one left.

THE WISHING TREE

Rub the stump

Apollo Theater, 253 West 125th Street
apollotheater.org
Tours must be scheduled in advance, contact historic.tour@apollotheater.
org or 212-531-5337. Tour reservations are offered to groups of 20 or more.
Individuals and groups with less than 20 participants can join an existing tour
if one is scheduled on your preferred date
2, 3, B, C and D trains/125th St

The big acts that have crossed the Apollo Theater stage are countless. But so are the small ones: the unknowns, the would-have-beens, the newly discovered. On Wednesdays for over seventy years the Apollo has hosted "Amateur Night," where anyone can perform to a raucous crowd. Next to the wings, on its own pedestal, sits an unlikely object: a section of a tree stump. The Wishing Tree, according to Apollo tradition, must be rubbed for good luck before testing your talent onstage. The hopefuls have polished the wood to a shine. Some of them stepped into the lights, took up the microphone, and moments later became Whitney Houston, or Ella Fitzgerald, or James Brown. Others stayed who they were: just people. Still, the stump contains dreams.

The theater's history echoes the history of Harlem. Originally a burlesque house, under the management of Jewish partners it became the first venue in New York to introduce black performers to white audiences. "The way black people danced," says historian and Apollo tour guide Billy Mitchell, "the way we played our music, our theater, our poetry, our intellect, our activism – our whole swagger, as they say. Our white brothers and sisters wanted to see black people perform." Once they did, they wanted more: American culture changed forever. And this wider success of black culture inspired the unknowns of Amateur Night who took to the stage, rubbed the stump, and prayed for discovery.

The roots of the Wishing Tree go beyond the Apollo, and beyond the Harlem Renaissance, stretching deep into black city lore. The stump is one section of a great elm that grew on 131st Street, in front of the old Lafayette Theater, in the early 1900s the foremost African-American venue in the country. Performers thought that standing in the tree's shade, or touching its bark or wearing its twigs and leaves would bring work, and luck. After the Wishing Tree was felled in 1934, pieces were sold off for souvenirs and firewood.

BEAR AND FAUN

A park for predators

Morningside Park
West 110th to 123rd Streets, Manhattan to Morningside Avenues; fountain
located at about 114th Street
nycgovparks.org/parks/morningsidepark
1 train/Cathedral Pkwy or 116th St – Columbia University;
A, C and B trains/Cathedral Pkwy or 116th St

Cicy statues make amateur historians of everyone: you get to consider the attitudes of former times through public images. Often something gets lost along the way. An illustration can be found in Morningside Park: for coming on a century, visitors have been trying to figure out the message of a bronze fountain just north of the duck pond.

"It's a boy," says a girl of about 8, holding a dripping plastic cup to the fountain's spigot. "And that bear is gonna eat him."

This is the general interpretation, and it hasn't been helped by the statue's location. Morningside Park, now mostly pleasant, was for decades a Thunderdome of crackheads and purse snatchers. Anyone who has lived in the neighborhood for more than twenty years can remember avoiding the place, but the park's rotten fame goes all the way back to gangs in the 1920s, and its proximity to the students of Columbia – the park is basically a ribbon of green between Ivy League and Harlem slum – has made for some interesting violence over the years. By the 1960s, Morningside was judged by the *Times* the least-used park in the entire city, a place where even cops were afraid to enter. One article describes a waterless cast bronze fountain "showing a huge bear peering eagerly over a ledge, beneath which a frightened faun is crouching."

If there ever was a time when the fountain conveyed a theme other than dread, it didn't last very long. It was dedicated in 1914, a gift to the city from banker Alfred Seligman. The artist, Edgar Walter, was a student of Rodin and a noted animalier with a thing for bears. He sculpted bears with fauns, bears with nymphs, bears with hunters, even, according to one review of his studio show, "an extremely attractive bear enjoying a meal of salted pork." The fountain depicts a scene that would be, in another park, potentially amusing: the faun (a faun with hooves and horns, not a boy) has taken shelter from the rain and gets surprised by the cave's owner, whose interests are proprietary, not dietary.

Mitch, a dog-walker who crosses the spot several times a day, enjoys the park's improved safety but still doesn't get the statue. "I don't know how anybody could think that's cute," he says. "It looks like that boy's about to die."

THE HIDDEN OWL OF
ALMA MATER

A sculptor with a thing for birds

Low Memorial Library, Columbia University
116th Street and Broadway
1 train/116th St – Columbia University

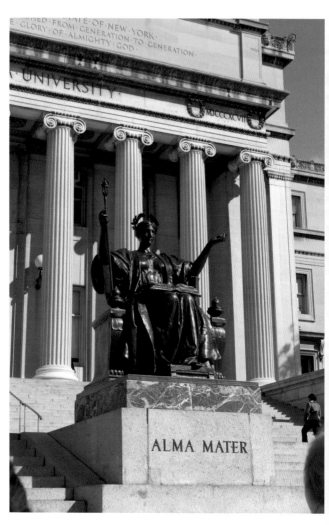

On the steps of Low Library at the center of the Columbia University campus stands a statue most people know. *Alma Mater* has been the symbol of the school for over a century. Head ringed in laurel, 12 feet high, she raises her arms from her massive throne and surveys the quad with a bronze power stare, as though entranced by her own awesomeness. The grandeur is nicely offset by a quiet, secret detail: an owl that peers out from a hiding spot deep in the folds of *Alma Mater*'s gown.

The owl has a thematic logic behind it. *Alma Mater* symbolizes the cultivation of the student mind (in Latin the name means "nurturing mother"), but the figure is actually Minerva, Roman goddess of wisdom and war, and her mythical companion is the owl Glaucus. The owl's night vision makes it a natural sage: the eyes cut through the darkness. The work is a trove of other symbols: the gown represents academics, lamps swirling from the armrests are labeled *Doctrina* (learning) and *Sapientia* (knowledge), the scepter in *Alma Mater*'s right hand is topped with the crown of King's College, a reminder that Columbia began as a Royalist college (1754).

You might think: the other hand would make an excellent perch for an owl with night vision. But then it would be in the service of the institution. The owl is so hard to find, it connects to the very personality of the sculptor, Daniel Chester French: when you finally spy it, it's like receiving a secret handshake that spans decades. French was fascinated with birds; his first love was not art, but taxidermy. As a youth he was described as "of sunny disposition, bright and witty [...] but by no means decided as to his future work," and his earliest sculptural success was a pair of owls. He went on to become perhaps the greatest American sculptor of his time (it's enough to say: Lincoln Memorial).

There are dozens of Daniel Chester French works in New York City, among them the *Four Continents* on the steps of the Customs House (now the National Museum of the American Indian, see page 54).

Stars over Manhattan

Pupin Physics Laboratories
Columbia University
outreach.astro.columbia.edu
212-851-7420
1 train/116th St – Columbia University

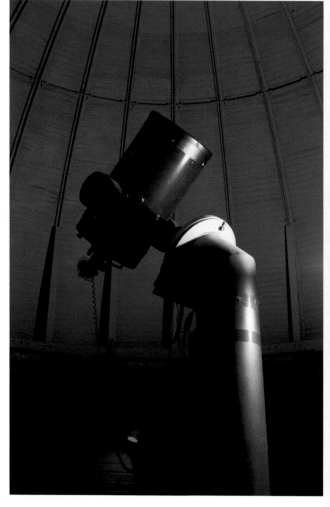

The metropolis makes a poor spot for a telescope. Light pollution creates a haze around New York that swallows starlight, some of which spent millions of years getting here for nothing. In the relative dark of upper Manhattan, Columbia's Rutherfurd Observatory on the roof of Pupin Physics Laboratories is one of the city's best astronomical vantages. Come for the Outreach Program and you'll rediscover the spinning vault of planets and constellations.

The evening begins with a 30-minute lecture by students and professors on a specific nook of astronomy: sunspot records of ancient Asia, gamma ray telescopes, exploding stars. One thing you learn is that astronomers are unfailingly nice. "You get a half-hour to tell people what you think is cool about astronomy," says graduate student Christine Simpson. "It's fun." What happens after the lecture depends on the weather: on cloudy nights there's a slideshow; if it's clear, you take an elevator to the roof, where the dark green dome of the telescope awaits you.

"What the atmosphere does to starlight is very interesting," says Neil Zimmerman, an Astronomy Department PhD. He's just a voice in the dark; a long line of visitors coils around him. "It's pretty. It actually distorts the image, so you'll see more than just a point of light." Tonight the large telescope is pointed at Sirius, the brightest star visible from Earth. You can already see it, a sparkling dot in the chink of open sky. In the eyepiece of the telescope the star becomes a brilliant blot that dodges and wobbles, rimmed in bending colors, and weirdly fluid, as though shining through bathwater.

There are two smaller telescopes on the roof: a domed one pointed at the cluster of fetal stars in the Orion Nebula, and an open one pointed at Saturn. The gas giant appears as a bright streak, but the cant of the rings is clearly visible. "Astronomy is my *passion*," says a man with a pair of binoculars around his neck, and from the look in his eyes he's not kidding. "Anybody mind if I check on New Jersey real quick?" he says. "No?" – and whips the telescope over to the Hudson.

Splitting the first atom

Pupin Physics Laboratories is where the first atom was split. New York's role in the early work on the atomic bomb is the source of the code name "Manhattan Project."

RIVERSIDE CHURCH CARILLON

The heaviest tuned bell in history

490 Riverside Drive
trcnyc.org
212-870-6700
Thursday to Sunday 9am–5pm
1 train/116th St – Columbia University

Riverside Church, the tallest church in the U.S., was designed and built like a skyscraper. The stone hangs on a steel cage; construction, funded by John D. Rockefeller, began in 1927 and was completed only three years later. The sturdy frame does more than support the tons of ornamented masonry: inside the tower is the world's biggest carillon. The bass bell that marks the hour, the Bourdon, is the single heaviest carillon bell in history.

Although regular visits to the bell tower and the observation deck are a tourism casualty of 9/11, it's still possible, with persistence, to arrange a special tour with the visitor center. But the best way to see the tower is to accompany Ralph, the assistant maintenance engineer, while he does his daily check of the building. Ralph is a large man in a permanently good mood; he makes noise as he walks – keys jingling, walkie-talkie crackling – but moves lightly up and down the corridors and stairs of the church he knows as well his own home. "I love this place," he says. "I'm proud to work here, and I'm sure Mr. Rockefeller would want us to share it."

The elevator stops at the twentieth floor; a small stair leads to the carillon and open air. The bells hang in a wash of white noise: distant traffic from the street far below, wind beating from the north, the rattling metal shutters of the observation deck above. The Bourdon – 20 tons of expertly tuned bronze – is on the lowest tier; around and above it are arrayed seventy-three increasingly smaller bells. The combined weight: over 100 tons. In the middle is a cubicle where the bells are connected by levers and pulleys to a system of bars laid out like a piano keyboard. Despite the enormity of the bells, the action of the clavier is almost instantaneous. "Look," Ralph says, touching the highest keys – and immediately a pair of pure notes peal out. "That one," he nods at the lowest key (and biggest bell), "you've got to put a little more force into."

Here to make a regular checkup of the carillon is John Witkowiak. "They're the best bells I've ever heard," he says with an expert's bluntness. Witkowiak, a third-generation carillon caretaker, notes the tower's size. "Massive beams," he says. "Everything's riveted." Suddenly it's 1 o'clock, and the place goes crazy: the bells make your bones vibrate. Witkowiak, undaunted – or mostly deaf by now – turns around and gets back to work.

RIVERSIDE LABYRINTH

Still mysterious after a thousand years

490 Riverside Drive
trcnyc.org
212-870-6700
Thursday to Sunday 9am–5pm
1 train/116th St – Columbia University

On the floor of the Riverside Church chancel you'll find an interesting hallmark of the building's medieval roots: a stone labyrinth.

Labyrinths first started appearing in the floors of Christian churches (although they predate them) around the year 1000. One theory holds that meandering along the loops and switchbacks served as a proxy journey for devout Christians who couldn't make the pilgrimage to Jerusalem: the hassles of travel in a conveniently concentrated form. If bumping around a maze sounds like a surer path to rage than to spiritual fulfillment, keep in mind that labyrinths are patterns, not puzzles. Everyone who walks the labyrinth walks the same inevitable route: there's only one.

Completed in 1930, Riverside Church is modeled after Chartres Cathedral in France and inherited the labyrinth along with the architecture. Chartres has the most well-known church labyrinth in the world: over 40 feet in diameter, it fills the entire nave of the cathedral. The design in the floor of Riverside is mostly symbolic: formed by contrasting polished marbles, it's only 10 feet across – borderline unwalkable. Still, since the 1990s the church has attracted labyrinth enthusiasts with a larger, portable version that can be spread out on the floor. The practice began with Riverside Church member Richard Butler, who first helped create a paper labyrinth for Easter Holy Sunday, and later had the design painted on canvas. "I experience a clearing of my mind," Butler told the *Times* about walking it.

Labyrinths are a wider phenomenon. Diana Carulli, an artist who has designed large public labyrinths in Union Square and other parts of the city, says there's a growing public need for walking around in circles. "Labyrinths go through these tremendous revival periods," she says. "They work through strengthening your core in some mysterious way."

The Chartres labyrinth

Riverside's Parish Life Ministry hosts labyrinth walks on a more or less quarterly basis. Anyone can come and try it.

BUTTERFIELD STATUE

Monumental hassle

Sakura Park
Riverside Drive from Claremont Avenue to West 122nd Street
From dawn to 1am
1 train/125th St

Sakura Park, just north of Riverside Church, is the home of the monument to Union Army general Daniel Butterfield. Butterfield's accomplishment: he composed the bugle call "Taps," which signals lights out to American troops and haunts the funerals of military veterans. Seems simple enough. But look what a mess.

To begin with, the man probably never composed "Taps" at all. During the Civil War, Butterfield directed his bugler to play the tune in place of the customary rifle shots at lights out, and the practice soon spread through both the Confederate and Union armies. The use and timing of the song was definitely Butterfield's contribution, but the melody was based on one published decades earlier. (Bugle-call historians, usually a docile lot, have been fighting about this for years.) Aside from the "Taps" question, the general probably had a lousy character. While serving as Assistant United States Treasurer under Grant, he became involved in a scheme to make a fortune by manipulating the gold market. The resulting panic was ugly enough to be dubbed Black Friday (September 24, 1869).

The statue itself has a messy history. The sculptor, Gutzon Borglum, was sued by the executors of the will of Butterfield's widow because the monument wasn't "colossal" enough. Also, it didn't look like the general. The widow wanted the head to be based on existing bronzes; Borglum instead used a photograph of Butterfield that failed to capture, according to the widow, "the strength always discernible in his face." Borglum was sued for $32,000 (more than half the commission). The artist filed a countersuit, and eventually won. According to the Parks Department sign next to the statue, Borglum was so disgusted by the process, as a parting shot he signed the top of Butterfield's head – "the

only part of the original statue they didn't make me change." But the crowning hassle might be your own if you take the trouble to verify this. Either the signature is very small, or pasted over with pigeon droppings or – more likely – just a legend.

AMIABLE CHILD MONUMENT

Always inclosed and sacred

Riverside Drive at 123rd Street
1 train/125th St

The smallest cemetery in New York City contains a single grave. The granite monument, inside a small iron fence, bears the message: "Erected to the Memory of an Amiable Child, St. Claire Pollock, Died 15 July 1797 in the Fifth Year of his Life." People are still moved by the bittersweet memorial; you'll often see tributes left here: stones, wildflowers, even toys.

The straightforward power of the Amiable Child Monument is thrown into relief by how thoroughly it has been upstaged by the most conspicuous burial place in the United States: nearby Grant's Tomb. Wanderers often stumble upon the Amiable Child by accident when they cross Riverside Drive after a visit to the 150-foot granite behemoth that sits on top of the dead president. The difference between the two monuments is one of kind, not just degree. This stretch of shoreline was once the country residence of linen merchant George Pollock who lost his son to a drowning accident in the Hudson River. When Pollock sold the property only two years after St. Claire's death, the burial plot was left out of the deed: he asked the new owner to "confer a peculiar and interesting favor by allowing me to convey the inclosure to you, so that you will consider it as part of your own estate, keeping it, however, always inclosed and sacred." And so it has been kept since 1797. By comparison, construction of Grant's Tomb was set back years over questions of location, funding, and design; New York wanted a structure that would dazzle the ages, outsiders resented sending a cent of funding to the "millionaire city." The 1897 inauguration – on the centennial of St. Claire's death – featured a parade of 60,000 soldiers and civilians, and was attended by a million people.

Grant's Tomb is still the area's main draw for visitors (although a recent poll revealed that only 10% of New Yorkers have ever seen it). Meanwhile the urn continues to work its humble reversal: a beacon not to awe, but feeling.

Originally white marble, the urn was replaced with a copy in 1897, and again in 1967. Photos from a century ago show the gravesite was flanked on the west side by benches that offered a clear view of the Hudson River (now obscured by trees), the supposed site of the boy's death.

FREEDOM TUNNEL

Life under the grid

Easiest approach: St. Clair Place (129th Street) west to the Henry Hudson Parkway off-ramp; follow fence until you find a gap
Transport: 1 train/125th Street
WARNING: The Freedom Tunnel is an active train tunnel, and entering it on foot is potentially dangerous as well as illegal

Mutants scurrying in the city's sewers and subway tunnels, howling in the permanent dark among the rats and the dripping cement, gearing up for the coming apocalypse or just eating each other...of New York's many gritty legends, underground dwellers make the most vivid nightmares. But some of the legends are true. And you can readily visit one place that for years was home to a scattered community that chose to live not off the grid but in the shadows under it: the Freedom Tunnel.

The tunnel runs under Riverside Park from 122nd to 72nd Streets. After the heyday of train travel (see page 172) it was taken out of service and gradually became a permanent shantytown: by the early 90s the population was in the hundreds. For many the privacy, shelter, and security of the underground life was a better deal – rodents and cold notwithstanding – than the streets or the city-run homeless shelters. In the documentary *Dark Days* one tunnel-dweller explains: "Anybody could walk by you while you're sleeping on a bench and bust you in the head. At least down in the tunnel you ain't got to worry about that. 'Cause they ain't nobody in their right mind would come down there." The dark was a kind of fatal lure; many spent years in the tunnel, emerging only at illness or death.

In 1991 Amtrak reopened the tunnel, and a long and bitter eviction followed. Today you can walk the full fifty subterranean blocks without seeing a soul. A stroll down the urban cave is one of the most memorable activities the city offers, but explorers take note: it's also trespassing. Access to the north entrance is over, under, or through the chain link fence between the off-ramp of the Henry Hudson Parkway between 129th and 122nd Streets and the train tracks west of it. The rectangular entrance looks dauntingly black on approach, but inside the tunnel is a regular and ethereal light: at every cross street a grate high overhead lets in a glow – often colored green or orange by piled leaves – which brightens areas of graffiti like a succession of works in a museum. The tracks gleam off darkly in either direction. It's cool, and dusty, and quiet except for the inconsequential sounds from the busy world above.

The tunnel is named for Chris "Freedom" Pape, a graffiti artist who painted here in the 80s and 90s.

OUR LADY OF LOURDES CHURCH ⑮

Gothic, grand, second-hand

472 West 142nd Street
212-862-4380
1 train/137th St – City College or 145th St

Whehen Our Lady of Lourdes Church was finished in 1903, a critic wrote: "It is enough to make the beholder stare and gasp." He was talking as much about the church's appearance as the method of construction. At that time, New York's attitude toward unwanted architecture was: topple it, crush it, cart it away. The forward-thinking man behind Our Lady of Lourdes took a different approach: rescue and recycle. The church is a brilliant freak, a Frankenstein composed of four other buildings.

When Rev. Joseph McMahon was charged with erecting a new Roman Catholic church on 142nd Street, this far uptown was backcountry: splendid marbles and Gothic flourishes were not in the budget. Instead of skimping on his vision, enterprising McMahon looked to lower Manhattan for what was coming down. He hustled to make deals with owners of demolished buildings and soon accumulated a mountain of priceless scrap: iron beams and windows from an orphan asylum, stonework from the mansion of department store magnate A.T. Stewart (see page 106), the back wall of St. Patrick's, which had to be removed to construct the cathedral's Lady Chapel, and – the real coup – almost the entire façade of the venerated National Academy of Design. Considered the finest art establishment in the U.S., the academy near Madison Square was New York's temple of painting and sculpture, with contrasting Tuckahoe marbles and Italian Gothic arches based on the Doge's Palace in Venice.

Our Lady of Lourdes is now just one building among dozens packed neatly into 142nd Street. The staff in the offices next door aren't familiar with the construction: consecration and time have erased the church's odd beginning. One of the employees offers a tour into the back. Sunlight angles through the narrow passage, grazes the palatial stonework of the south side, and falls tenderly on a rank of overflowing garbage cans. Underneath the church is the "grotto" or, if you come for Spanish service, la gruta: a chapel slathered with gobs of plaster in imitation of the French cave Our Lady of Lourdes is named for. The air down here does in fact have a dark, cool, watery quality. After punching on the lights around a Madonna in her craggy niche, the guide asks, "It's nice, no?"

For an even more ambitious recreation of the Lourdes grotto, see page 290.

HAMILTON GRANGE

A New York home for a Founding Father

414 West 141st Street
nps.gov/hagr – 646-548-2310
Visitor center: Wednesday to Sunday 10am-4pm; guided tours are available on
a first-come, first-served basis
1 train/West 137th St; A, B, C and D trains/145th St

Of all the Founding Fathers, Alexander Hamilton is the striver, the go-getter, meritocrat – the New Yorker. Born in the West Indies, he arrived a poor orphan bastard, and within five years was personal aide to George Washington. He had a sixth sense for finance, and his concession to Thomas Jefferson – moving the nation's political capital to Washington D.C. but maintaining New York as the banking center – resounds even today. It follows that the man left traces in the city. You can raise a glass at Fraunces Tavern where he kept his first offices as United States Treasurer or visit the site of the oldest bank in the country, which he founded. You can stand on West 42nd Street and look just over the Hudson to Weehawken, where Hamilton dueled with Aaron Burr – or at the foot of his grave at Trinity Church. A surprising number of New Yorkers, especially those who see everything above 110th Street as a kind of exotic hinterland, are unaware that his last and only home is here, too.

Hamilton named the house the Grange after his grandfather's estate in Scotland. Part of why it's often ignored is a years-long restoration, finished in the fall of 2011. Then there's the unsettled character of the house itself: it has been moved – the entire thing – twice over the years, once four blocks west to a tight fit next to St. Luke's Episcopal Church (where a bronze statue of Hamilton still stands) and more recently to West 141st Street where the house was reoriented so it would better fit against St. Nicholas Park.

Hamilton's reasons for building this country home were chiefly parental. He had seven children in 1802 when the Grange was finished, and the long distance from New York – at that time almost completely contained in what we'd call downtown today – meant less risk from the city plagues of cholera and yellow fever. The house is small but comfortable: Hamilton called it his "sweet project," and likely saw himself

dying there, old and content. Instead, he walked out early in the morning on July 11, 1804, to meet the Vice President of the United States in the country's most famous duel.

AUDUBON'S GRAVE MARKER

Bird killer (and painter)

Trinity Mausoleum and Cemetery
770 Riverside Drive
trinitywallstreet.org/cemetery-mausoleum
212-368-1600
Daily 9am–4pm
A and C trains/155 St; 1 train/157 St

Although the Washington Heights area offers some clues – Audubon Terrace, Audubon Avenue – the fact that "America's greatest naturalist" John James Audubon made a home here is news to many people. Audubon might as well be a myth: he seems to have lived in some harmonious and colorful dimension inhabited chiefly by birds. But the man died a New Yorker. Born in Haiti, raised in France, American by citizenship, Audubon spent years in thankless toil and poverty trying to create a perfect thing: a complete visual record of America's avifauna. When the project finally won him the fame he deserved, the painter bought an estate above 155th Street and lived there until his death in 1851.

The land of Trinity Cemetery was once part of this Audubon estate, and the naturalist's grave is one of the most impressive you'll find there: a 7-ton Celto-runic cross carved from a solid block of bluestone, 19 feet tall and covered with birds. Give it a careful look and you'll discover an aspect of the naturalist's career that most people would never suspect. On one flank of the stone base appear bas-relief painter's tools – palette, brushes, and maulstick – framed by leafy sprigs and flowers. But on the other side you'll find a powder horn, game bag and crossed hunting rifles. Audubon was by necessity an ace hunter first and an artist second: he killed pretty much every bird he ever painted. You almost can't find a portrait of the man where he's not holding a gun. He shot the birds, arranged them in vivid poses with the help of twisted wires, backdropped them with a grid to correct proportion, and then took his time with the art.

Birds of America

Audubon's *Birds of America*, first printed in 1827, contains almost five hundred different birds, including several species that have since gone extinct – the great auk, the pinnated grouse. When the man died, he left his estate to his wife, who had largely supported him while he tramped for years through America's backwoods. When the widow fell on hard times she sold the book's original watercolors to the New-York Historical Society for $2,000. Most of the copper plates for the engravings ended up melted at a scrap dealer. At a London Sotheby's auction in 2010, a complete edition of Birds of America became the most expensive printed book in history when it sold for $11.6 million.

PORTOLAN CHART

America, terra incognita

The Hispanic Society of America
Broadway between West 155th and West 156th Streets
hispanicsociety.org – 212-926-2234
Library: Tuesday–Saturday 12pm–3:30pm
Admission free
1 train/157th St; C train/155th St

If there's anything more compelling than a map of the world, it's an ancient map where things are patchy and strange, and whole continents of *terra incognita* fade off into the margin. The Hispanic Society of America Museum has one hidden away in the library: a giant portolan chart on parchment from 1526 by Juan Vespucci, nephew of the great Italian explorer Amerigo.

Created for the purposes of trade, the portolan charts are the first no-nonsense maps of the known world. The one in the Hispanic Society is believed to be the official Spanish exploration atlas called the *padrón real*, or royal register. "When sailors returned from America to Spain," says library curator William Delgado, "they had to draw the contours of the coast that they saw, and make a report." The resulting chart, regularly updated, was a state secret: the New World glimmered in the imaginations of contending European powers like a vast tract of solid gold. The person in charge of compiling the fresh information was called the *piloto mayor* or master navigator. The explorer Amerigo Vespucci held the title until his death in 1519, when it fell to his nephew Juan. The master navigator had to perform a political balancing act: both correctly record the buzz of new discovery and keep a lid on it. At some point, Juan tripped. "He got fired," Delgado smiles, raising his eyebrows at the 500-year-old scandal.

Vespucci's map still has an appealing air of secrecy about it. For one, it isn't kept in the main museum, but in the attached library. There you have to whisper your desire to an assistant, who will direct you to a curtained wall and, with a certain drama, pull the cord to reveal the known world of half a millennium ago. Europe is well-defined. Africa too, but the blocky elephants were drawn by someone who had clearly never seen one. Brazil is patrolled by mysterious dragons. Most striking is the nascent accuracy of the Americas: the Gulf of Mexico and the Indies are precisely drawn, and Florida appears as a peninsula and not the island it was once believed to be. As you would expect from a chart made by sailors, the details are in the coasts. Inland America grows vague: just a wash landscape of gloomy blue hills that fade into nothing, the very depiction of the unknown.

BRUSH STAIRWAY AND OLD POLO GROUNDS

The last trace of Manhattan baseball

Coogan's Bluff at Edgecombe Avenue and West 158th Street
1 train/157th St; A and C trains/155th St

An iron stairway on Coogan's Bluff once looked over the New York Giants baseball field, the Polo Grounds. Hidden behind teetering fences, half-buried in dead leaves, and leading nowhere, the Brush Stairway speaks as clearly as a gravestone: Manhattan baseball is long gone.

Baseball was born here. In fact Manhattan is woven into baseball's very geometry: the diamond came about in Madison Square in the 1840s, where office clerks began playing after work. The original game (called "rounders") had five bases, but the square was too small so they took one out and made it four. New York's first team, the Knickerbockers, codified the rules of the game in 1845, and baseball madness quickly followed: within a decade the sport was declared the national pastime.

So many fans came out for the first Polo Grounds game, hundreds couldn't get in. According to James D. Hardy's *The New York Giants Baseball Club*, they "climbed to the top of Coogan's Bluff and watched from there, a site that promptly acquired the name of dead-head hill." This bluff remained a favorite place to catch a free game throughout the Polo Grounds' career until the field was demolished in 1964. In addition to the Giants, the stadium was also home to the Yankees and the Mets for shorter periods, and site of "The Shot Heard 'Round the World," Bobby Thomson's immortal homer against the Brooklyn Dodgers.

Today all that's left of the ball field is this stairway creeping down the bluff, and an iron message laid in the concrete landing by Giants owner John T. Brush. Standing there you can see the traffic along Harlem River Drive where Dominican taxi drivers park and gather around a food van. One of the older drivers remembers watching games from dead-head hill. "Sure," he says. "If you can't buy a ticket, you go right up there." He turns around to look over the drive at the identically dismal brick projects that now occupy the stadium's spot. "Long time ago." When asked if the food at the van is any good, he makes a friendly scowl: "Not really" – and then drives off.

This is the second site of the Polo Grounds; the first was on 110th Street and was in fact originally used for polo.

MANHATTAN PETROGLYPHS

The antidote to Instagram

Highbridge Park
At the request of the artist, the exact location can't be printed here
The petroglyphs are incised into the north face of an outcrop of schist rock in
Highbridge Park, between Edgecombe Avenue and Harlem River Drive, south
of 165th Street
A and C trains/163rd Street—Amsterdam Avenue

A petroglyph is an image created in relief on a stone surface by scraping or carving. A Paleolithic man in the year 30,000 B.C.E. gouges the outline of a horse into the wall of a cave with a bear's rib bone: that's a petroglyph. A guy from Minnesota with a masters degree in fine art chisels a helicopter into a rocky outcrop of upper Manhattan: that's ... a little different, somehow. Petroglyphs are a form that went out of fashion with the invention of writing. You don't expect to see new ones, particularly not here, and particularly not depictions of jet planes, hot air balloons, space shuttles, or satellites. The effect is distinctly odd, and it's hard to know what to do with it. Chalk up a victory to Kevin Sudeith, self-defined "petroglyphist," and perhaps vandal.

Sudeith has work all over, from California to Nova Scotia, on commissions and public art pieces. The petroglyphs in Manhattan are a personal riff, and to find them you need to climb rocks and whack through poison ivy and pokeweed. It's part of the attraction. Coming upon the carvings, most of which are small enough to cover with your hand, is a private ordeal. This art form doesn't share well. You have to go to the rock: the rock will not come to you. You could call it the antidote to Instagram.

An experienced draftsman, Sudeith first glimpsed the potential of the petroglyph form while visiting Australia. He saw a wall of rock art there with layered images: one part thousands of years old, another depicting a European man on a horse. This collapsing of history clicked with him, and his goal since has been to create art that not only endures, but could also form a connection with a local person around the site. It's a way to be both timely and timeless. "The thing with petroglyphs," Sudeith says, "is they exist on their own terms. Once they're made, they don't need an art world to find an audience. It will come at some point. When exactly doesn't really concern me — now or in a hundred years, both work equally well. And if nothing happens, a petroglyph will just sit there quietly. But it's definitely *something*. It will keep being that regardless of me, or my career. And that's enough."

THE LITTLE RED LIGHTHOUSE

The master of the river

Fort Washington Park
Riverside Drive at 179th Street under the George Washington Bridge
nycgovparks.org/parks/fortwashingtonpark/highlights/11044
A train/181st St; follow the Henry Hudson Greenway from Riverside Drive

In the summer of 1951, traffic along Riverside Drive suddenly began to slow down when it hit a certain section at the foot of the George Washington Bridge: drivers pausing to get a glimpse of a cherry-red lighthouse. It had been announced that the lighthouse, a familiar sight on the banks of the Hudson River for thirty years, would soon be sold off for scrap iron. The resulting fuss was all over the papers.

Leading the fuss were children. Since 1942 they'd been emotionally bonding with the tower through a popular book, *The Little Red Lighthouse and the Great Gray Bridge* by Hildegarde Swift and Lynd Ward. The story is about a contented lighthouse, "round and red and jolly," that saves ships from the fogs and currents of a treacherous stretch of the Hudson. The lighthouse marvels at its own importance: "Why," it thinks to itself, "I am the MASTER OF THE RIVER." This much of the story is true: the Hudson had seen so many accidents in that area – where a spur of land called Jeffrey's Hook juts out – it had been marked by lanterns as early as 1889. When the 40-foot red lighthouse was constructed in 1921, its powerful lamp and fog bell saved lives and cargo.

Ten years later the George Washington Bridge opened. Next to the brilliantly lit metal behemoth, the lighthouse went from heroic to merely cute. This crisis of identity is the real subject of the children's story. "Very likely I shall never shine again," it thinks. "And it was VERY, VERY SAD." If you think an illustration of a weeping lighthouse is too silly to be touching, go find a copy of the book. Things end well: the huge, cold bridge assures the lighthouse that the ships still need him, and a storm soon proves the bridge right. In the huge, cold city, things were different. The little red lighthouse really had become obsolete: the Coast Guard announced its imminent sale for scrap, and kids lost their minds. One psychiatrist of the Citizen's Committee on Children said that the lighthouse had become a symbol of security, giving "reassurance that even though you are little in a big world you won't be annihilated." Children wrote letters, some even sent pocket change. And, in an act of almost wondrous compliance, the city listened. The Parks Department took over the lighthouse, spruced it up, and opened it to the public. It's the only lighthouse left on Manhattan.

AMERICAN REDOUBT MARKER

Where the Patriots lost Manhattan

Fort Washington Park
From the street: Take 181st until it stops at the Parkway; cross over on the pedestrian bridge. Follow the path south down to the water. Look for the short trail on the left with sign reading "American Redoubt Marker."
From the bicycle path on the water: After passing under the George Washington Bridge, look to the right for the trailhead. If you cross over the railway, you've gone too far
A and 1 trains/181st St

As noted elsewhere in this book (see page 20), New York City is strangely disconnected from the American Revolutionary War. Everybody knows Brooklyn; few can tell you about the Battle of Brooklyn. Perhaps because New York's military monuments plot a path of defeat. Here in 1776 the patriots learned painful lessons (Brooklyn was the first major battle after the Declaration of Independence) and lost, and lost, and lost. Washington made a daring escape over the East River to Manhattan, had to flee up the island when he was pursued, then fled yet further into Westchester when he was overrun. The English set up an occupying force that lasted until the end of the war. The site of the last American defeat on the island is on a promontory of schist in the shadow of the George Washington Bridge. For over a century an oblong boulder has marked this spot, "American Redout 1776" chiseled into its face.

General Howe, the British commander, was impressed by the last-ditch defenses along this stretch of rocky shore; he noted that they'd been "fortified by the rebels with incredible labor." In an alternate history the American forces might have beaten the British back, reversing the tide and curtailing the war by seven years. It's this other story shining through that makes monuments to defeat so interesting. We're compelled to cast our minds back to the moment of action, when nothing was certain and the actors were on the very point of time's arrow. A whole web of contingencies flows from this lumpy boulder.

The setting of the redoubt (the spelling on the stone is archaic) makes this exercise in imagination easier. You're just a stroll from a subway station, within hearing distance of the cars and trucks banging over the bridge and along the parkway, but it's a realm of oak and rock and bird. The modern city infrastructure looms, but there are glimpses through the trees where you see only river and the blank bluffs of the opposite shore – New Jersey, where the patriots would escape to, and where they'd suffer, and freeze, and growl, and refuse to give up.

LOEWS 175TH MOVIE PALACE

23

A spell of mysterious adventure

4140 Broadway at West 175th Street
unitedpalace.org; check for open service schedule
212-568-6700
A train/175th St; 1 train/168th St

In the Golden Age of Hollywood, New Yorkers saw films in sumptuous movie palaces. Most of them have been demolished, or are falling to dust, or survive as no more than façades. Perhaps the greatest one ever built still stands, proud and enigmatic, on 175th Street.

When you first see it, you know you're looking at something rare, but the theater's style is unclassifiable. It's been called "Indo-Chinese," "Mayan Revival-Oriental," "Cambodian Neo-Classical." *Times* reporter David Dunlap shotgunned the entire architectural dictionary at it with "Byzantine-Romanesque-Indo-Hindu-Sino-Moorish-Persian-Eclectic-Rococo-Deco." Outside it looks vaguely like an ancient temple. Inside the walls shimmer with gilt: goddesses, cherubs, elephants, deities.

The palace is considered the grandest offering by architect Thomas W. Lamb, who is not remembered for restraint. "His buildings were pretty sober until about 1927," says Craig Morrison of the Theater Historical Society of America. "Then all of a sudden: kablooey." Lamb wasn't alone: for movie palace architects, crazy was the rule. "We sell tickets to theaters, not movies," said theater chain owner Marcus Loew. In 1924, Loew bought a controlling interest in Metro-Goldwyn-Mayer studios – in other words films were made to drive the venue business, not the other way around. Movie palaces became fantasies of distilled exotic, casting, in Lamb's own words, "a spell of mysterious adventure."

Today you can visit Loew's 175th, but you can't see a movie there. In 1969 the abandoned palace was bought by Frederick "Reverend Ike" Eikerenkoetter, who renamed it the United Palace Theater and repurposed the space as headquarters for his radio and television ministry. Ike, who drove a different color Mercedes every day of the week, preached that poverty was the root of all evil, and made millions flogging a bland and shady method called "Thinkonomics." But the reverend is forever redeemed in the eyes of theater enthusiasts: "It's an absolutely beautiful restoration," says Morrison.

Ike died in 2009, but his church still holds open service on Sunday afternoons. The preacher delivers a feel-good sermon to the first four or five rows while all around, the ornate walls and balconies, and the high curved ceiling drawn from a dream of the Orient, gleam in the low light.

24

TOP OF THE HIGH BRIDGE TOWER

Once a month, a guided tour all the way up

High Bridge Park
Between West 155th and Dyckman Streets, Edgecombe and Amsterdam Avenues
nycgovparks.org/parks/highbridgepark
Tours once a month; call for details: 212-304-2365
A train/175th St; 1 train/181st St

Most New Yorkers familiar with High Bridge Park know it only from the window of a rushing car: a 200-foot-high stone tower that suddenly comes and goes above the trees on Harlem Drive. Many never even get that close. And scarcely anyone knows that not only is the tower visitable, it's climbable: once a month, the urban rangers of the Parks Department unlock the door and offer a guided tour all the way to the top.

After spiraling up the iron stair to the observation level, you'll see stretched out before you the Harlem River valley, and beyond a surprisingly green Bronx. Directly below, the river is spanned by a relic of the Croton Aqueduct: the red brick stripe of High Bridge itself. This bridge, the city's oldest, was the last leg of the aqueduct's 40-mile journey to Manhattan (see page 66).

The bridge was off-limits for decades before re-opening in 2015. "Some of you born before the seventies may remember it as a place to throw rocks at the traffic down below," says today's urban ranger, Jerry Seigler. He wears the standard-issue hat and on his belt hang a walkie-talkie, a baton, and handcuffs. If anybody remembers, they keep quiet. Ranger Jerry leads the group down the steps again and out to where the old bridge meets the rocky hillside of High Bridge Park.

It unfolds that the guided tour extends to the whole of the riverfront, which is serviced by trails and unexpectedly wild: dense greenery of vines, mossy rocks, and tall trees. It also unfolds that Ranger Jerry is a well of information. He knows social history (in the 19th century the park was a favorite spot for horse buggy racing), geology (the bedrock we see on the surface formed miles below, millions of years ago), botany and/or alcohol (mugwort weed is a component of beer production), Indian hunting tricks (deer were driven into the river and drowned)... In fact, Ranger Jerry might know everything.

The group hikes down a shaded track of clay. Except for the gravel of broken glass underfoot, it could be Appalachia. "This is one of my favorite trees," the ranger says, leading the way to a giant London plane with a gaping hole in the trunk. "One day I found somebody living here." We wait for this "somebody" to turn out to be an adorable raccoon, but Ranger Jerry really means somebody: a homeless man with a leaning mattress, a battery-powered TV, and a shopping cart chained to a tree.

BENNETT PARK

The highest natural landmass in Manhattan

Fort Washington Avenue and West 183rd Street
nycgovparks.org/parks/bennettpark
1 train/181st St

The New York skyline is drawn in architecture: you can easily forget that the spires and rises of the vertical metropolis are just the icing on a titanic stonescape of underlying geology. Manhattan is mostly composed of two kinds of rock: schist – the ashy, glittering stone that you can see in the outcrops of Central Park – and marble, found only in the north at Inwood. The rock undulates along the length of the island, swooping down over a hundred feet deep in Midtown and climbing to a peak in Washington Heights at the small outcrop in the middle of Bennett Park. A plaque embedded there gives the exact elevation: only 265 feet above sea level.

Still, the hill had strategic advantages. In the summer of 1776, George Washington reconnoitered the site and ordered the construction of a fortification, "a kind of citadel." In the park you can still see, outlined in stone, the footprint of a five-bastioned earthwork that was called Fort Washington in the general's honor (and is the namesake of Washington Heights and Fort Washington Avenue). After a series of close calls and setbacks, the Americans were hemmed in by a combined force of Redcoats and Hessians that outnumbered them four to one. General Howe, the British commander, unhelpfully pointed this imbalance out. The Americans dug in anyway and waited for the attack.

It came on November 16. From his position on the opposite shore of the Hudson, Washington could peer up at the fort through his spyglass and see Hessians bayoneting Americans to death. "Such is my situation," he wrote, "that if I were to wish the bitterest curse to an enemy on this side of the grave, I should put him in my place, with my feelings." The battle was bloody, and decisive: the British occupied Manhattan until the war's end.

America's first woman soldier

When Margaret Corbin, "the heroine of Fort Washington," received a military pension, she became America's first woman soldier. During the battle she helped her artilleryman husband until he was killed; she then shot the cannon herself. In nearby Holyrood Church there is a tablet honoring her.

Due to the same feature of geology, this part of Washington Heights is also the location of Manhattan's deepest subway tunnel. The lowest stop on the island: 181st St on the 1/9 line.

MOTHER CABRINI SHRINE

The first American Catholic saint

701 Fort Washington Avenue
cabrinishrinenyc.org
212-923-3536
Tuesday–Sunday 9am–5pm
A train/190th St

Frances Xavier Cabrini, the first American citizen to be made a saint by the Roman Catholic Church, lies in this shrine in Washington Heights. The sight of a dead person under glass can make visitors uneasy.

"Oh, they're spooked out, some of them," says Rose, the shrine secretary. "There's her skeleton, and some skin. But that's not what makes you a saint. A saint is the *miracles* they do." Rose, a Puerto Rican woman with a good laugh balanced by a dry administrative edge, has worked at the shrine for seven years. "You become ... I won't say a counselor, but you listen to people's problems."

The problems the Mother Cabrini shrine specializes in are those of immigrants, and in this respect New York is her natural place. Cabrini understood immigrants because she was one. After founding an Order in her native Italy, she arrived in the city in 1889 with a group of sisters, landing in the notoriously squalid Five Points in the Lower East Side. The residence was filthy, loud, and skittered with pests: at night, one of the sisters would stay up to defend the others from rats. The Italians were widely viewed at that time as a variety of sub-human. "The field is so vast to do good for our poor Italians who are abandoned and very much looked down upon," Cabrini wrote. "They cannot bear the sight of [us]." Much of Cabrini's charity work focused on children: schools and orphanages. When asked to take up hospital duties as well she resisted until, as Rose tells it, she was visited in a dream by the Virgin Mary "who had her sleeves rolled up to 'do the work you don't want to do yourself.'" Rose widens her eyes with awe at a personal rebuke from the mother of Jesus. "So she said 'All right, all right.'"

In all, Cabrini founded more than sixty institutions, among them a medical center on 22nd Street (now closed). She became a U.S. citizen in 1909 and was canonized in 1946. In the papal brief the saint is formally recognized as "the heavenly patroness of immigrants." Rose fingers through a stack of paper and pulls out a recent letter from a Dominican woman: she begs desperately for an early release from prison so she can rejoin her children. The letter is written directly to the saint and the tone is familiar, but Rose is the one who'll answer it.

Mother Cabrini isn't completely here: the unsqueamish Church divvied her up. The heart is in Rome, the head in Codogno.

THE LAVAUDIEU TORSO
OF CHRIST

An antique scarecrow

The Cloisters Museum
99 Margaret Corbin Drive, Fort Tryon Park
metmuseum.org/cloisters
212-923-3700
Thursday-Tuesday 10am-5pm
A train/190th St

An unassuming wooden torso of Christ hangs on a bare wall in The Cloisters Romanesque wing. Incomplete, scarred, and stained by the centuries, it must be one of the least noted among the museum's artworks. But the sculpture has an outrageous story that sums up with comic precision the whole tale and purpose of The Cloisters as a cultural institution.

"If you're looking for bizarre places that are really awe-inspiring," says a Cloisters docent, "this would be at the top of your list." The awe is owed to the thousands of works of medieval art; what makes it bizarre – and unique among American museums – is the layout. To visit The Cloisters is to stroll through a clever patchwork of authentic monastic architecture: tons of carved stone were shipped from Europe to create it. This period-specific exhibition space was the brainchild and passion of George Grey Barnard, an American sculptor who studied in Paris and amassed a heap of European art – the kernel of the present collection. He had a passion for medieval sculpture that was rare at the time. "Now we recognize it as something very interesting," says the docent, "but it wasn't always so."

If the States were cool on the Middle Ages, the attitude in France was practically hostile. During the French Revolution, the National Assembly took over church property and sold it to private citizens. Abbeys became farmhouses, chapels became barns, statues were crammed into the gaps of old walls. That's how the religious stonework of Europe made its way into an American collection: it was there for the taking.

The docent stands by the torso and pauses to linger on the specialness of its appeal – a build-up to the punch line. "There's a great sensitivity to the anatomy of the human figure: bone, muscles, pulling skin. It's extraordinary for the twelfth century, and it's long been recognized as a really rare find." Barnard came upon the ancient torso near the Lavaudieu abbey in the Auvergne region. "He bought it from a French family," the docent says, "that had been using it out in the field. Dressed up. As a scarecrow."

DYCKMAN FARMHOUSE

The last farmhouse on Manhattan

Broadway and West 204th Street
dyckmanfarmhouse.org
212-304-9422
Friday 12pm–4pm, Saturday 10am–4pm
A train/Dyckman St or Inwood – 207th St; 1 train/207th St

Where the trees block out the lampposts and the fire escapes, you can look up at the Dyckman Farmhouse on the corner of Broadway and West 204th Street and see the rural 18th century. Upper Manhattan was then nothing but farmsteads and quiet creeks, and the hidden remains of Indian villages. For over two hundred years this plain white house, the last real farmhouse on Manhattan, has been an unchanging island of the past. Built by William Dyckman in 1784, the house was never modernized on the assumption that it would be torn down sooner than later. In the early 1900s there was talk of moving it to nearby Isham Park, but descendants of William stepped in to keep the house where it stands and open it to the public.

Now the museum staff goes to extravagant lengths to keep the farmhouse frozen in time. The upstairs has been maintained as it was when the house was converted into a museum in 1915, while the downstairs parlor and sunken kitchen are as accurate for a period farmhouse as historians today can possibly make it. "Our concept of the past constantly changes," explained former director Susan De Vries. "Any historic house museum is going to be a layering of history, and we acknowledge that those layers are important."

If you can glimpse the past by squinting at the house from the outside, inside is a thorough time warp. The decorations and furniture have been restored or reproduced at great pains, and the closer you look, the realer it gets: on the table a hand of cards is fanned out next to a half-drunk glass of Madeira wine; Missus' knitting lies on a chair in the corner; from the wall ticks and chimes a period clock. Downstairs is a warm kitchen, with a fresh loaf of bread on the table and diced carrots waiting to be thrown in the pot. The Dyckman Farmhouse has stopped. The only thing missing is the Dyckmans. The only thing out of place is you, a curious ghost from the future.

Leading to the cellar kitchen there's a patch of rock foundation with what looks like a strange ideogram carved into the surface: three superimposed squares connected by lines. It's actually an ancient board game, Nine Man Morris, and might have been chiseled there for the Dyckman children.

MILESTONE NO. 12

The silent sentinel

Isham Park, south entrance
Broadway and 211th Street
nycgovparks.org/parks/isham-park
1 train/207th St

There is a strange red sandstone block embedded in the wall at the entrance of Isham Park. The only features setting it apart from the rough granite all around are the regular shape and the muddy color of its crumbling face. Millions pass the block, on foot or on wheels, without a pause: to them it's nameless. To New York historians it's a relic known as Milestone No. 12.

Milestones are unique and suggestive monuments. On the one hand they're humble rocks that bear one simple message in a series; on the other they can summon in an instant galloping horses and coach horns and clouds of romantic dust. They are also collectible. Manhattan is 14 miles long, and tracing the fates of the fourteen original markers has lured many researchers into weedy roadsides and forgotten basements, and into the stacks and maps of libraries.

The original milestones were installed in 1769 during a project headed by deputy postmaster Benjamin Franklin, who realized a need for regular postage fees. Franklin crept, with an odometer of his own invention, along the road connecting New York and Boston. This colonial artery, called the Boston Post Road, had already been in use for a hundred years, but it was the markers that made it. "A road was regarded with dignity and respect," wrote milestone expert and Historical Society curator Richard J. Koke, "when it was lined with well-cut stones."

As streets widened and shifted with the evolving map of the city, the milestones were uprooted and forgotten. Many are gone for good; others have been rediscovered in private gardens, in landfill, embedded in the front steps of houses. No. 10 is in the New York Historical Society collection; No. 11 is at the Morris-Jumel Mansion; Nos. 13 and 14 are still lost.

No. 12 first stood on Post Road at 190th Street; in 1813 the distances were recalibrated when mile zero became the newly-completed City Hall and the stone was moved (and perhaps recut, no one knows). The message chiseled into the face, "12 Miles from N.York," was probably blasted off by the potshots of vandals. Sometime in the 1800s the stone was placed in the retaining wall where it stands today: worn, wordless, ignored, and as old as anything you'll find in Manhattan.

THE LAST SALT MARSH

Primeval Manhattan

Inwood Hill Park, northernmost Manhattan
nycgovparks.org/parks/inwoodhillpark
A train/Inwood – 207 St; 1 train/215 St

Study the northernmost tip of Manhattan on a map, and you'll see it's dented by a small inlet. There, within Inwood Hill Park, is the last saltwater marsh left on an island that was once fringed with pretty much nothing but. The marsh is an ecological time capsule tucked away among the last natural scenery on the most rigidly developed spot on earth.

The essence of a tidal salt marsh is change. At high tide the bay is unexceptional: a body of water fringed with grasses and seawalls of split stone. At low tide it reveals a different nature, becoming a glistening mudflat where channels of water snake out toward Spuyten Duyvil. Birds stoop and peck over the mud, leaving tracks of dimples like stitches in fabric as they jab at holes for fiddler crabs and in the shallow pools trembling with mummichogs.

It's not exactly a forgotten oasis. The tide is the globe's clockwork, and the animal life, which has a knack for ignoring development, goes about its timeless pursuits—but the shore has been shaped by modernity, and even if you drift into a vision of the past, the moans of passenger jets high above will reel you back. What the marsh offers is subtle instruction in preservation. On the north shore of the inlet, there's a station where the city park rangers can tell you as much about the tides, plants and animals of the inlet as you care to learn. Ranger Sunny Corrao looks out over the flats on a bright summer day and talks about the marsh's role as a last of its kind. "People who are coming specifically for that know about it," she says. "Others just see it as a peaceful spot."

Although there's still just enough at high tide to row a canoe, the water was deeper in the 1930s when most of Inwood Hill Park was built: the mud is partly sediment laid down over the decades. It's a favorite spot for birders: you can see egrets, great blue herons, plovers, geese, ducks. Once in a while a goose will give a single echoing honk; then all the browsing geese fly away as a sudden team, wingtips slapping the surface. They leave behind an impostor pigeon (the sign: DO NOT FEED THE PIGEONS) to pick among the shore rocks by itself, as at home in a precious salvaged landscape as in a gutter.

INDIAN CAVES OF INWOOD HILL

Shelter in Manhattan's last great forest

Inwood Hill Park
Between Dyckman Street, Hudson River, and Harlem Ship Canal
nycgovparks.org/parks/inwoodhillpark
A train/Dyckman St or Inwood – 207th St; 1 train/207th St or 215th St

Not counting herds of mastodons (see page 254), nothing is harder to square with the current state of Manhattan than the communities of American Indians who hunted here (bears, deer, turkeys) and fished here (especially oysters) and even, some historians have proposed, paddled canoes straight across the island by connecting rivers. But that was then. You can think of the urban development of Manhattan as a wildfire lit in the Battery in the 1620s that gradually crackled its way uptown before burning out just shy of the island's very northwestern tip. There stands Inwood Hill, Manhattan's last great forest, and the only place to imagine how the island appeared to the earliest New Yorkers, the Lenape.

Inwood Hill Park's main attraction as prehistoric Manhattan is the Indian Caves. Natural overhangs in the rocky ridge that leads down to the waterfront provided temporary shelter to camping Lenape, and in one spot the caves, which were once deeper than they are today, make a through-and-through around massive boulders. The first archeological work in the area was conducted in the late 1800s by two enthusiastic amateurs (the only category of archeologist at the time), William Calver and Reginald Bolton, who combed northern Manhattan for artifacts. Calver later wrote that the opportunities for fishing and game hunting, along with the natural rock shelters, made northern Manhattan "unmatchable in the features possessed for the accommodation of primitive life" – a judgment that has gone uncontested since.

One can marvel that the frenzy of urban development has spared not only a piece of Native American history but also the original scenery. Tulip trees of stupefying height, forested hills alive with birds (tanagers, cardinals, hawks, and in winter even bald eagles) and, up in the winding trails, no trace of the modern world except for the tiny rumble of a passenger jet far overhead.

The word "Manhattan" is of Lenape origin, but the meaning is unclear. "Manna-hata" was recorded by Hudson's first mate Robert Juet in 1609, and a year later the name first appeared on maps. Possible translations include "island" (Lenape: *menatay*), "place to gather wood for making bows" (*manahatouh*), and the far-fetched "place of general inebriation" (*manahactanienk*).

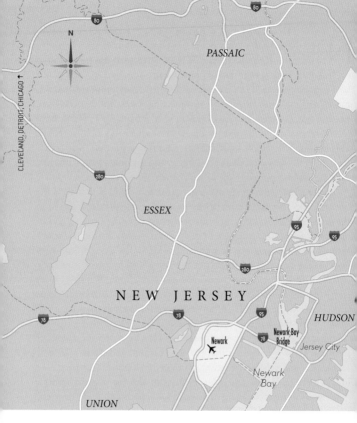

Bronx and Queens

THE CROTON TRAIL

New York, lost civilization

The Bronx portion of the trail starts at the top of Van Cortlandt Park, where Hancock Avenue meets Forest Avenue (Yonkers) and descends to High Bridge at the Harlem River (at 170th Street)

I n the late 1830s, New York took on its greatest public works project: connecting Manhattan, which suffered from a scarcity of fresh water and from all that goes with it (disease, fire hazard, drunkenness), to the sprawling Croton River 40 miles to the north. The path of the original Croton Aqueduct is dotted by remnants: gatehouses, paths, towers, and Gotham's oldest bridge. Follow them and you'll get as close as you can in the city to discovering ancient ruins.

The strangest piece of aqueduct infrastructure is also the most remote: the stone weir in Van Cortlandt Park in the Bronx. A weir is a station of flow control: here water could spill off, fresh air could waft in, and the underground tunnels could be accessed. This one is special because you come to it in the middle of a nature trail, like a sun-worshipper's temple suddenly appearing in the jungle. The stone is old enough to be well-crumbled in places; an elm tree grows right out of the roof, and even the graffiti has the jumbled charm of a forgotten alphabet. If you've got an eager imagination, you'll sense the specter of History pacing around; if not, there's a city slicker's fill of trees and birds. Dedicated aqueduct fans will, of course, swoon.

The Van Cortlandt Park website advises that the Croton Aqueduct trail is "cut by Major Deegan Freeway," which is like saying that the way to England is cut by the Atlantic. In fact, for explorers of these parts, the ramps of whooshing traffic are the primary bummer. The best place to pick up the trail again is probably Aqueduct Avenue, which starts at Kingsbridge Road and makes a pretty straight shot (the Parks Department calls it "Aqueduct Walk") to East Burnside Avenue, where there's a prominent stone gatehouse. The Bronx portion of the trail ends at the Harlem River at Sedgwick Avenue and 170th Street: put your feet there and it will be plain enough why. There stretches the oldest bridge in the city, High Bridge, built specifically for this massive works project, to deliver fresh water from the mainland to a parched Manhattan.

THE GRAND CENTRAL TEST PILLARS

Overgrown monuments to transit

Van Cortlandt Park, Old Putnam Trail

© MTA

In the Bronx, in the woods, off an old railroad line, the Grand Central test pillars are a miniature Stonehenge-like assemblage of monoliths which still sit in Van Cortlandt Park, over a century since serving their purpose.

The strange, roughly 10-foot-tall blocks are the samples New York Central Railroad owner and shipping magnate Cornelius "the Commodore" Vanderbilt ordered to consider for use in the exterior of his commuter rail hub, Grand Central Terminal. In 1903, as the terminal's construction began, the now defunct company placed 15 pillars – twelve granite, two limestone and one marble – along the tracks of its Putnam passenger train branch, each submitted by firms from Maine to Indiana, their tops carved in dual bands to assess how the exposed portions would handle the elements and which would fare best overall through eternity.

By the time the above-ground portion of the terminal began being built in 1910, the stones had been taking New York's weather head-on for years, and the victors were selected: Of the 15 contenders, the winners were a granite slab from Stony Creek, submitted by Connecticut's Norcross Brothers, and Indiana limestone from Indiana's Perry, Matthews & Buskirk. Both were used to cover the face of Grand Central's head house on Park Avenue between 42nd and 43rd streets, the granite on the ground floor and the limestone – which was selected mainly for its affordable cost rather than its durability – on the much larger upper portion.

Grand Central was completed in 1913, but 13 of these test pillars still stand (two of the three Milford pink granite slabs are gone, and although they were quite possibly removed due to redundancy, their disappearance remains a mystery).

In the decades since their installation, the stones became a canvas to not just the climate but also time's ceaseless passage, graffiti, and haphazard paint jobs done by a short-on-money Parks Department seeking to cover up the graffiti.

In 2017, grant money was given for the rather sorry-looking slabs to have a makeover, and they received much-needed repointing, old mortar replacement and a fresh lease on life.

Today, a sign and set of stone steps mark their quiet, dignified continued existence in the brush between Van Cortlandt Park's tennis courts and lake, next to what has long ceased to be train tracks and is now a nature trail.

> Cornelius, one of the richest Americans of all time, died in 1877, but a bronze statue of him continues to stand guard on the Terminal's south side.

WEST 230TH STREET

Stairway to the suburbs

1 train/225th St – Marble Hill or 231st St

West 230th Street in the Bronx zags under the clatter of the elevated train at Broadway, skirts the northern edge of Marble Hill, and after a stretch of arid concrete magically turns into a stairway that climbs straight into the trees.

Step streets look like streets on the map, and are often marked with the standard Department of Transportation signage, but they're stairs: strictly for pedestrians. There are a few such streets in West Bronx; 230th is the longest. The stairs start at Irwin Avenue, and cross two other avenues – terraces on the way – before cresting at Netherland. There they flatten out and become a conventional street again.

Vanishing into greenery isn't 230th Street's only trick. The odd stair offers a succinct lesson in Bronx variety, especially to those whose mental image of the borough is a waste of drugs and flame. If all you see of 230th Street is the deafening area around the subway, you've only seen one side. On the other is the hilltop community of Riverdale. It's a suburban postcard up there: private houses, trim yards, SUVs. What the street does is cut a neat path from chaos to clover.

Start down on Irwin Avenue. Around you are two gas stations, the hissing air hoses of a car repair shop, a loner on a skateboard ("I've never been up there," he says of the heights), and a lot of asphalt. Two brick projects flank the stair entrance. Climb the steps one level to Johnson Avenue: you've just seen your last fire escape. Move up another level to Edgehill Avenue: there's your first private garage. On the last leg to Netherland Avenue you'll begin to see yards, brick and half-timbered houses, slate roofs. Finally, at the top: rustic stone walls, cherry trees sprinkling blossoms on the lawn, dads hollering at kids to get in the car, and happy dogs.

You've hardly moved 500 feet, but it might as well be as many miles. One woman who lives at the top allows that Riverdale is "the most expensive neighborhood in the Bronx," but complains that sometimes "they" get in by the stairs. Another woman with a bag of groceries has plodded the steps every day for twenty-two years; asked when is a good time to come, she says, "Oh, anytime. But not late at night." Why, dangerous? "Well," she says, "I haven't heard anything, but I don't want to be the first."

MARBLE HILL

A piece of Manhattan north of the river

1 train/Marble Hill – 225th St

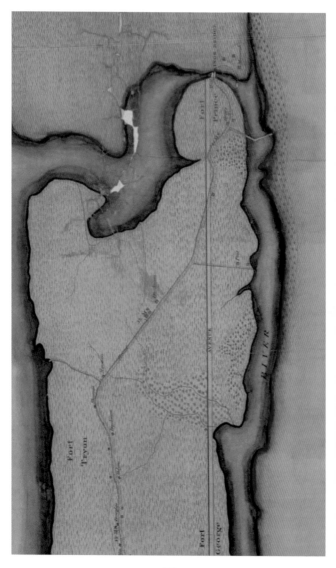

Ask the people who live in the small community of Marble Hill whether they consider themselves residents of Manhattan or the Bronx and you'll hear different answers. "What?" says a man washing his car on Fort Charles Place. "It's the Bronx. Who told you different?" A woman walking her dog on West 225th says she feels "technically in Manhattan," but tells friends she lives in the Bronx. Two out of three teen boys standing in front of a brick project shout "Bronx!" – the third, who speaks only Spanish, smiles ambivalently. "I just call it Avalon," says a mellow gentleman in a pair of Wayfarers held together with a paper clip. "It's whatever you want it to be."

Marble Hill's debatable status goes back more than a hundred years. Look on a map and you'll see that the neighborhood follows a curve: Terrace View bends into West 228th, which bends south again into Broadway. These streets mark the original course of Spuyten Duyvil Creek: Marble Hill used to be a bump on the northern tip of Manhattan. In 1895, the Harlem River Ship Canal was dug right through the bump, making Marble Hill an island; later the old Spuyten Duyvil was filled in and the neighborhood became physically attached to the Bronx and, by extension, the continent.

Not everyone here knows about this. And the confusion is official. Marble Hill is politically part of New York, not Bronx County, but residents vote in Manhattan elections at polling stations north of the river. The local area code is 718 (Bronx) but residents' numbers appear in both Manhattan and Bronx sections of the phone book.

In the playground at the north end of the neighborhood there is an inscribed stone set in the asphalt: an impossible Manhattan-Bronx boundary marker. An older man at a concrete chess table has this all figured out. "It's Manhattan," he says firmly. "When they call you to Bronx jury duty, they go by the zip code. You just send it back." When asked how long it takes officials to make a proper summons, he adjusts his baseball cap on his head and grunts: "Never."

Marble Hill's name comes from the Inwood marble that starts cropping up in northern Manhattan. You can see the stone in the crags where the neighborhood meets the river. The local Indians were also inspired by marble: they called the area Saperewack, "the glistening place."

SUPERMAN PORTRAIT AT LEHMAN COLLEGE

A national treasure, missing for fifty years

Lief Library, Lehman College, Bronx
250 Bedford Park Boulevard West
718-960-7766
Call for opening hours
4 train/Bedford Park Blvd – Lehman College

W hen you enter the library of Lehman College, you can see at the far end of the reading room a large portrait of Superman. It's the classic pose, what might be called Man of Steel at Ease: feet planted wide, fists on the hips, with cape blowing behind and a smile that says he's a good guy, but a good guy who's not above socking the bad guy in the jaw. Put aside for a moment why the portrait hangs in a college in the Bronx ("What does he have to do with education?" as one librarian put it) and ponder this fact: the image is the first full-length portrait of Superman. The artist didn't copy that classic pose: he invented it.

The original publisher of DC Comics, Harry Donenfeld, commissioned the painting in 1940, two years after Superman first appeared in Action Comics #1. Originally intended to be the basis of fan-photos for the radio show *The Adventures of Superman*, the painting later hung behind Donenfeld's desk. When the publisher retired in 1957 he quietly took it with him, and for half a century nobody at DC Comics knew where Superman was.

In 2009, artist and writer David Saunders tried to track the portrait down. His interest was less the superhero than the illustrator who formalized him: H.J. Ward. Saunders was preparing a book on Ward, and the deeper he got, the more he felt sure of the image's singular influence. "I realized: this was the most important painting this guy ever did," Saunders says. "How could I do a book without it?" After months of dogged sleuthing, including writing letters to every person in the U.S. with the last name Donenfeld, Saunders eventually picked up a crucial clue: a Donenfeld family member recalled that the painting had ended up in a New York college. "David wasn't sure which," says Janet Munch, head of Special Collections at the Lehman library. "So he wrote to all of us. And I told him we had the painting here." For years it hung in one of the vice-presidents' offices, a donation from Donenfeld's widow. By the time it found its way to the library, no one at Lehman knew the painting was a national treasure.

Saunders' book, *H.J. Ward*, came out in late 2010. At Midtown Comics in Times Square, Raphael Soohoo (the shop's "Superman guy") says: "I've only been aware of this painting since last year. We all think we're super fans until we find something new that completely changes everything."

STRAUS GRAVESITE

We lived together, so we shall die together

Woodlawn Cemetery
Between Jerome, Bainbridge, and Webster Avenues and East 233rd Street,
Bronx
thewoodlawncemetery.org
718-920-0500
Daily 8:30am–4:30pm
4 train/Woodlawn; 2 and 5 trains/233rd St

The story of the spectacular *Titanic* disaster has been profitably mined for a century; this gravesite in Woodlawn Cemetery expresses a dignified moment amid the frenzy. Ida Straus, wife of Macy's department store co-owner Isidor Straus, decided to go down with her husband rather than save herself on a lifeboat. The two had been married forty-one years. Isidor's body was later retrieved by a cargo ship, and he lies here; Ida was never found, and the gravestone also serves as her cenotaph. The Straus story is referenced by an ashlar block carved into the form of a galley ship. Chiseled into one side is a passage from the *Song of Songs*: "Many waters cannot quench our love – neither can the floods drown it."

Much of what is known about the final moments of Ida and Isidor is due to a coincidence: John Badenboch, a Macy's grocery buyer, happened to be on the *Carpathia*, the ship that changed course to attempt a *Titanic* rescue. The grocer spoke with survivors and sent a full report to Percy Straus, the couple's son. "Mother was asked by an officer in charge," Badenboch wrote, "and urged by your Father to get into one of the life boats. She refused to do so and insisted that the maid take her place." This maid, a recent hire, later filled in more of the story when she tried to return a fur coat to the Strauses' oldest daughter. Ida had given the woman the coat as a farewell, saying she had no more use for it. The Strauses remained on board together as the lifeboats filled up; Ida actually had her foot in one, believing that Isidor would follow, but when officers then barred men from boarding she pulled away and delivered the line that has become famous in *Titanic* lore: "I will not be separated from my husband; we lived together, so we shall die together."

Percy Straus sent news of the tragedy to his family in a cable: "Mother refused to leave Father danger realized too late both showed perfect courage and composure to the end."

At Broadway and West 106th Street, in a small park named for the Strauses, there's a bronze statue of a woman peering dreamily into the flowerbed. There used to be a pool there, and the statue (and her intended reflection) are called *Memory*.

The *Titanic* was meant to dock in New York, at Pier 59 on the Hudson River (see page 158).

CANOEING THE BRONX RIVER

A watery dream in the middle of the borough

May to September
Check website for schedule: bronxriver.org
The Bronx River Alliance hosts free paddles during the summer as well as paid and private excursions

The Bronx River, narrow, calm, and only 24 miles long, runs down the middle of the borough. You can step out of the striped shadows of the roaring elevated train, walk just 100 yards of asphalt and concrete, and come upon a fluvial dream: wooded banks hopping with whitetail rabbits, an air aflutter with birds, and the slow water slipping south under the hanging branches of ancient trees. Once you've witnessed this, you'll find yourself struggling to convince other New Yorkers that it exists. The river, named after Jonas Bronck, who built a life in the area during the earliest days of Dutch settlement, in turn lent its name to the whole borough. It touches the city's historic core, and while you'll be content to walk the banks, the best way to see it is floating in a canoe.

"It's not *exactly* like it was," says Linda Cox, executive director of the Bronx River Alliance, which has committed itself to the river's appreciation. "It was straightened in places, mostly for the trains." If this is a defect, it's being gradually corrected as shoring efforts give the stream what Cox calls "natural sinuosity." While you're paddling lazily under a slowly advancing canopy of willow and oak, and see turtles and darting minnows in the shallows, you won't be annoyed that things aren't curvy enough: you'll be too busy redefining an entire metropolis. "People who discover the Bronx River," Cox agrees, "start to see the city differently."

The Alliance offers various canoeing trips, some of them free to the public and confined to one area of the river, others for a small fee that will get your pioneering blood up: long descents through the woods, and then industrial flats, and eventually out into the Long Island Sound. As is true for virtually every organization that seeks to revitalize interest in the city's nature, the Alliance has had a positive impact on wildlife. "We're like the *capital* of that," says Cox. A few years ago a bizarre animal waddled into these waters and found it good: a beaver. The last ones to make a home in the Bronx River died two centuries ago, wiped out by the fur trade that was the basis for the city's very foundation. Asked if she gets more satisfaction from people discovering the river by canoe or the rebounding nature, Cox says, "Luckily, I don't have to choose! You can have both."

PRIMEVAL FOREST

The largest remnant of original forest

New York Botanical Garden, Bronx
2900 Southern Boulevard
nybg.org
718-817-8700
Tuesday–Sunday 10am– 6pm
Metro-North Railroad from Grand Central: Harlem Local/Botanical Garden;
subway: B, D and 4 trains/Bedford Park Blvd

You can see the canopy of giant trees as you head down from the entrance of the Botanical Garden. Next to the trail that leads inside, there's a sign to make the curious visitor pause. "You are standing," it reads, "at the edge of the largest remnant of original forest that once covered most of New York City. As you travel through this area, you will walk along Native American hunting trails, see marks left by glaciers, and pass under trees dating back to the American Revolution."

As "original forest," this is the most ancient spot you can visit in the entire city. It sits in the center of the 250-acre Botanical Garden, surrounded by other attractions ("Cherry Collection," "Daffodil Hill") which seem trivial next to the authority emanating from this wild heart. Old-growth or primeval forests are defined by never having been logged or otherwise interfered with, allowing for tall, ancient trees that bring about special conditions on the ground. In the contest for light, three distinct zones are created: above, the canopy, where the leaves of the tallest trees spread evenly and block most of the sun; the understory below, with shrubs and smaller trees that wait for a gap to open overhead when an old tree dies; and the forest floor, with seedlings, grass, and wildflowers.

Aside from the scant sunlight penetrating the canopy, old growth forests are striking for the decay that takes its natural course, busily turning wood into soil. "On the trail, there's a gigantic tulip tree that just fell a couple of days ago," says one of the rangers. "After a while all you'll see is a hump covered with debris." He points the way down the trail and, a quarter of a mile later, there it is: a fallen giant, its pale root system a dozen feet across and still gripping the soil and rock it ripped from the ground.

The forest teems with fauna, too. One thing the New Yorker is likely to notice: the many grey squirrels along the trail, while not especially timid, have never learned to panhandle. Chipmunks forage among the dead leaves, cheeping like birds. Hawks fly low, the air audibly breaking around their beating wings. Near the trailhead there's a human couple, standing as still as statues and staring open-mouthed at a nearby tree. In it a likewise frozen pair of owls stare back.

LORILLARD SNUFF MILL

America's first tobacco company

New York Botanical Garden, Bronx
2900 Southern Boulevard
nybg.org
718-817-8700
Tuesday–Sunday 10am–6pm
Grounds are free all day Wednesday and Saturday 10am–11pm
Metro-North Railroad from Grand Central: Harlem Local/Botanical Garden;
subway: B, D and 4 trains/Bedford Park Blvd

The map offered by the Botanical Garden features a "Stone Mill." If you hunt the old building out, a sign will inform you that it was constructed in 1840, that it ranks as "one of New York City's most picturesque structures," and that the material is locally-quarried schist. What you won't learn: what it was *made for*. The mill, a National Landmark, has recently been restored and at the same time its history has been pointlessly sanitized. For hundreds of years people called this place the Lorillard Snuff Mill. It's the country's oldest tobacco manufacturing facility.

Snuff, the powdered form of tobacco that was snorted in a more or less civilized manner by 18th-century gentlemen, was more than just ground tobacco. One of the varieties sold by the mill's namesake Pierre Lorillard called for stemless Virginia leaves soaked in rum, then stored at 100 degrees for twelve days, powdered, and left to breathe for another four months before the addition of tamarind, vanilla, tonka bean, and chamomile. This sounds like something you'd sooner sprinkle on ice cream than put in your nose, but Lorillard knew what he was doing: snuff became the family business, and the tobacco company he started in 1760 (America's very first) still sells cigarettes today. The commercial space was in Manhattan. The snuff mill and a dam next to it were bought by Lorillard's sons in 1792 to keep up with demand (the present structure replaced the original mill at the same site).

It's worth remembering that the tobacco trade was a shaper of early America. The Dutch grew it on Manhattan, and the Indians might have, too. As the Bronx River flows serenely by, one of the garden trams approaches slowly and stops on the Stone Mill Road bridge to give passengers a good look at this endangered agent of history. "They changed the name," says the driver confidentially, "because of the connotation of, you know ..." letting the specters of cancer and heart disease hang in the air. "But I've been born and raised with the Snuff Mill, and in my mind, that's what it is."

The word "tobacco" entered the English language in the late 1500s by way of the Arawak Indians encountered by Columbus and his crew. The fine points are disputed, but the source is likely a forked pipe the Indians used to draw smoke into their nostrils. It was called a *tobago*.

MONKEY HOUSE, BRONX ZOO

Beastly grandeur

2300 Southern Boulevard, Bronx
bronxzoo.com
Monday–Friday 10am–5pm; weekends and holidays 10am–5:30pm
bus: BxM11 from Madison Avenue directly to the zoo gate; subway: 2 and 5
trains/West Farms Sq – East Tremont Av

In the middle of Astor Court, in the old heart of the Bronx Zoo, you'll find a bronze plaque with a few lines by Lord Byron: "There is a pleasure in the pathless woods, There is a rapture on the lonely shore, There is society where none intrudes, By the deep Sea, and music in its roar: I love not Man the less, but Nature more." This has to be the most insulting plaque in New York. There are no pathless woods at the zoo. It's full of every kind of intrusion, the deep sea is substituted by a tank full of begging seals, in every direction Nature is artificially framed for man's pleasure. If the beasts drowsing in their boxes ever rise and attack us, hopefully the plaque is the first thing they'll rip up. The ideal location for revolt headquarters would be the Monkey House: it's the one place in the zoo that gets things precisely right.

Strange to say, fears of violent uprising are built into the zoo. The Greek-temple animal houses by Heins & LaFarge are excellent examples of the City Beautiful movement of the turn of the century, which hoped to inspire the growing numbers of slum-trapped poor, through exposure to classical ideals, to be more moral creatures – or at least not burn the city down in riots. It's a hard policy to criticize, but what we see today as beauty for its own sake contained, in the early 1900s, a note of social control.

The Monkey House seems to be making a sly statement about all this. Decorative primates gambol freely around the terracotta cornice, swinging and feeding on plants. But at the entrances on either side, they form a noble tableau: orangutans of different ages fill the pediment; at the center the oldest and wisest holds up a stick of bamboo, like a legislator displaying his authority. The finials at the top are lordly baboons. Because they so closely resemble us, everything monkeys do seems to invite irony, but the Monkey House raises animals to a level that is distinctly human, in an architectural vernacular meant to flatter our best idea of ourselves. Meanwhile, inside, neurotic macaques paw themselves and fling poo.

Sculptor Alexander Proctor used two live hamadryas baboons as models for the proud finials. In a sad twist, the models later became inmates: when he was finished, Proctor donated them to the zoo.

POE COTTAGE

A final home for poor Edgar Allan Poe

2460 Grand Concourse, Bronx
bronxhistoricalsociety.org/poecottage
718-881-8900
Thursday and Friday 10am–3pm, Saturday 10am–4pm, Sunday 1pm–5pm
B and D trains/Fordham Rd or Kingsbridge Rd

Edgar Allan Poe left biography all over the city, and in return the city crept into his writing. Usually more associated with Baltimore, where he had family, and died, the writer first made New York his home when he was only 22, and repeatedly returned, eventually buying a small country cottage in the Bronx. Now it's a museum, Poe Cottage, in an area that has spent the last 150 years becoming locked in concrete and asphalt. On the adjacent streets there's a halal butcher, a Thai grocer, a *farmacia*. Poe Square, where the cottage sits, is where the Bronx as you know it meets the Bronx as Poe did.

The writer's fame is the only reason the house survived. It's a rare bit of luck. "The house is unique in New York," says the guide. "It's the only one where you can actually see life as it was lived in the mid-19th century by a relatively low-income family." Poe arrived poor, looking for some peace away from the city for his wife Virginia, who had tuberculosis (she eventually died in the house); he stayed poor until the end, when he was found stumbling and delirious in the streets of Baltimore where he'd returned on a trip. The list of possible causes of death is a sort of biography in itself: heart attack, meningitis, cholera, rabies, syphilis, epilepsy.

The cottage was his last home in the world. A bronze bust that used to stand in the middle of the square is now perched in a corner of the cottage's tiny living room (where a desk, some books, and an inkwell have been installed to evoke the literary ghost); it wears the expression you see in photographs of Poe: something between worry and regret. He liked to take walks on the ramparts of the old Croton Reservoir ("particularly beautiful") and precisely predicted, when the grid was only just being felt north of 14th Street, the transformation of the city: "In some thirty years," he wrote, "every noble cliff will be a pier, and the whole island will be densely desecrated by buildings of brick."

The Mystery of Marie Roget

One of Poe's best-known stories, *The Mystery of Marie Rogêt*, is considered the first piece of crime fiction based on actual events. In the story the body of young Parisian Marie Rogêt is found floating in the Seine. Rogêt is based on Mary Rogers, a beloved lower Broadway tobacconist's clerk who was known as "the beautiful cigar girl." She was found dead in the Hudson in 1841, perhaps victim of a botched abortion.

THE HALL OF FAME

The original collection of great Americans

Bronx Community College
2155 University Avenue, Bronx
bcc.cuny.edu/halloffame
718-289-5170
4 train/Burnside Av or 183rd St; B and D trains/Tremont Av or 183rd St

The term "hall of fame" so pervades American culture it seems sourceless – but the source is here, on the campus of the Bronx Community College. The idea of a shrine to luminaries is ancient of course, but when it was inaugurated in 1901 as part of what was then a campus of New York University, the Hall of Fame of Great Americans became the national template.

The "hall" is actually a vaulted colonnade designed by Stanford White – famous in his own right – to flank and curve around three neoclassical buildings, also of his design, on the west side of the campus. As you walk the 630-foot length, you cross the bronze stares of ninety-eight remarkable Americans. A core group of thirty was included in 1901, with a plan to induct others every five years.

Fame is a fluid corollary of greatness; while the inclusion of Thomas Jefferson or George Washington is a given, you might frown at the head of dentist William Thomas Green Morton (the first person to use ether as a general anesthetic). The busts are grouped in themes such as Leaders, Scientists, Teachers. And Authors: here the Hall of Fame fills a need neglected by Central Park's baffling "Literary Walk" (Columbus, Shakespeare, two Scotsmen, and otherwise uncelebratable Fitz-Greene Halleck): Mark Twain, Edgar Allan Poe, Walt Whitman and Nathaniel Hawthorne get their due.

The busts are considered the finest such collection in America. Certain stand out. There is the stunned expression of Daniel Webster, a touchingly somber Lincoln gazing at the ground, and Susan B. Anthony, whose face seems determined even for statuary. If the blank green gazes begin to tire you out, seek out William Tecumseh Sherman. His portrait by the great Augustus Saint-Gaudens (honored with his own bust in the Artists category) feels nearly alive. Magnificently scruffy, Sherman looks like he was just roused from a haystack. Saint-Gaudens made the bust in 1888 as a study for his equestrian monument in Grand Army Plaza. The artist asked the Civil War general if he wouldn't mind buttoning his collar and adjusting his tie. Sherman growled: "The general of the Army of the United States will wear his coat any damn way he pleases." And, as you can see, he did.

LIGHTHOUSE AT THE TOP OF 950 UNIVERSITY AVENUE

A former company logo

960 University Avenue
Bronx, NY 10452

I f you drive on the Major Deegan Expressway, look up as you pass through the Highbridge section of the Bronx. There is a curious detail at the very top of 950 University Avenue: a lighthouse that looks over the Bronx and Manhattan.

Built in 1929, the complex was once the headquarters of H.W. Wilson, a publishing company, known for its *Readers Guide to Periodical Literature*. The lighthouse was part of the company logo, symbolizing the mission of H.W. Wilson: "To give guidance to those seeking their way through the maze of books and periodicals, without which they would be lost."

Although it's hard to see from the Deegan, the lighthouse rests on an opened book and had a working beacon. The interior of the building had pneumatic tubes, the once ubiquitous means of delivering mail in New York City. H.W. Wilson merged into EBSCO Publishing in 2012 and the building was bought by Tuck-it-Away storage, after Tuck-it-Away lost its headquarters in Harlem in an eminent domain battle with Columbia University.

Tuck-it-Away spent over $2 million refurbishing the building and converted it into offices and storage units. The company painted the lighthouse orange to mirror the colors of the company branding. Nick Spraygren, the CEO of Tuck-it-Away, told the *Bronx Times* in 2013, "By having this prominent light, people will become even more aware of us. We can spread the word and spread the light of what our mission is ... When H.W. Wilson left, they left a tremendous amount of office cubicles and desks." He also said at the time, "We are very bullish on the Bronx."

Unfortunately, Tuck-it-Away storage went out of business and in 2018, the brick complex was reclad completely in concrete and repainted in white, gray and green as part of a conversion into Extra Space Storage. During this time, the lighthouse remained orange. In 2020, Spraygren's son sold the five-building complex for $28.5 million to Prime Storage Group. The lighthouse remains, although it has since been repainted entirely black. The logo of the Prime Storage Group, a white key with the initials PS inside a shield, is emblazoned on it.

LORELEI FOUNTAIN

From Düsseldorf to ... South Bronx?

Joyce Kilmer Park
Between Walton Avenue and Grand Concourse, 161st to 164th Streets, Bronx
nycparks.org/parks/joyce-kilmer-park
B and D trains/161st St – Yankee Stadium

161st Street climbs east of the long corridor of elevated train tracks up to the Bronx Supreme Court. Just opposite the courthouse is a white marble statue that locals pay so little mind, it's nearly impossible to find anyone in the area who can tell you about it. The statue portrays Lorelei, a woman of legendary beauty. But the legends are German, and part of the reason the statue is overlooked is because it really has no business being in America, let alone South Bronx.

Lorelei is originally the name of a rock outcrop on a stretch of the Rhine River where the current is lethal. The name was loaned to a mythical temptress who perched there and sang as she combed her golden hair, luring – unknowingly but unfairly – distracted sailors to their death. The myth was put into verse by poet Heinrich Heine, whose portrait you can see on the marble statue in the Bronx: its proper name is the Heinrich Heine Fountain. Surrounding the central figure are mermaids, one of whom sits on a skull. This, you'll notice, still has nothing to do with New York.

Heine was from Düsseldorf. In 1888 a public subscription paid for the fountain, but the city of Düsseldorf immediately refused it on the grounds, according to many sources, that Heine was Jewish. "Dislike of the Jews," said a *Times* article about the rejection, "in some Germans amounts to a mania." Contributing factors were Heine's cutting satires of German authority and his love of France (he once described himself as "a German nightingale nesting in Voltaire's wig"). Another *Times* writer said the sculpture was simply poor, and if the Düsseldorfers were asses for rejecting a statue because it portrayed a Jew they were doubly so for letting it get out that this was the reason.

For years the marble fountain went unclaimed. Then in 1893 it was bought by the Arion Society, a local German-American group. The press found a way to make the fountain's ugliness a national virtue. "The fountain is not, indeed, a very great work of art," notes the *Times* after the purchase, "but as a symbol that America will not accept from the old country its prejudices of race it has its own value" – and a proper, if curious, place in New York City.

NEW FULTON FISH MARKET

The country's largest fish market

800 Food Center Drive
newfultonfishmarket.com
718.378.2356
Monday–Friday 1am–7am
Bx6 bus/Food Center & National Food

The old Fulton Fish Market was on the shore of the East River just south of the Brooklyn Bridge, and for well over a century spiced downtown with the racket of mongers, the stink of the sea, and the Mafia. It was the last outdoor market of any significance in Manhattan, and visiting according to its graveyard schedule was a favorite activity among night owls with a yen for the hectic. The New Fulton Fish Market, built in 2005, is even larger, but you have to weigh your interest against the enormous pain in the ass of getting there. The industrial flats of South Bronx are tough during the day; at four in the morning they're downright ominous. But that's when New Fulton is hopping. New York's restaurants and retailers send out armies to buy meat and produce while the city sleeps.

The market is a single, vast hangar: the largest wholesale fish outfit in the nation. It might also qualify as the largest refrigerator. It's always cold here; the guys wear hip boots and wool caps and gloves, and shift cardboard boxes full of ice and pollock, or wrestle out chilled swordfish onto tables. There is a swagger to the workers – most have a wicked steel fishhook balanced on their shoulder – that seems out of place under the endless rows of fluorescent light, because it really belongs to the sea. The fish business remains wild: the supply chain, unlike one that leads from a ranch or a farm, is unknowable. "It's been windy up and down the coast," says seller Bobby Weiss, noting a meager catch this early Friday morning. "The wind is a lot more of a factor than the weather—it's all about the wind direction. Shark's one seventy-five," he says to a buyer (all Fulton conversations are friendly, and all eventually get cut off like this).

A walk down the vast length of the hangar is an obstacle course of crates, loading palettes, sodden cardboard, baskets, and small hills of crushed ice. At every moment, brightly colored forklifts veer and vroom, bearing boxes of seafood or heading off to the truck docks to load up. Tuna from Central America. Kingfish from the Gulf. Oysters from New Zealand. It's a machine with a million parts; the entire world leads to it. And it's a little more interesting for being so vast and at the same time so hidden from the rest of Metropolis.

NORTH BROTHER ISLAND AND THE AUDUBON ECOCRUISE

Reclaimed by nature

nycaudubon.org/events-a-adventures
212.691.7483
Available June to September; other cruises available throughout the year
Launch at Pier 17
2 and 3 trains/Fulton St or Wall St

North Brother is a small island under the Bronx in the upper sprawl of the East River. Once location of the hospital that housed New York's quarantined and incurables, half a century ago it was given over to nature, which wasted no time in taking over. Today North Brother is unvisited, uncontrolled, and shaggy with wild trees. The ruins give the place a forsaken character – but only from a narrow, human perspective. For the city's cormorants, which nest there, it's home. There are three ways you can see this mysterious place. One, be a cormorant. Two, trespass, and exasperate a cormorant. And three, take the excellent EcoCruise hosted by the water taxis, and led by smart people from the Audubon Society.

New York water taxis, never the first conveyance that occurs to visitors or locals, are, aside from a beautiful way to see the city, an ideal way to watch estuarial nature. Which, as it happens, is rife. "Acre for acre," says the guide over a microphone on the upper deck while the boat throbs through the snapping wind upriver, "estuaries are the second richest ecosystems on the planet." (The first: tropical rain forests.) The taxis are catamarans, and so draw hardly any water, allowing the pilot to pull as close as you can get to the city's small islands without a kayak. These wooded humps rise like forgotten realms, and there's a satisfaction in watching the local birds transact the timeless business of fishing and feeding their young, undetected by the swarms of New Yorkers doing *their* business in the bowers of concrete and glass on the shore at either side.

The guide is full of remarkable facts. Cormorants dive as deep as 100 feet in search of fish, which means they can explore the darkest deeps of the East River with ease. Off Mill Island we spot the very symbol of the Audubon Society: the great egret, a frilly bird pushed to near-extinction by, of all things, hat makers: the decorative plumes were once more valuable by ounce than gold. When the taxi nears North Brother, the wind suddenly whips up as the river opens out to Long Island Sound. "This," says the guide, "is what sixty years of unchecked nature looks like." The photos of North Brother when it was still occupied by people show a flat, well-tended expanse of lawn crossed with paths. That civilization might as well have been a thousand years ago: the roofs of ruined buildings are now just visible through a real New York City jungle.

HELL GATE

Indian legends and treasure ships

Best seen from Wards Island Park or Astoria Park
4, 5 and 6 trains/125th St, then M-35 bus/Charles Gay Center (Wards Island
Park); N and Q trains/Astoria Blvd (Astoria Park)

A t the northern tip of Manhattan, things turn diabolical. On the one side you've got Spuyten Duyvil, the tidal strait between Manhattan and the Bronx whose name is mangled Dutch for either "Devil's whirlpool," or "to spite the Devil" – a reference to a folklore character who swam the strait during a tossing storm and got his leg tugged by Satan himself. On the other side is the awesomely named Hell Gate passage, the waterway between Ward Island and Astoria, Queens. The origin of the term Hell Gate is contested as well. From Dutch *Hellegat*, it could mean "bright passage," "Hell channel," or even "Hell-hole." This last translation might have been borrowed by the Dutch from the local Indians, who, according to legend, were so impressed with the waters of Hell Gate they believed them to be the entrance to the netherworld. But the Dutch might as easily have coined the term fresh: those waters are the deadliest in New York.

During the occupation, a British major called it "a horrible whirlpool, the vortex of which is called the Pot, and drawing in and swallowing up every thing that approaches near it." In 1780 the British frigate HMS *Hussar* sank in the channel, and the ship's freight of millions in gold and silver still glitters in the daydreams of treasure divers (the wreck has never been found). By 1850, it was estimated that every year about a thousand vessels ran aground in Hell Gate, and a fair amount of those sank. The U.S. Army Corps of Engineers began clearing the strait of dangerous rocks with explosives, a process that would stretch well into the 20th century.

But the real force behind the danger of Hell Gate isn't hidden rock: it's the tidal chaos. If you want to know what might compel a Lenape Indian to locate the churning portal to the underworld in the channel, it helps to have the perspective of someone like Antonio Burr, the commodore of the Inwood Canoe Club, the oldest kayak and canoe club in Manhattan. "I'll tell you what happens there," says Burr, who has paddled the water many times. "The Long Island Sound is at a different height than the other waterways, and the tides between the East River, the Sound, and the Harlem River don't coincide. Those waters *swirl*. If you wash out of your kayak in Hell Gate, you're in trouble."

THE MARRIAGE OF MONEY AND REAL ESTATE SCULPTURES

A real hidden gem

In the East River, to the west of James McManus field
Roosevelt Island, NY 10044

While the popular destinations on Roosevelt Island include FDR Four Freedoms Park and the abandoned smallpox hospital, if you head in the opposite direction you may happen upon some quirky sculptures by Tom Otterness. But you'll have to look over the water's edge, as the sculptures come out of the water.

Installed in 1996 and titled *The Marriage of Real Estate and Money*, the sculptures make quite a statement, situated between the dueling residential developments on both Roosevelt Island and Midtown East. Otterness, a Kansas-born American sculptor who is based in Gowanus, Brooklyn, is known for his cartoonish bronze figures that are both playful and political. He riffs on capitalism, featuring bankers with money bags for heads, workers holding hammers and other quirky characters.

The three Roosevelt Island sculptures depict respectively: a coin attacked by a moneybag coming out of the mouth of a man, a house wearing a skirt attacked by a money-inspired lobster, and a house and coin getting married. While Otterness certainly has many other more high-profile installations in New York City (and around the world), including *Life Underground* at the 14th Street subway station (see page 150), which depicts various scenes including an alligator reaching out from underneath a manhole cover to snatch a man for dinner, and *The Real World* in Battery Park City, *The Marriage of Real Estate and Money*, is a real hidden gem because you really have to look out to notice it.

TROMA HEADQUARTERS

Forty years of schlock

36–40 11th Street, Long Island City, Queens
troma.com
718-391-0110
Free tours weekdays 12pm–6pm; schedule at tours@troma.com
F train/21st St – Queensbridge

Troma Entertainment calls itself "perhaps the longest running independent movie studio in United States history." For forty years the company, founded by former Yale classmates Lloyd Kaufman and Michael Herz, has produced and distributed a shocking amount of schlock. The first successes were racy gag films (*Squeeze Play*, *Waitress* – they're now marketed together as the "Sexy Box"), but Troma really broke out with *Toxic Avenger* (1984), something like the *Citizen Kane* of special-effects-based low-budget mutant horror comedies. It's the tale of a wimpy mop-pusher who falls into a barrel of green nuclear waste and emerges with superhuman strength and bubbling skin. Vengeance ensues.

Make an appointment, and Troma will give you a tour of its Long Island City headquarters. The pull-down grate at the entrance bears a large painting of the mutant from *Avenger* ("Toxie"); above someone has dabbed "Welcome to Tromaville" – the name of the fictional town where many of the movies are set. Upstairs is production, downstairs distribution. The titles on the DVD boxes are a crash course in the Troma aesthetic: *Poultrygeist*. *Fat Guy Goes Nutzoid*. *Klown Kamp Massacre*. "This used to be a storehouse for a Chinese restaurant supplier," explains the guide, Kyle Corwin. He smiles vaguely at a steel sink in the corner where, for no obvious reason, lie a hook, a bone saw, and a pair of handcuffs. Then he leads the way through a sliding freezer door to the film reel and cassette stacks: hundreds of movies. The message seems to be: Make something. Don't make *Out of Africa*, necessarily. But something. "The demographic is basically, like, 13-year-olds," Corwin says. "And up." When Corwin isn't showing people around, he's an editor. He says one of the unwritten production guidelines is nudity within the first 10 minutes. Blood and dismemberment are also a plus.

If it sounds like Troma has made itself the prisoner of a formula, it's a formula that can accommodate an undercover cop whose secret power is Japanese theater (*Sgt. Kabukiman, N.Y.P.D.*), a gay snow monster (*Yeti: A Love Story*) and whatever Bloodspit is about. In fact, for forty years Troma has specialized in doing whatever the hell it wants. "We opened doors in '74," says Corwin. "Same people running it, hasn't changed hands, never got bought."

BROOKLYN GRANGE

The good earth, overhead

37–18 Northern Boulevard, Queens
brooklyngrangefarm.com
Farm open to visitors Saturday 10am–3pm (spring to fall)
E and M trains/36 St

Brooklyn Grange is a farm on a roof. Most visitors access it through a café at street level which has its fruits and vegetables delivered, perhaps uniquely, from upstairs. When a waiter passes with a mixed salad, the owner says, "Yep," and points at the ceiling. "Everything on that plate came from up there."

The old six-story building, formerly a manufacturing plant, is square and sturdy, and has a footprint that is, as if an agricultural future were glimpsed in the architect's dream, almost exactly one acre. There are a few similar buildings on Northern Boulevard left over from a heyday in car building. Only this one has orderly rows of soil – over a million pounds of it – on top. There's also a chicken coop, beehives, wildflowers, and a small stand where you can buy the farm's produce: tomatoes, lettuce, kale, peppers, ground cherries, garlic. It's not a gimmick: the aerial field, created in 2010, is sustainable and even profitable. Rooftop farms work.

"We use this mixture called Rooflite," says Bradley, the farm manager, scooping up a handful of earth specked with flinty rock. "It's a good growing medium because it's got these porous stones." Not that weight is an issue: the industrial roof, which was specially prepared with layers of absorbent felt and runoff collecting measures, could withstand four times as much. The soil is enriched with compost; the farm creates its own with a solar-powered system. You can see how this works yourself on any Saturday during the growing season (spring to fall), and aside from the peculiar charm of taking an elevator to a tended field, you'll find it worth visiting for the view. The Manhattan skyline dominates the horizon; the city grid and the orderly rows of vegetables turn out to be a natural match.

The Grange has a companion project in the Brooklyn Navy Yard, and together they're the largest rooftop farms in the world. While you're stooped over weeding or picking turnips, you might forget that you're 100 feet up. "It's funny, yeah," says Bradley. "Oftentimes I don't look at this all day" – motioning towards a glittering cityscape that includes the Citigroup Tower, the Empire State and Chrysler buildings. "Then, I love it when everybody goes home at the end of the day and I have time to myself with the plants and check out the view as the sun goes down."

THE PANORAMA

A gargantuan miniature

Queens Museum of Art
New York City Building, Flushing Meadows, Queens
queensmuseum.org
718-592-9700
Wednesday–Sunday 11am–5pm
7 train/111th St

t's unfair to call the Panorama a "scale model." Even "largest architectural scale model in the world" – a title it has held for half a century – seems stingy. This miniature metropolis spreads over an area greater than two basketball courts and comprises in all 895,000 individual buildings. The project is so grand, an air of beautiful lunacy hangs over it.

Now an attraction at the Queens Museum of Art, the Panorama is a relic from the 1964-65 World's Fair. 1964 was in the heat of the space race, echoed in the Flushing Meadows map: Court of the Astronauts, Promenade of Infinity, Lunar Fountain. As is always the case, this Fair's vision of the future was strewn with priceless duds: one pavilion featured a full-scale "ultramodern" home built completely underground. "Among the desirable features," the guidebook reads, "is complete privacy." The Panorama was a hit: thousands of visitors paid their 10 cents to hover over the gigantic model in a simulated helicopter ride.

But you might expect, in place of this scrupulous scale model, a dashing New York City of Tomorrow, with hovercraft docks and pneumatic railways gleaming under a glass dome. This didn't fit the plans – or the personality – of Fair director Robert Moses. "It was definitely a Robert Moses project," says David Strauss, a Queens Museum director. "It was his way of showing the world what he'd done to create the epitome of a modern metropolis."

Moses, the city's most brilliant, prolific, and despised urban planner, was a scale-model person, not a people person. He saw New York as a complicated toy, and New Yorkers as obstacles to the comfort of his real love, the automobile. In the model for his notorious expressway proposal, Moses fitted a happy Greenwich Village neighborhood with handles so it could be neatly banished from the map. The Panorama was a chance to create a New York that was mentally manageable, clean and precise, and totally devoid of humans.

But without crabby Moses, the Panorama never would have been. It took 100 craftsmen three years to complete, and is so exact (Moses demanded a margin of error of less than 1%), well into the 1970s city planners would make the trip to Queens to measure projects against this perfect scale replica. Today the Panorama is reason enough to visit the Queens Museum of Art, and remains one of New York City's true marvels.

STEINWAY PIANO FACTORY

Living machines

1 Steinway Place, Long Island City,
Queens
steinway.com/about/factory-tour
For tours call: 718-721-2600
N and Q trains/Astoria – Ditmars Blvd; the factory is a 10-minute walk up
38th St

Photo courtesy of Steinway & Sons

Steinway & Sons, makers of fine concert pianos, is perhaps the oldest manufacturing business in New York City. There are places at the factory compound that still have hitching stanchions for horses. The core building techniques of Steinway pianos have hardly changed over the years, and many of the company's groundbreaking patents have run out because they've been in use for over a century. "I'm just now starting to be seen as one of the regular staff," says the guide, Bob Bernhardt. He's a retired senior engineer with thirty-three years at the company.

The Steinway tour is thorough: it covers every aspect of piano building, and by the end of it you'll have walked a couple of miles. The factory has a peculiar beauty. It's raw, clamorous manufacturing, but the product is so sensitive it's practically alive. You can see the place as a progression from very loud to very quiet: from howling saws and knocking hammers to the buzz of sanders and the swish of hand-rubbed varnish, all the way, finally, to a soundproof chamber where a tone adjuster bows over the assembled instrument and responds to subtle vibrations normal mortals can't even hear.

"The tone adjusters are sort of the prima donnas around here," says Bernhardt. He's so accustomed to the excellence of Steinways, he can deliver a whole string of amazing details without much change in tone. The bridge is cut by hand because machines have no feel for the subtlety required, a matter of thousandths of an inch. In the Veneer Room there is 3 million dollars' worth of premium woods at any one time: the raw lumber of a Steinway is often valued higher than a competitor's retail price. The rim is kilned after pressing to arrive at a precise moisture content – "unless of course the piano is going to a tropical area," Bernhardt notes, "then it'll be adjusted for humidity." Even the parts sawn by robot are finished by hand, because wood is not dead: it changes with the temperature and the weather.

Secret marks

There are whole dynasties of piano builders at the company. Families have secret marks that they leave inside the instruments so they'll be recognized if it ever comes back for service – after 50, 80, 100 years.

MARINE AIR TERMINAL

Flying boats and lost art

LaGuardia Airport, Queens
airport-laguardia.com/terminals.php
718-533-3400
Many possibilities; use the MTA Trip Planner: tripplanner.mta.info

W ithin the LaGuardia Airport complex, about half a mile from the airport proper you'll find a low, modest building that seems frozen in the 1940s. The Marine Air Terminal is a hangover from the earliest days of passenger air travel, when flying was still novel and had a classy romance about it. "Marine" and "Air" may seem to sit awkwardly together but the name refers to the hybrid planes that serviced this terminal: great propeller-powered "flying boats" that landed on the water and taxied to gangplanks stretching from shore.

Every detail here invites bitter comparison with the current airport experience – part shopping mall, part Gulag – that has made flying a byword for grief. The terminal is small and light. The doors bear linear chrome motifs of winged globes, a nod to Pan Am, the company that kicked off the age of international air travel. The waiting area is perfectly circular, with a great oculus letting in natural light. You sense the sea and the sky.

Two Canadian commercial pilots stand by their luggage in the middle of the polished floor, just looking up. "Pilots have a soft spot for flying boats," says one. "You read all these history books about the guys who flew for Pan Am – it's amazing what they did." Like making repairs in the middle of the ocean, or navigating by the stars. "It was adventurous."

The terminal is also an art landmark: a 12-foot high mural runs the entire circuit of the waiting hall interior. Over 230 feet long, *Flight* by James Brooks is the largest painting created under the Work Projects Administration (WPA), Roosevelt's public projects agency. The mural, depicting man's quest for flight through the ages from Icarus to the Wright Brothers to Boeing, has a peculiar history. The Port Authority administrators, touched by the anti-Communist fever of the 1950s, detected a note of progressivism in the theme and had the mural painted over. *Flight* didn't see light again until a restoration in 1980.

> The Marine Air Terminal is the only airport dating to the earliest period of American air travel that is still active today.

LOUIS ARMSTRONG HOUSE

A humble address for a jazz god

34 – 56 107th Street, Queens
louisarmstronghouse.org
718-478-8274
Tuesday–Friday 10am–5pm; weekends 12pm–5 pm
7 train/103rd St – Corona Plaza

When you hear Louis Armstrong sing or play trumpet, there's a golden quality that makes it easy to assume he was a good man. After a visit to the Louis Armstrong House Museum in Queens you'll be convinced he was a great one.

"Armstrong is the king," says guide Al Pomerantz. "He's the first American superstar." Pomerantz is tall and wears a permanent smile; as he walks you through the rooms, he fidgets with barely containable enthusiasm. This is a tribute museum to make fans swoon. Not only is the low-ceilinged brick house the only one Armstrong ever owned, he lived here for almost thirty years and died in his sleep in the upstairs bedroom. Sitting on the sofa, cutting turkey at the dinner table, watching TV ... whatever jazz legends do at home, Armstrong did it here.

As the 40-minute tour unfolds, two themes emerge. First, an almost uncanny success. During his fifty years in the business, Armstrong dominated music: recordings, radio, concert broadcasts, film, television – they wanted Pops in everything. Then there is Armstrong's knack for wearing this superstardom lightly. Born in the poorest neighborhood of New Orleans, Armstrong grew up believing that he'd never have a house of his own: his wife Lucille bought this one while he was away on tour. When the musician pulled up to the address, he asked the taxi driver to keep the engine running in case it was too good to be true. By that time he was already a millionaire.

"Pops could have lived anywhere," says Pomerantz, "but he chose a working-class neighborhood." One of the gems of the museum is a breezy letter by the musician outlining his love for the simple pleasures of strolling these streets, greeting neighbors, stopping at the barber shop. On a wall of the den hang two photographs: one of Armstrong's triumphant reception in Paris and the other of Pops goofing on the front porch with the neighborhood kids. There you have the whole man. "I am here with the black people," he said, "with the Puerto Rican people, the Italian people, the Hebrew cats, and there's food in the Frigidaire. What else could I want?"

QUAKER MEETING HOUSE ㉖

New York's oldest house of worship

137 – 16 Northern Boulevard,
Queens
nyym.org/flushing; check for service/tour schedule
718-358-9636
7 train/Flushing – Main St

On a busy boulevard in Flushing, Queens, stands a quiet example of early settler architecture. The wooden Quaker Meeting House was built in 1694 as a place where Friends (as Quakers call themselves) could gather in peace, and has served that purpose ever since. It's the oldest house of worship in New York.

Tours are conducted on Sundays directly after service, but the service is a worthwhile experience in itself. Quakers will welcome you. On the back of the door hangs an ancient poster: TO THOSE ATTENDING OUR MEETING FOR THE FIRST TIME, with the suggestion: "Do not be anxious about distracting thoughts, but ride through them to the still centre."

The ride is curious. The congregants – not more than a dozen – sit on the benches with head up and eyes closed, and enter what resembles a trance. The meeting house calls this state "expectant waiting." There is no talk of any kind, except at rare moments where a Friend will rise and deliver a brief, personal message. The focus is on the individual: no one is the minister; everyone is the minister. This simplicity is echoed in a pointed lack of decor. The walls of the small prayer hall are white plaster, and totally bare except for metal candle holders; the wooden benches are unvarnished, and date from the Revolution (the British burned the originals). Outside the open window is lawn and hydrangea, and the small sounds of the boulevard – motorcycle, jet, honk – are not those a Quaker who sat here three hundred years ago would recognize, but they enhance rather than distract from the pocket of antique silence within. When the hour's up, the Friends rise and shake hands all around, visitors included, with a glad "Good morning!" No recitation of holy writ, no gory prophecies, no obsession with Hell and sin; the very divinity of Christ is a matter of debate. They don't even call the place a church.

"It's very democratic," says one of the Friends over coffee and cookies after the service. One of the new visitors, a young woman from Thailand, says she was reminded of Buddhist meditation. "I can see that," the Friend nods, and reaches for another ginger snap.

GEORGE FOX STONE AND THE FLUSHING REMONSTRANCE

A memorial to a pair of trees

Sidewalk at 36–40 Bowne Street, Queens
bownehouse.org
7 train/Flushing – Main St

The angular granite rock that rises like a tooth from the sidewalk of Bowne Street is a unique monument: it memorializes a pair of trees. "Two immense oaks," according to Katharine Nicholson's *Historic American Trees*, "under whose shade George Fox, founder of the Society of Friends, preached to the Indians in 1672."

The Friends, commonly called Quakers, formed in England around 1650. Those who made their way to America were treated roughly. In Boston they were hanged in the streets, in New Netherland the first Quaker preacher was clubbed and jailed, and Friends were forbidden from assembling. Still, the movement took hold in Flushing. In 1657 the citizens there, disgusted by the harassment, composed a protest letter that has come to be known as the Flushing Remonstrance. It pled for religious acceptance and mutual respect, "which is the true law both of church and state." This noble document is considered the precursor to the Bill of Rights, but it didn't impress New Netherland director Peter Stuyvesant: his reply was to toss out the Flushing government and imprison the man whose house served as the Quaker meeting place.

This homeowner, John Bowne, wasn't even a Quaker at the time. His house still stands on the other side of Bowne Street; the oaks were in his garden. To read that George Fox "preached to Indians" gives the impression he roamed the dewy forest with a Bible and a smile, but although he liked Indians ("courteous and loving") and even stayed with them during his two years in America, the famous sermon under the oaks took place outdoors because the Bowne house was too small for the hundreds of Flushing residents who came to listen.

The oaks lived until a storm toppled them in 1863. They were half a millennium old. The granite block has marked the site since 1907.

NEARBY

Behind the Bowne house, on 37th Avenue, stands the Kingsland Homestead, headquarters of the Queens Historical Society. Next to it is the site of the first weeping beech tree in America, brought from Belgium as a sapling. The huge disheveled tree you see today was grown from a cutting of the original: with its tendril branches and drooping leaves, it looks at least as much like a sea monster as it does a tree. If you visit it, feel free to give a kick to New York's most passive-aggressive signage: "You are being videotaped. Smile!"

THE GANESH TEMPLE

Please do not touch the deities

Hindu Temple Society of North America
45–57 Bowne Street
nyganeshtemple.org
718-460-8484
Monday–Friday 8am–9pm; opens at 7:30 am on weekends
7 train/Flushing – Main St; then Q45 Jamaica-bound bus at Main St and
Roosevelt Av, get off at 45th Av and Bowne St

Y ou know a New York City house of worship is about to offer a unique experience when you see, just inside the grounds, a granite basin with the sign: COCONUT BREAKING AREA. Gopal, a native of Madras who now lives in Queens, has come to the Ganesh Temple with his wife and takes a moment to explain. "It's for *pooja*. It's the way you pray to the god. *Pooja* is when you stand in front of him and say his praise and offer him flowers and fruit and so on." Asked if the temple serves only the devotees of Ganesh, the elephant-headed god of the vast and complex Hindu pantheon, Gopal shakes his head. "You can go pretty much to any Hindu temple. This one is to Ganesh, but philosophically speaking, god has no form." This is a strangely attractive thing to hear from a man who holds a dripping coconut.

The Ganesh Temple rises suddenly like a carved mountain from the endless residential streets of Flushing. Patterned after architecture in Maharashtra, India, the pleasing proportions and fine texture of detailed sculptures conceal a rigid underlying logic that has remained constant for centuries. Ganesh is the first Hindu temple in the United States built according to these ancient rules. Hundreds of traditional tradesmen worked on the building and almost all of the material, including the black granite of the principal shrine, was shipped from India.

Respectful visitors are welcome inside; Westerners are likely to find it a feast of the exotic. Barefoot priests pass quietly, or ring bells, or chant, or converse in one of four main languages – Tamil, Telugu, Malayalam, and Kannada. At the center of the main room the principal shrine spreads like the root of a hill, and rises straight through the ceiling, its sunlit peak visible through skylights. The walls are lined with cordons; behind them are smaller shrines. In each shrine is a god. Ornate sculptures little over a foot high, they're decked in vivid colors and garlands; some hold folded dollar bills in their gesturing hands. The sign reads: "Please do not cross this line and/or touch the deities." Note: not the image of the deity, but the deity itself. The Hindu temple is a fluid zone where the boundaries between man and the divine dissolve – even in Queens.

THE GRAVE MARKER
OF THE MATINECOC INDIANS

A lost people on Northern Boulevard

Zion Episcopal Church
243-01 Northern Boulevard, Queens
zionepiscopal.org
718-225-0466
Monday–Wednesday and Friday 9am–12pm, Sunday services at 8 and 10 am
7 train/Flushing – Main St; then Little Neck-bound Q12 bus, get off at
Northern Blvd and 243rd St

In the graveyard of the Zion Episcopal Church in Douglaston, Queens, you'll find a large granite boulder that appears to have been split by a growing oak tree. The boulder is actually a grave marker: many bodies lie beneath it. If you look closely, you can read these epic words chiseled into the stone: HERE REST THE LAST OF THE MATINECOC.

The Matinecoc were an Indian tribe, and of any corner of Queens, Douglaston probably most deserves a particularly bloody Indian curse. The townlet is quiet and pretty (it once applied for a kind of general landmark status) and seems insulated from worry. The Zion Episcopal is a small white clapboard structure with a steeple that perfects the generic notion of "church;" there's brick and shingles in every direction around it. "It'll be on the right-hand side as you go towards the firehouse," says the young woman by way of directions, and the words make Manhattan seem like a noisy dream. And there it is: a grave marker to a lost people.

The spot is not obviously cursed, just a little depressing. Today hardly anyone has heard of the Matinecoc, but they were the first Long Islanders, along with a host of others that have left their names – just the palest of ghosts – on the map: the Canarsie, the Manhasset, the Montauk, the Massapequa, the Rockaway. Early European colonists associated the different groups ("tribe" is often judged too broad a definition) with the land they lived on. The Matinecoc had settled the series of inlets on the northwest side of Long Island, including the area of Little Neck Bay where Douglaston is today.

How the church came to have a grave marker to an entire Native American society is a tale of urban renewal like a thousand others, with this difference: what was busted up and paved over was a last remnant of New Yorkers whose history went back not decades, but millennia. In 1931, the city widened Northern Boulevard, and in the process destroyed a Native American cemetery. Thirty bodies were reinterred in the churchyard under the rock and the oak: the mark of the Matinecoc.

THE ALLEY POND GIANT

New York's oldest living thing

East Hampton Boulevard: the trailhead is on the left just before you cross the Long Island Expressway (heading south)
Q30 bus/Horace Harding Exp/E Hampton Blvd

The oldest known living thing in New York City is also the tallest: a tulip tree in eastern Queens. Getting there requires some pluck, and like much of what is striking and natural in the city, the tree seems forgotten, or lost. It grows next to a snarl of expressways in a corner of Alley Pond Park, and if you make the trek to sit for awhile in its speckled shadow you'll hear, beneath the birdsong, a constant background wash of hissing traffic. But the trip is worth it.

This area of Queens will be unrecognizable to most as a part of Gotham. It's a realm of one-story brick houses that all resemble each other, and so make an effort to stand out with some genteel addition: a plastic deer, a chrome banister, concrete lions. Where East Hampton Boulevard crosses the Long Island Expressway there are, to one side, towering traffic signs and retaining walls and a caged overpass. It's the other side you want: a trailhead with thistle, cattails, and butterflies. At first you'll think that you've been lured into a facsimile of nature: the trail is asphalt and all of the green is on the other side of a black chain link fence. But after a few paces the fence ends. To your left is a deep forest. In it are trees that remember Indians.

The Alley Pond Giant stands only 50 yards or so straight in. After passing a runoff of tumbled rock, you'll head through territory in a hurry to get wild. The ground is spongy with leaves and tulip blossoms; rare ferns sprout in curling clusters, and the damp bark slips from fallen branches when you walk on them. There are several immense trees here, but you'll know when you've found New York's tallest. The Alley Pond Giant has its own fence enclosure; next to the hollow bole is a Parks Department sign trimmed in spiderwebs and beetles: "This tuliptree (Liriodendron tulipifera) is the tallest carefully measured tree in New York City with a height of 133.8 feet. It is also probably the oldest living thing in the City at an estimated age of 400 years or more. This tree is perhaps the last witness to the entire span of the City's history from a tiny Dutch settlement to one of the great metropolises of the world. If we leave it undisturbed, it may live among us for another hundred years or so."

LIVING MUSEUM

The finest collection of art in New York City

Creedmoor Psychiatric Center
80–45 Winchester Boulevard, Queens
omh.ny.gov/omhweb/facilities/crpc/facility.htm
Call to schedule a visit: 718-264-3490
F train/Jamaica – 179th St; then take the Floral Park bound Q43 bus at Hillside
Av and 179th, get off at Hillside Av and Winchester Blvd

Creedmoor has been a psychiatric facility since 1912. Generations of eastern Queens parents have been telling rowdy children that if they don't clean up their act they'll end up there. The main building is the tallest in the area, a yellow brick monolith that has the gravity of an evil castle. But on the other side of Union Turnpike is a pleasant grassy campus. There you'll find the Living Museum, the first American museum dedicated to the art of the mentally ill.

The space was founded in the 1980s on the principle that patients do better when they have something to be other than patients – namely, artists. According to program founder Janos Marton, it's a natural fit anyway. "There is no difference," he says, "between creativity and mental illness." Marton looks like he could be a patient trying a little too hard to fool you into believing he's the real Dr. Marton: he has long white hair, a perceptive stare, and an Austrian accent. When a tabby cat jumps onto his open date book, he sits back with a sigh: not shooing it off, but not petting it either. The desk is an oasis of administrative clutter amid a riot of artistic clutter, and patients continually come and go – with problems, with ideas, with silence. At first the doctor seems reluctant to discuss the Living Museum, but mostly, it turns out, to avoid confirming silly generalizations about mental illness. His opinion, once expressed, is categorical. "This is the finest collection of art in New York City," he says with quiet emphasis. "It's because the artists here are authentic. That's what everybody's trying to be."

And perhaps better than spending time with the work – two floors, every wall hung with paintings, every corner filled with installation and sculpture, tables strewn with clay figures and found objects – is spending time with the creators. Some are outgoing, others keep busily to themselves. Some are perceptibly off, others barely eccentric. Most instructive is when another first-time visitor arrives, and sees you as just another face in the wallpaper of crazy, and puts on a certain smile – just a little too bright, just a little condescendingly sane – that you'll hope you weren't wearing yourself a few minutes earlier.

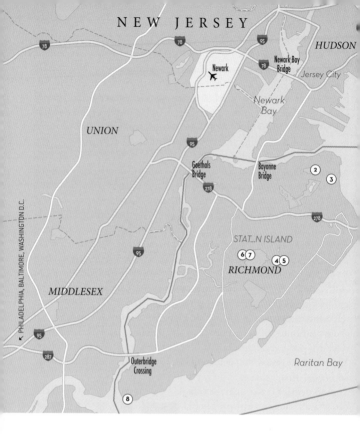

Staten Island

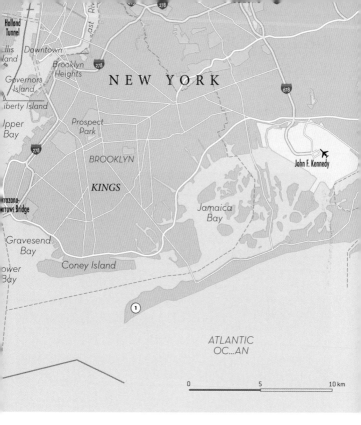

BREEZY POINT

Secret, beautiful, inconvenient

Queens
nyharborparks.org/visit/brpo.html
2 train/Flatbush Av, then Q-35 bus/Fort Tilden; A train/Rockaway Beach, then Q-22 bus/Fort Tilden; car: paid parking at 222nd Street Ferry; ferry: NY Water Taxi/Riis Landing

Breezy Point is plain on the map: it's the very tip of the Queens peninsula that stretches under Brooklyn and encloses Jamaica Bay. But the place is not exactly easy to get to. "It's the real best-kept secret in these parts," says a man in a bar at Rockaway Beach. "That's why the people there are a little ... chilly."

The chilly people fear invasion. But the Point is unlikely to become overrun with New Yorkers anytime, ever: it has the natural defense of being totally inconvenient. The peninsula is part of the Gateway National Recreation Area and so government property. The streets that lead there are public, as is the beach – but the rest is a large private co-op. This means non-members generally have only three ways to access the place: 1) walk or ride a bike the length of the beach from a point further east; 2) arrive by sea; 3) confuse the locals.

Once you get there, the payoff is big. Sailboats and motorboats cross paths across the open Atlantic. Breezy Point is one half of the inlet to New York Harbor; the other, Sandy Hook, is visible on the other side. Everything to the north is Lower Bay, and as you stand on the point the misty vistas of Staten Island, southern Brooklyn, Jersey City and Manhattan overlap in unexpected ways. Most interesting is a chance to see the icons of Coney Island – the Parachute Drop, Wonder Wheel, and Cyclone – from the sea. Faraway Manhattan rises behind yellow-green dune grass, but is so small the jagged skyline is strikingly tender, softened by distance to a palette of airy pastels.

The very tip of the Point – the end of the peninsula – is marked by a jetty of granite block. The only person on it today is a barrel-chested Russian in a wetsuit, frowning down at a white fish. The fish has a bleeding hole in it. "Is a fluke," the man says. "This is problem of spear fishing: too big, too small, the fish die anyway. I think this is not a fair rule." (By law fluke have to be at least 20.5 inches or you throw them back.)

What urban noise might reach this far is muted by the constant swish of the surf: the jets of JFK pass in apparent silence overhead. As the waves roll in, they are dodged by great flocks of scurrying terns and plovers. The birds, among four protected local species, nest in grassy dunes closed off from the public, and their presence is all the proof you need that for the most part humans leave Breezy Point alone.

CHINESE SCHOLAR'S GARDEN

Staten Island: the best place in New York City to see China

1000 Richmond Terrace, Staten Island
snug-harbor.org
718-448-2500
Tuesday–Sunday 10am–5pm
At Staten Island ferry terminal, S-40 bus (Gate D)/Snug Harbor

The best place in New York City to see China isn't in Chinatown, it's on Staten Island. The Chinese Scholar's Garden at Snug Harbor is an acre of flowing water, rocks and trees that might as well be Asia. Even the sky, framed against the upturned eaves of the pavilions, looks foreign.

The site's impact is heightened by the oddness of the approach: you buy your ticket in a small gift shop in the Botanical Garden and pass out the back into a trail that cuts through swishing bamboo. Confucian scholars' gardens were a regular feature of southern China during the 15th century; this one was constructed in the late 1990s by forty expert artisans from Suzhou Province. Every detail here is designed to be the object of contemplation. Everything bears a message. The flowering plum trees bloom in late winter and so evoke loyalty in hard times. The water and rocks are arranged for contrast: yin and yang, horizontal and vertical, soft and hard. A small footbridge arches over a waterfall, forming a grotto underneath; in classical Chinese poetry the arrangement is said to provide a gateway to the mystical. Down in the wash a photogenic crane perches on a rock: silent, patient.

"The crane is long life," says a middle-aged Taiwanese tourist who introduces himself as William. "If you see it, you have good luck." William knows mainland China and Suzhou Province well; he seems to have appeared here in the capacity of quality control. Overall, he's impressed. "It's very, very good," he nods. "Almost perfect." In front of one pavilion a rough stone mosaic is set in the path: cranes and pine trees, a combination that augurs continued happiness. "The pine," he explains, "in warm weather, cold weather – always green." Around the border are circles that mimic the shape of old Chinese coins. "If you have health," William says, "it's good. If you have money also ..." he cuts off with a smile: no need to interpret the universal.

The Confucian scholar's garden is unique in the United States. Planned over a fourteen-year period, the Chinese artisans who built it lived on site for six months.

Where Europeans first set eyes on New York

Tompkinsville Park, Staten Island
nycgovparks.org/parks/tompkinsvillepark/
At the Staten Island Ferry terminal, walk south on Bay St to Tompkinsville
Square (10 minutes)

In the year 1525, the following scene took place just off Staten Island: "They came towards us very cheerfully, making great shouts of admiration, showing us where we might come to land most safely with our boat. We entered up the said river into the land about half a league, where it made a most pleasant lake ..."

The pleasant lake was New York's Upper Bay. The cheerful greeters were Lenape Indians. The chronicler is Giovanni da Verrazzano, who was the first European ever to set eyes on the land that would be New York. Unsure of the safety of the channel, he anchored his ship in the Narrows, the tidal strait between Brooklyn and Staten Island that is now spanned by the Verrazano-Narrows Bridge. Just a little inland from that spot was a natural spring; if he took water, it's likely he took it there.

Today "The Watering Place" is marked by a stone and a plaque. If Verrazzano might have come here, the Dutch certainly did. Their early descriptions of the area are as admiring as the Italian's: constant references to safety and fertility, richness, sweetness, colors. The first accounts of New York invite comparison with the current version. The Watering Place is now hemmed in on one side by a view of the shining Upper Bay that Verrazzano was too timid to enter (and is now crossed by the Staten Island ferry fifty times a day), and on the others by every variety of fast food. The park behind it attracts a weird mix of bums and kids. Two men drinking beer from cans in paper sacks are surprised to learn about the existence of the stone a dozen paces away, and take to arguing about where the original spring might have been. Then one straightens up with a frown.

"Why you asking us about this anyway? Folks around here don't know anything about this stuff. You need to go to a *library*."

The other man hisses a belch. "I don't need a library," he murmurs, to no one. "I got a fucking photographic memory."

The Verrazano-Narrows Bridge has officially misspelled Verrazzano's name by cutting a z, reportedly due to a clerical error.

MOSES MOUNTAIN

A one-of-a-kind view and a slap in the face

Greenbelt Park
nycgovparks.org/park-features/virtual-tours/greenbelt/moses-mountain
718-667-2165
Trailheads, maps, and parking at High Rock Park at the end of Nevada Avenue,
Staten Island

As noted elsewhere (see next page), Greenbelt Park running through the middle of Staten Island is one of the city's great unsung wonders. The natural beauty there is so impressive, it was deemed worth ruining by the greatest and worst parks commissioner in New York history: Robert Moses. Moses was as single-minded as an evil robot. His answer to the urban planning riddle: rip it up and lay a clean, wide strip of asphalt over it. He came close to wrecking the Greenbelt, and the park's highest point, Moses Mountain, is both a reminder and a back-handed tribute. This hill is entirely composed of the rubble left over from Moses's aborted plan for a cross-Staten Island parkway.

It wasn't the only time a Moses project was thwarted by citizens who saw a future mazed with car traffic as less than ideal. The commissioner's plans to expand a parking lot along Central Park and run a sunken boulevard through Washington Square and the West Village were defeated; the Greenbelt protest was helped by a nudge from State Governor Nelson Rockefeller. By the time the Greenbelt section of the parkway was abandoned in the late 60s, rock had been blasted, roads dug up, houses razed. The earth and debris hauled off to this location, eventually topping out at 260 feet, still has the feel of unfinished business, even though the whole mess has gradually turned as green as Peru. As you climb up, you can see crags of old asphalt jutting from the dirt, and the cement pipes of uprooted sewers.

But the real wonder of Moses Mountain is the view out when you've scrambled up to the summit. It's here that the tease in the name people have given this spot is keenest. Instead of an endless chain of cars creeping through the forest, you see gulls wheel lazily over an unbroken landscape of billowing emerald. It's the kind of view that's missing nothing, but would look very nice with, here and there, the long bowing neck of a grazing dinosaur. It's the only place in all of New York City where you can stand at the top of a landmass and see a horizon that is nothing but trees.

NEW YORK'S WILDEST PLACE   ⑤

Remotely fascinating

sigreenbelt.org
718-667-2165
Trailheads, maps, and parking at High Rock Park at the end of Nevada Avenue,
Staten Island

In the hive of Metropolis, there are expanses of wild: great parks, beaches, and lonely urban wastes like abandoned airfields. But there must be a place that is more remote from the buzz of people than any other—New York City's wildest spot. According to one writer (Bruce Kershner), it's on Staten Island. There, in the middle of one of the city's truly great parks, the underappreciated Greenbelt, is a spot that is 1,488 feet from any public street or house. Is this the record? If you accept it as the goal of a day's adventure, you won't care. Inside the Greenbelt, you are gone.

Logical that the wildest spot would be on Staten Island: the place is only partially tamed. Sidewalks tend to disappear in the interior, and the ground cover seems to come in three varieties: mugwort, poison ivy, and another kind of poison ivy you didn't know about yet. The "Forgotten Borough" is fully one-third parkland, and the Greenbelt is the prize. "This is New York City's last self-supporting ecosystem," says Pete Ziegeler, who wears National Park Service green. He trudges around the soppy rim of a pond, ducking under bushes to get an uninterrupted view of the other shore, which, on this golden afternoon, might have been arranged by a sentimental landscape painter. Ziegeler works at nearby Great Kills Park, but when he clocks out he comes here. At another pond, where the swamp trees rise out of the shallows and the water is dimpled by water skippers, a patient researcher takes photos. "It's for a survey of dragonflies," the man says. "So far about twenty-seven different species have been found in this area. Give or take."

To a New Yorker's gridded experience, this might as well be the Russian Taiga. Kingly trees—oak, sweetgum, hickory, beech—permeate a weird terrain, the so-called kettle ponds and bogs that are the legacy of the last ice age. It's within reach of public transportation: the whole trip of subway, ferry, and bus will cost you $2.50. That's a bargain for a trek that starts at a noisy intersection and ends, just a couple of hours later, on a fallen tree over a bog grunting with toads. The wildest spot is on the most easterly bank of Hourglass Pond. You can find it, probably, by using the trail guide and following the blazes on the trees. If you don't, you've still done something that counts as pretty particular.

STATEN ISLAND RANGE LIGHT ⑥

A landlocked lighthouse

103 Edinboro Road
Staten Island, NY 10306

"Landlocked lighthouse" sounds like an oxymoron, but the Staten Island Range Light on Lighthouse Hill in Staten Island has been the metaphorical beacon of a charming and historically rich neighborhood for over a century. Located four miles from the nearest coastline and

seven miles from the Staten Island ferry's stop, the elegant lighthouse is still in operation, thanks to its location at 231 feet above sea level.

Built in 1912 and originally powered by a kerosene lamp, the yellow brick and limestone lighthouse (also known as the Richmond Light) has been running on a 1,000-watt bulb and a Fresnel range lamp since 1939, aiding ships in the Ambrose Channel, between Staten Island and Brooklyn, the primary lane for shipping in New York harbor.

The beloved local historian Joe Esposito kept the light from 1992 to 2001, accepting no salary in exchange for his labor until a heart attack led to his retirement. According to the *New York Times*, Coast Guard officers stop by every three months just to make sure the light is still on. The original lighthouse keeper's house is now a private home.

The lighthouse became the subject of a tussle between the New York City Landmarks Preservation Commission and the federal government in 1968 over granting landmark status. Because the lighthouse is technically on federal land, the proposal was met with resistance, as such a designation would place the lighthouse under New York City jurisdiction. The Commission won, declaring it "a building of which New Yorkers are proud" and cementing its significance to New York history. The Landmarks Designation report notes that in addition to its "distinguished" architecture, the Staten Island Range Light "stands as a reminder of the men and women in the lighthouse service who have devoted their lives to the safe entry and departure of ships in and out of this great American port."

The Lighthouse Hill area feels more like a quaint New England community than somewhere in New York City. Many of the houses have a colonial influence and the lush greenery feels like a rare pocket of nature in the big city. The streets are lined also with Victorian and turn-of-the-century manors steeped in New York history. For example, back when Lighthouse Hill was known as "Richmond Road," it was home to the "Richmond Seminary for Young Ladies," a finishing school for wealthy young girls from around the country.

Famous residents of Lighthouse Hill include Pulitzer Prize winning poet Edwin Arlington Robinson, a favorite of Teddy Roosevelt, and Arthur Andersen, who is known not by his name, but by his voice being that of the Lucky Charms Leprechaun. Lighthouse Hill is also home to the only Frank Lloyd Wright home in New York City, Crimson Beech, and the Jacques Marchais Museum of Tibetan Art (see following double page).

THE JACQUES MARCHAIS MUSEUM OF TIBETAN ART

A miniature duplicate of the Potala of Lhasa in a surprising corner of the boroughs

338 Lighthouse Avenue
tibetanmuseum.org – 718 987-3500

On a Staten Island hilltop, in a sleepy residential neighborhood, nestled among suburban-looking stand-alone homes, hidden behind a fieldstone wall sits a small monastic complex which is one of the oldest examples of Himalayan-style architecture in the US.

The Jacques Marchais Museum of Tibetan Art has occupied its perch atop what is one of the Eastern Seaboard's highest points since 1947, when Ohio-born child star Jacques Marchais and her third husband decided to create a permanent home for her extensive collection of Tibetan art.

Marchais's story begins with a tumultuous midwestern childhood, a career as a stage performer and two marriages, after which she moved to New York, opened a gallery in Manhattan, wed a chemical factory

owner, bought a house on Staten Island and grew her collection of Tibetan art and artifacts to, eventually, more than 5,000 pieces.

Seeking to display her life's work in a context which did it justice, Marchais and her husband bought the land next door to their home and, with the help of a local stonemason, constructed a compound inspired by a 16th-century Tibetan monastery, a miniature duplicate of the Potala of Lhasa, palace of the Dalai Lama.

"No one had anything what-so-ever to do with the designing and planning...I was a Lone Wolf from the beginning to the end," Marchais wrote in her notes of developing her vision with hardly any help.

Marchais passed away mere months after the completion of her sanctuary in 1948. She was 61 and never actually visited Tibet, but her homage to its culture has maintained long past her death.

"She didn't create a museum – she created a cultural center. A space for inner reflection," says Nico Simoni, current executive director of Marchais' "Jewel on Hillside," her "Potala of the West."

The space – which is listed on the National Register of Historic Places – remains a peaceful oasis of prayer flags, altars and Buddha statues, its gardens a landscaped retreat of seasonal Himalayan plants and stone paths, its two buildings as much museum as tranquil refuge, a shrine to a distant region and its culture, transporting visitors to a far off corner of the Earth many miles from the manic bustle of New York City.

In looking at black and white photos of the center's early days, it is striking how little has changed: The Jacques Marchais museum appears then much as it does now — the trapezoidal windows, decorative wooden posts, a replica of a Chinese temple's rooftop cupola. It is the once rural surrounding area that time has rendered nearly unrecognizable.

King or country?

298 Satterlee Street, Staten Island
conferencehouse.org
718.984.6046
The house can be visited April to December; the reenactment takes place every
year on September 11
S59 or S78 bus/Hylan Blvd – Craig Av; Staten Island Railway train/Tottenville
(last stop)

On a hill overlooking the southern tip of Staten Island stands the city's oldest manor, the Conference House, which hosts a curious ritual. Every year in mid-September reenactors gather in their buckle shoes and bonnets to recreate an episode in local history when the fate of America was decided during the course of a single lunch.

We're in September of 1776. Under the shade trees there is an elegant table: British commander Howe—or the actor who wears his wig and breeches—has invited Benjamin Franklin, John Adams and Edward Rutledge from the Continental Congress to discuss an immediate end to the Revolutionary War. You might get swept up in the play. "Are you ready," asks a man in full military kit, "to fight for king and country?" He has a contemporary glint in his eye, but other reenactors maintain a glassy earnestness: "I am but a poor farmer," says an elderly man in the green coat of a Loyalist; he sided with the British, he claims, because he can't stand the thought of more violence after the gruesome Battle of Brooklyn two weeks ago. When asked how he thinks the historic meeting will turn out, the man wobbles and blinks. "I would not hazard a guess," he says, and then nibbles some hardtack from a Ziploc baggie.

Reenactment is more often miss than hit; the Conference House does it right. Smiling women stir iron pots of apples and bacon over smoky flame, wiping tears from their eyes on the hems of their aprons. There are butter-churners and quilt-makers and men firing muskets at the sky. The air is filled with dulcimer music and the tang of burnt wood. At the appointed hour a fife and drum trill from the direction of the beach: the Yanks have arrived, as they do every year, in a rowboat from New Jersey. After trooping from the landing and up the hill, the proud rebels seat themselves uneasily around the table ("The menu," says a young lady reading over a loudspeaker, "included good claret, tongue, ham, and mutton"). Commander Howe makes civilized and condescending overtures of compromise which foxy Ben Franklin rejects on principle, while John Adams appears to fight an urge to vomit. "And so the Americans," the young lady announces, "resisted the temptation to compromise their ideals of liberty." The drum rattles, the fife tweets, and the delegates head back to their rowboat, trailed by whooping kids.

ALPHABETICAL INDEX

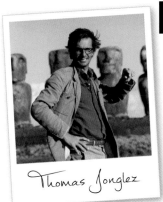

Thomas Jonglez

It was September 1995 and Thomas Jonglez was in Peshawar, the northern Pakistani city 20 kilometres from the tribal zone he was to visit a few days later. It occurred to him that he should record the hidden aspects of his native city, Paris, which he knew so well. During his seven-month trip back home from Beijing, the countries he crossed took in Tibet (entering clandestinely, hidden under blankets in an overnight bus), Iran and Kurdistan. He never took a plane but travelled by boat, train or bus, hitchhiking, cycling, on horseback or on foot, reaching Paris just in time to celebrate Christmas with the family.

On his return, he spent two fantastic years wandering the streets of the capital to gather material for his first "secret guide", written with a friend. For the next seven years he worked in the steel industry until the passion for discovery overtook him. He launched Jonglez Publishing in 2003 and moved to Venice three years later.

In 2013, in search of new adventures, the family left Venice and spent six months travelling to Brazil, via North Korea, Micronesia, the Solomon Islands, Easter Island, Peru and Bolivia.

After seven years in Rio de Janeiro, he now lives in Berlin with his wife and three children.

Jonglez Publishing produces a range of titles in nine languages, released in 40 countries.